...broke House Library
...bury Grove

...1 (Renewals)
...witchboard)
...ous) http://opac.unl.ac.uk

C000127172

RECALLS

You may be asked to return this book
BEFORE THE DATE STAMPED
if it is reserved by another reader.

PN 9189359 3

THE APPEAL OF INTERNAL REVIEW

Why do most welfare applicants fail to challenge adverse decisions despite a continuing sense of need?

The book, based on research funded by the Nuffield Foundation, addresses this severely under-researched and under-theorised question. Using English homelessness law as their case study, the authors explore why homeless applicants did—but more often did not—challenge adverse decisions by seeking internal administrative review. They draw out from their data a list of the barriers to the take up of grievance rights. Further, by combining extensive interview data from aggrieved homeless applicants with ethnographic data about bureaucratic decision-making, they are able to situate these barriers within the dynamics of the citizen-bureaucracy relationship. Additionally, they point to other contexts which inform applicants' decisions about whether to request an internal review. Drawing on a diverse literature—risk, trust, audit, legal consciousness, and complaints—the authors lay the foundations for our understanding of the (non-)emergence of administrative disputes.

THE APPEAL OF
INTERNAL REVIEW

*Law, Administrative Justice and the
(non-) emergence of disputes*

DAVID COWAN

AND

SIMON HALLIDAY

WITH

Caroline Hunter, Paul Maginn
and Lisa Naylor

HART PUBLISHING
OXFORD AND PORTLAND, OREGON
2003

Published in North America (US and Canada) by
Hart Publishing
c/o International Specialized Book Services
5804 NE Hassalo Street
Portland, Oregon
97213-3644
USA

© David Cowan and Simon Halliday 2003

The Authors have asserted their right under the Copyright,
Designs and Patents Act 1988, to be identified as the authors of this work.

Hart Publishing is a specialist legal publisher based in Oxford, England.
To order further copies of this book or to request a list of other publications
please write to:

Hart Publishing, Salter's Boatyard, Folly Bridge, Abingdon Rd, Oxford, OX1 4LB
Telephone: +44 (0)1865 245533 Fax: +44 (0) 1865 794882
email: mail@hartpub.co.uk
WEBSITE: http//:www.hartpub.co.uk

British Library Cataloguing in Publication Data
Data Available

ISBN 1-84113-383-3 (hardback)

Date	02/12/2003 NL
Fund	CPE
	ORD
Class no	344.03 / COW
Accession no	9189359⅔

Typeset by John Saunders Design and Production
Printed and bound in Great Britain by
Biddles Ltd, www.biddles.co.uk

Preface

This book is born out of a discussion at the Socio-Legal Studies Association annual conference in 1999 (in Loughborough) between Dave Cowan, Caroline Hunter and Simon Halliday. We all had an interest in homelessness, law, administrative justice and decision-making, and had a background in researching these issues. In particular, Dave had done some early work about informal internal appeal systems which had been developed in the early 1990s in homelessness cases. Caroline and Dave together had conducted a survey of local authorities in 1998 which demonstrated a cause for concern in that few homelessness applicants were using the (then) new internal review system under the Housing Act 1996. After our discussion at the conference we decided to resurrect a proposal for funding and set in train a research programme. A number of research questions emerged, but the overriding concerns were to seek to understand why a few unsuccessful homelessness applicants pursue their grievances, and the vast majority do not. This book provides a set of findings about this which we hope will be useful for future research and policy development in the field of social welfare and administrative justice.

The research took place in two local authorities in England, which we call 'Southfield' and 'Brisford'. They are discussed in chapters three and four respectively. We are grateful for their willingness to take part in the research, their openness during it, and their discussion of our findings after it. We also interviewed 94 people who had made homelessness applications. Their experience forms the bulk of the rest of this book. We are grateful to them for sharing that experience with us. Thanks are also due to the local solicitors and advice workers in the two sites who were also prepared to be interviewed.

We were fortunate to be able to employ two researchers of high quality—Paul Maginn and Lisa Naylor. Lisa worked in Southfield, and Paul in Brisford. They carried out all the observations of local authority practices and conducted interviews with homeless applicants. It is the quality of their work and their tenacity in obtaining interviews which provides the basis for this book. Caroline, Dave, Simon and Lisa conducted post-observation interviews with local authority personnel. Simon managed the fieldwork on a day-to-day basis, and we all met up as a team to discuss emerging issues and the direction of the research on a quarterly basis. Caroline and Dave repeated their 1998 questionnaire in 2001, the findings of which are discussed in chapter two.

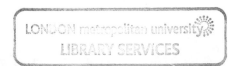
LONDON metropolitan university
LIBRARY SERVICES

Other research commitments unfortunately took Caroline, Lisa and Paul away from the project at the end of fieldwork, though Caroline was able to write the section on homelessness law in chapter two. Data analysis and the writing of the remainder of the book's text, accordingly, were carried out jointly by Dave and Simon.

This book would not have been possible without having received a grant from the Nuffield Foundation. We have felt extremely fortunate to have had funding from the Foundation, not least because of its generosity and willingness to top up the grant, enabling us to complete the project. We are also grateful to Richard Hart and Hart Publishing for agreeing to publish our findings and for being so pleasant a publishing company to deal with.

During the life of this project, Finbar Cowan was born. Dave would like to dedicate this book to him, to Helen and Jake, and to his friends who, like Anna, said they would be interested in reading it.

Much of the data analysis and development of the text took place during periods when Simon was a visitor at the Law Faculty of the University of New South Wales, Sydney. He is grateful to Jill McKeough and her colleagues for the provision of research facilities and for the warmth of their welcome. Thanks also to Bronwen Morgan, a colleague at the Centre for Socio-Legal Studies, for reading and commenting insightfully on various parts of the draft text. Simon dedicates the book to Peggy.

Dave Cowan, Bristol
Simon Halliday, Oxford
October, 2002

Contents

List of Tables   xi

1 INTRODUCTION   1
   (Non-)Emergence of Disputes in Welfare   2
   Methods   7
      Recruitment Strategies for Homeless Applicant Interviewees   7
      The Outcomes of the Recruitment Process   8
      Numbers of Interviewees Who Had Failed to Pursue Internal
         Review   10
      Assessing the Interview Sample   11
   Structure of the Book   17

2 HOMELESSNESS LAW AND INTERNAL REVIEW IN CONTEXT 19
   Social and Political Context of English Homelessness Law   19
      History of Homelessness Law   19
      Contemporary Social and Political Context of Homelessness
         Law   20
      Political Context of Implementation   21
      Introduction of Internal Review to Homelessness Law   22
   The Legal Provisions   24
      Entitlement: Assessments Decision-Making   25
      Housing Duties: Allocations Decision-Making   27
      Miscellaneous Duties   28
      Internal Review   28
   The Use of Internal Review   30
      Volume of Internal Reviews   31
      What are Reviews About?   33
      Success Rates   34
      Internal Review Procedures   35
      Third Party Advice/Assistance   36
      County Court Appeals   37
   Conclusion   37

3 SOUTHFIELD COUNCIL   39
   Introduction   39
   Assessments Decision-Making   39
      Contrasting Models of Decision-Making   40

Single Men and Childless Couples: Residential Team   42
Single Men and Childless Couples: Casework Team   48
Single Women   49
Families   53
Conclusions about Assessments Decision-Making: The Risk
    Authority   58
Allocations Decision-Making   61
Singles   62
Families   65
Conclusions about Allocations   67
Internal Review   67
Refusals: Singles   67
Refusals: Families   70
Statutory Internal Review   73
Conclusion   77

4 BRISFORD COUNCIL   79
Introduction   79
Assessments Decision-Making   79
Introduction   79
Decision-Making Practices   82
Conclusions About Assessments Decision-Making: The Audit
    Authority   88
Allocations Decision-Making   92
Temporary Accommodation Section   93
Allocations Team   96
Internal Review   99
Assessments Internal Review   99
Allocations Internal Review   104
Conclusion   110

5 UNDERSTANDING THE FAILURE TO PURSUE INTERNAL
   REVIEW   111
Introduction   111
Ignorance of the Right to Internal Review   112
Applicant Does Not Receive the Decision-Letter   112
Applicant Receives but Does Not Read the Decision-Letter   113
Applicant Reads but Does Not Understand the Decision-Letter 114
Internal Review Scepticism   118
Lack of Independence   118
Lack of Trust   119
Negative Advice of HPU Officers   130
Scepticism about External Review/Appeal Processes   130

Rule-Bound Image of the Decision-Making Process   131
  Introduction   131
  Blamelessness of Bureaucrats   133
  Situating Legal Consciousness within the Bureaucratic Practices   134
  Plurality of Legal Consciousness Narratives   137
Applicant Fatigue   138
'Satisfaction' with Decision   141
  The Initial Offer of Housing   142
  After the Initial Offer of Housing   143
Applicant Does Not Want/Need Substantive Benefit   145
  Applicant Finds Other Accommodation   146
  Applicant is Granted Discretionary Housing   147
  Applicant Only Sought Temporary Accommodation   147
Conclusion   148

6 UNDERSTANDING THE PURSUIT OF INTERNAL REVIEW   151
Introduction   151
Aims and Motivations in Pursuing Internal Review   152
  Reversal of Original Decision   152
  Calling the HPU to Account   153
  Delay of Eviction from Temporary Accommodation   154
  Ignorance of Having Sought Internal Review   155
  Conclusions about Motivations in Pursuing Internal Review   156
Grounds of Review   158
  Inaccuracy   158
  Unspecific Sense of Unfairness   165
  Comparative Sense of Unfairness   167
  Pursuing Internal Review with No Grounds of Review   168
  Conclusions about Grounds of Review   168
Confidence and Scepticism in Pursuing Internal Review   169
  Confidence   170
  Scepticism   170
  Confidence Co-Existent with Scepticism   172
Conclusion   173

7 LAWYERS AND OTHER COPING STRATEGIES   177
Introduction   177
Alternative Coping Strategies   180
  Advice and/or Information   180
  Non-Legal Representation/Support   183
  Going it Alone   184
Why and How Did Applicants Access/Fail to Access Legal
  Assistance?   184

Motivations in Seeking Legal Assistance   184
Conditions Affecting the Seeking of Legal Assistance   187
Finding a Lawyer   190
At What Stage was Legal Assistance Sought?   191
The Effect of Legal Representation on the Practices of Internal
    Review   192
Juridification of Homelessness Decision-Making   194
Shifting the Character of Administrative Justice   196
Conclusion   197

8 CONCLUSION   199
Introduction   199
Decision-Making in Southfield and Brisford   199
Explaining and Predicting Disputing Behaviour   202
The Interaction Perspective and Policy   204
    Communication   204
    Trust, Faith and Scepticism   205
    Image of Decision-Making   206
    Length and Complexity of Bureaucratic Process   206
    Coerced Choice   207
Internal Review and Administrative Justice   207
The Research Agenda   209
    What Configuration of Factors Facilitate the Take-Up of
        Grievance Rights?   209
    The Importance of 'Audience'   210
    Impact of Legal Representation   210
    Interaction Perspective   210
    The Emotional Dimension   211

Bibliography   213

List of Tables

1 Number of Interviewees who Failed to Pursue Internal Review   10

2 Combined Analysis of Interview Sub-Sample in Terms of Gender and Ethnicity   13

3 Analysis of Brisford's Interview Sample in Terms of Initial Decision Type   13

4 Estimated Frequency of Representation (Lawyer and Non-Lawyer) in Internal Reviews   36

5 Estimated Frequency of Representation by Lawyer in Internal Reviews   36

6 Ideal Types of Bureaucratic Decision-Making   42

7 Overview of Assessments Decision-Making—Southfield Council   59

8 Subject Matter of Internal Reviews—Southfield Council   74

9 Overview of Assessments Decision-Making – Southfield & Brisford   89

10 Subject Matter of Internal Review Requests: Brisford Oct 2000 – Sept 2001   100

11 Assessments Internal Reviews by Outcome—Brisford Council   101

12 Allocations Internal Reviews by Outcome—Brisford Council   108

13 Interaction Perspective on Failure to Pursue Internal Review   149

1

Introduction

Shortly before Christmas 2000, Andrew Holt applied with his girlfriend, Pamela McKenzie,[1] to Brisford Council for somewhere to live. Andrew was 35 years old, Pamela was 29. Both had histories of drug use but had recently been through detoxification programmes. They each also suffered from other medical problems. They were unemployed and in receipt of welfare benefits. They were sleeping rough and were desperate to get off the streets as winter was setting in. Pamela was pregnant. Not long after making their housing application, however, Pamela tragically died in a fire. Andrew continued in his application for housing, but was eventually rejected as not having a 'priority need' as a homeless person. He was informed that he could have this refusal reviewed by a senior officer. There were no other housing options available to him and he was desperate for housing. During our taped interview with him he took hold of the microphone and pleaded for help from Brisford Council:

> I'll tell you what, keep this for the record, yes? Keep this one for the record and I'll tell 'em this then, I'll speak into your microphone: [Brisford] Council, will you please help me out? Will you please give me some permanent accommodation? Thank you very much. I would appreciate it. I will pay the rent. I will pay the bills and you know, I will be an absolutely model citizen. I will be an absolute model of a tenant for you, thank you very much. There you go.

However, Andrew never pursued his grievance with the Council. He did not take up the opportunity to have his decision reviewed internally, and so lost his right to have the decision reviewed subsequently in court.

The interesting and, in our view, surprising and worrying thing about this is that Andrew's reaction to the refusal of help, despite his desperate plight, is by far the normal response. The vast majority of homeless applicants specifically, and welfare applicants in general, fail to challenge adverse decisions despite their continuing sense of need. Surprisingly little is known about why citizens do not challenge adverse decisions from government agencies, though the repeated finding is that the take-up of rights to challenge refusals is breathtakingly low. Genn (1994), for example, cites the rate of challenge to refusal of social security payments as being less than one per

---

[1] Interview B16. These are false names

cent. This represents a spectacular failure of the administrative justice system and constitutes a major policy conundrum.

The value of a system of administrative justice must surely rest on the extent to which it is accessible, relied upon and used by aggrieved citizens (Harris & Eden, 2000). Additionally, of course, the low take-up of grievance rights suggests the need for an explanation in and of itself. The structure of the administrative justice system is premised largely on the notion of aggrieved citizens as rational actors who will pursue their grievances where the opportunities occur (see Le Grand, 1997). The data about the low take-up of grievance rights certainly explodes this myth, though the question still remains of why exactly the take-up is so low.

This book is about citizens' engagement with the administrative justice system. It presents a study of welfare applicants' interactions with welfare bureaucracies and explores their reasons for challenging – and, more often, failing to challenge—adverse decisions. The administration of English homelessness law is used as a case study. We present our findings about why homelessness applicants did—or did not—seek the internal review of adverse decisions, the first port of call when challenging a decision and the gateway to the external adjudicative process. Our aims are to provide some answers to why welfare applicants do, or fail to, take up their rights to grievance mechanisms within the administrative justice system; and to provide a solid foundation for taking related research issues forward.

In this first chapter we do three things. First, we explore the existing literature about the (non-)emergence of disputes with particular reference to the field of welfare and set the specific aims of our research. Second, we describe the methods we employed to carry out the research. Finally, we sketch out the structure of the remainder of the book, highlighting the other research issues explored in the text.

(NON-)EMERGENCE OF DISPUTES IN WELFARE

Socio-legal studies have long been concerned with the emergence and non-emergence of legal disputes. Felstiner, Abel and Sarat (1980) have set out an influential theoretical framework for understanding the emergence of disputes—the celebrated 'naming, blaming and claiming' sequence. They argued that for too long, the study of disputes had focused on the legal institutions most remote from society. Instead they urged an examination of the emergence of disputes—an exploration of the conditions under which experiences are transformed into grievances and, from there, to disputes:

> The sociology of law should pay more attention to the early stages of disputes and to the factors that determine whether naming, blaming and claiming will occur. Learning more about the existence, absence or reversal of

these basic transformations will increase our understanding of the disputing process and our ability to evaluate dispute processing institutions. (1980-81: 636)

Felstiner et al's conceptual structure remains highly influential, though it has received some criticism (Lloyd-Bostock, 1984; 1991; Merry, 1990: 92). Lloyd-Bostock and Mulcahy set up an additional theoretical model for under-standing complaining behaviour which they call an 'account' model (1994:141). Under the 'account' model, initial complaining is better regarded as an event in and of itself—a non-instrumental event calling someone to account for failure to meet the complainant's normative expec-tations. The goal of complaining here is not redress (compensation, restitu-tion, substantive benefit, etc), but rather to make a person or organisation acknowledge and account for fault of some kind. We discuss these explana-tory models further in chapter six when we examine our data about why some of our interviewees pursued internal review.

In the field of social welfare, generally speaking, research about disputes has often been policy-focussed, revolving around particular areas of social policy. Research on why welfare applicants fail to challenge adverse deci-sions is fairly sparse, comprising only a handful of projects (Genn & Genn 1989; Sainsbury & Eardley, 1991; Huby & Dix, 1992; Sainsbury et al, 1995; Sheppard & Raine, 1999; Harris & Eden, 2000; Blandy et al 2001). Such work has generally been a small part of wider considerations of a particular welfare benefit or tribunal process. The largest project is that of Genn and Genn (1989) who conducted a survey of unsuccessful social security appli-cants and asked them why they failed to appeal to a Social Security Appeals Tribunal. However, this aspect of the research was incidental to their larger project of assessing the effectiveness of representation at tribunals. The question of the non-emergence of disputes around welfare benefits, accord-ingly, has still not received sustained and intimate treatment.

It is helpful, nevertheless, to examine briefly the main themes which have emerged in the literature so far. The research about the failure to appeal to tribunals has recently been summarised by Adler and Gulland (2002). They subsume the findings about the 'practical barriers that prevent potential users from accessing tribunals' within four headings: (1) ignorance of rights or procedures; (2) cost; (3) complexity of the appeal process and absence of appropriate help; and (4) physical barriers.[2] Due to the fact that their focus was on tribunals, Adler and Gulland did not consider the work of Sainsbury and Eardley (1991) which examined Housing Benefit Review Boards, or Huby and Dix (1992) which looked at internal review as part of their wider study of the social fund. Adler and Gulland's focus also seems to have been

[2] Adler and Gulland additionally speculate about the impact of electronic access and the impact of amalgamation of tribunals.

curtailed by their remit to consider the practical barriers to the take up of tribunal appeal rights. However, Sainsbury and Eardley (1991) as well as Huby and Dix (1992) both draw attention to what might be termed 'attitudinal' barriers. Sainsbury and Eardley discuss the problem of 'cynicism', as a result of which potential review applicants failed to challenge housing benefit decisions because of a cynicism about their prospects of success. Huby and Dix additionally draw our attention to the problem of apathy whereby potential internal review applicants fail to pursue their grievances because they felt it was too much trouble or effort.

Our study has clear links to that of Huby and Dix's (1992) brief examination of the non-emergence of disputes in that it focuses on the pursuit and non-pursuit of internal review. The study of the failure to pursue internal review has a number of advantages when considering the non-emergence of disputes in the field of administrative law generally, and social welfare in particular. First, internal review represents the first rung on the ladder in terms of challenging adverse decisions. As we shall see in greater detail in chapter two, homeless applicants must pursue internal review before being permitted to seek external review in the County Court. This cementing of internal review as a compulsory first stage in the overall adjudicative process is quite a common feature of administrative law systems. In the UK, for example, prior to 1998, compulsory internal review was part of the grievance systems for a range of welfare benefits (disability living allowance, attendance allowance, Child Support, the social fund and housing benefit). The Social Security Bill 1998 proposed to extend the compulsory model to a much wider range of benefits, though this proposal was eventually withdrawn. Compulsory internal review still remains, however, for council tax benefit, housing benefit, and the social fund (Sainsbury, 2000) in addition to homelessness law. The requirement of internal review as a pre-requisite to external review is also a common feature of other administrative law systems and is particularly strong, for example, in Australia (Administrative Review Council, 2000). Further, it is not hard to imagine how it might increase in the future. As Sainsbury has noted:

> In deciding what decision-making arrangements to introduce for new elements of the social security system, policy makers and politicians have been more influenced by practical and political considerations than by any guiding principles derived, for example, from natural justice or administrative law. (2000:211)

Compulsory internal review has the policy advantage of cutting down on the numbers of claims being adjudicated in external fora. As we shall see in chapter two, this was a central reason for the development of a statutory right to review in the homelessness legislation. Such a policy may, as the UK government suggested in relation to the Social Security Bill 1998, prevent 'hopeless cases' from wasting the time of tribunals, or avoid dissatisfied applicants from being drawn into the tribunal process when they would have been satisfied with a simple explanation of the decision (Sainsbury, 2000). However, it is also clear that such a gated approach to adjudication would bring economic savings for the administrative justice system as a whole. Compulsory internal review, then, will have a clear attraction for governments seeking to promote efficiency and financial savings. Researching the failure to pursue internal review which is a prerequisite for external review has a particular significance, then, when considering the non-emergence of disputes. If one is interested in understanding the emergence and non-emergence of disputes, one has to look first at the foundations of the architecture of administrative justice. Despite internal review having the theoretical potential to be merely the first step in a grand hierarchy of legal redress, research has indicated that the majority of grievances do not proceed beyond the first stage of complaint (Sainsbury & Eardley, 1991; Dalley & Berthoud, 1992; Lloyd-Bostock & Mulcahy, 1994; Atkinson et al, 1999). As we shall see in the next chapter, the position in relation to homelessness law is no different. The high level of drop-out after internal review renders it considerably more significant in terms of administrative justice than the theoretical potential suggests.

Moreover, our study of the use and non-use of internal review is still important to a more general understanding of the non-emergence of disputes in welfare—even where the applicant has the right to appeal directly to an external body without the need to seek internal review. Research (Genn and Genn, 1989; Sainsbury et al, 1995; Harris and Eden, 2000) has repeatedly shown that many applicants fail to appreciate that a tribunal is an independent body. Although the analytical distinction between internal and external review may be clear to policy-makers or administrative law scholars, it seems not to be so for many users of the system. From the perspective of the welfare applicant, appeals to tribunals and internal review requests may amount to the same thing. Our findings about the failure to pursue internal review, then, may equally have pertinence for understanding the non-take-up of tribunal rights.

The second principal reason that the study of internal review has particular promise is that internal review represents what might be described as the 'Rolls Royce' of notionally accessible, 'consumer-friendly' grievance mechanisms. It scores particularly well against some basic standards of accessibility. As we shall see in more detail in chapter two, all that the aggrieved homelessness applicant must do to initiate an internal review is to ask for it within a limited time scale. It does not cost anything, legal representation is not required, no forms have to be filled in, the applicant does not have to attend a hearing. It is already free from most of the 'practical barriers' highlighted by Adler and Gulland (2002): cost, complexity, physical barriers. By looking at the failure to pursue internal review, then, we should get deeper into the core reasons for failing to challenge adverse welfare decisions. The richness of our qualitative data will allow us to gain more penetrating insights into the 'attitudinal barriers' touched upon briefly by Sainsbury and Eardley (1991) and Huby and Dix (1992).

Indeed, one of the principal contributions of our research is that it allows us to explore the (non-)emergence of disputes from an 'interaction perspective'. As we shall see in the chapters which follow, we suggest that one of the key contexts for understanding the (non-)emergence of disputes is the relationship between the applicant and the bureaucracy. By situating the failure to challenge adverse decisions in the applicant-bureaucracy relationship we obtain a much deeper understanding of the reasons why, for example, applicants may be sceptical of their prospects of success, or apathetic about seeking review. The study of the relationship between the applicant and the bureaucracy, and its significance for explaining the (non-) emergence of disputes, is an element which has been missing from existing research. This is no doubt a reflection of the fact that studying the failure to challenge adverse decisions has been incidental to a larger project. However, it leaves something of a gap in our understanding of why people fail to take up their rights of redress. As Bridges et al have noted (1998), research which focuses on the perspective of only one of the parties to 'legal' processes runs the risk of producing an incomplete and very partial analysis. Our research seeks to demonstrate the importance of the interaction perspective for understanding the failure to challenge adverse welfare decisions, and provides an example of how this kind of research may be conducted. Not only is our understanding of the (non-)emergence of disputes enriched, but an interaction perspective also feeds directly into the policy objective of increasing applicants' access to grievance mechanisms. It highlights bureaucratic practices which may unwittingly help to construct barriers to the use of grievance processes.

Our aim in this book is to provide a sustained analysis of the emergence and non-emergence of administrative disputes based on systematically obtained qualitative data. Our findings offer some fresh insights into this research issue and provide a solid foundation for taking the research agenda forward. Of course, as a qualitative study, our research is not capable of analysing the reasons why grievances are/are not transformed into disputes according to social group (eg class, age, gender, ethnicity, etc) Our role rather is to gain a picture of the various 'barriers to transformation' and to locate them within a careful conceptual framework. This, we believe, should be helpful for future study of the non-emergence of administrative disputes which has a quantitative element to it.

Our research aims, of course, must be matched by our research methods. It is to this matter that we now turn.

METHODS

Fieldwork took place for approximately one year in two sites which we have called Southfield and Brisford. In Southfield, fieldwork took place from June 2000 until May 2001. In Brisford it took place from October 2000 until September 2001. In both sites there were three phases of fieldwork. Initially, a period of observation took place over a period of 10 weeks. During this time the fieldworkers learned about decision-making behaviour and routines within the Homeless Persons' Units. This phase was followed by a period of interviewing with 'unsuccessful' homelessness applicants (those who had been refused assistance under homelessness law) and with aggrieved successful applicants (those who had been offered long-term housing with which they were unhappy). Finally, a number of taped interviews and focus groups with local authority officers and interviews with local solicitors and housing advisers took place. In relation to the local authority officers, these interviews allowed us to test further the themes which had emerged from the prior fieldwork phases. Interviews with local solicitors and advisers allowed us to gain external perspectives on the local authorities' decision-making practices.

Both Southfield and Brisford granted us unrestricted access to their routine operations. During the course of fieldwork, we observed daily routines, officer meetings and officer-applicant interactions. In Brisford, our fieldworker was able to interview homeless applicants informally about their experiences of applying for housing during the course of their interviews with homeless officers when the officer was away from the interview rooms. These interviews were not taped. Instead, notes were taken which formed the basis of the fieldworker's ongoing fieldwork diary. We were also able to view and analyse applicants' files as well as various policy documents.

Recruitment Strategies For Homeless Applicant Interviewees

Similar broad strategies for the recruitment of applicant interviewees were developed in both field sites. The broad strategy with which we began fieldwork was to send out an initial contact letter with every refusal of assistance letter issued by the Homeless Persons' Units (HPU). This letter requested an interview with the 'unsuccessful' homeless applicant for which we offered a small fee.

Such a strategy was more difficult in relation to 'aggrieved' successful homeless applicants – those who were unhappy with an offer of accommodation. The identity of such applicants would not be self-evident. Instead we had to rely on such applicants making themselves known to the HPU by way of complaining about the offer of housing. In both sites, as we shall see in the following chapters, the HPUs operated a pre-statutory internal review scheme to consider complaints about the unsuitability of offers of housing. Our strategy, therefore, in relation to allocations decisions was to contact applicants for interview after they had engaged with these pre-statutory review processes and their challenge as to suitability had been rejected. This, of course, exposes a gap in the data. We were only able to make systematic contact with aggrieved successful applicants after they had challenged the suitability of the accommodation offer. We were not able to interview those who may have felt aggrieved about an offer of accommodation but who did not challenge it. This was an unavoidable limitation of our research design.

However, as we shall see in more detail later, it was a limitation which was mitigated by two factors. First, our observational and interview data which focused on the HPUs' operations permit us to offer suggestions about why applicants may not challenge offers of accommodation despite feeling aggrieved. These suggestions are not, of course, grounded in applicants' descriptions of their own behaviour and motivations, but they do arise from grounded observational data about the working practices of the HPUs' officers. Having been explicit about the nature of the data, we offer these suggestions to readers with appropriate caution. Second, we were able to collect interview data about why such applicants did not pursue internal review, though only in the sense of statutory internal review as opposed to the HPUs' formal though non-statutory prior review process. In this way our design permitted us to enquire into why applicants dropped out of the overall grievance process, ie why they did not pursue their grievance onto the statutory internal review stage. This data is important and contributes to our overall understanding of the barriers to the machinery of administrative justice.

The Outcomes Of The Recruitment Process

Southfield

In Southfield, the HPU is split into four separate teams, housed in different buildings. More than 40 officers routinely send out negative decision-letters. Our fieldworker had to rely on these officers to include our contact letter with the negative decision-letters. However, it soon transpired that many letters were not being sent out. The number of officers and the geography of the various offices rendered the monitoring of the exercise very difficult. A new strategy was developed, therefore, whereby our fieldworker herself took control of the process of sending out contact letters. A weekly check of Southfield's computer records was made to ascertain the names and addresses of homeless applicants who had been refused assistance. Such information was updated weekly although a substantial number of records took two weeks or more to be updated and many were never updated. Given that this delay was compounded by the time taken for our contact letter to arrive, it seems likely that many potential interviewees had already moved on from the address in question by the time our letters arrived. The checking of the computer system offered, accordingly, a limited improvement to the recruitment process. Manual checks with the various teams of the HPU, however, also had to be made. This proved very time-consuming and slowed down the fieldwork process considerably.

We developed two additional strategies to contact potential interviewees. First, posters advertising the research were sent to 23 different agencies which worked with homeless people in the area. Agency workers were additionally asked to make clients aware of the research and to encourage clients to contact our fieldworker. No interviews, however, were secured in this way. Second, local solicitors and advice agencies who had represented homeless applicants in their dealings with the HPU were also asked to refer potential interviewees to our fieldworker. One interview was secured using this method.

Overall, however, the process of recruiting interviewees was more difficult than we had hoped it would be and the number of interviews obtained was slightly lower than we had anticipated. (We had anticipated the response rate to be between 12–15 per cent). In total, 30 interviews were conducted in Southfield. Nineteen of these interviews were with unsuccessful applicants—those who had been refused assistance. Eleven interviews were with aggrieved successful applicants—those who believed their offer of accommodation was unsuitable. It is not possible to frame this volume of interviews as a precise response rate. In total, our fieldworker attempted to contact 268 potential interviewees by letter over a period of seven months. Seventy-one of these letters related to offers of housing. The remaining 197 related to negative assessments decisions. These figures would suggest a response rate of 15.5 per cent and 9.6 per cent respectively, and an overall response rate of 11.2 per cent. However, additional letters were sent out by HPU officers in the early stages of fieldwork in relation to negative decision-letters, though it is not clear how many. We would estimate, therefore, that the overall response rate for Southfield was a little less than 10 per cent.

Brisford

Similar difficulties were encountered in Brisford. From the outset, our fieldworker took control of the process of contacting potential interviewees. However, he was reliant on the details of negative decisions being passed to him by Principal Officers who had to sanction these decisions. These Principal Officers were subject to the standard pressures of working in a busy and demanding environment and, just as in Southfield, it became clear that the details of many cases were not being passed down. Further, there was often a delay between the negative decision being made and the passing on of the required contact information to our fieldworker. All this resulted in a low initial response rate. However, after five months of fieldwork

Brisford set up a computerised 'negative decision' database. Our fieldworker was able to access the relevant contact information for all cases much more quickly, resulting in a substantial increase in responses from potential interviewees. A total of 398 contact letters were sent over a period of seven months. Sixty-four interviews were conducted. This represents an overall response rate of 16 per cent. Forty-four of the 64 interviewees related to assessments decisions, and 20 related to allocations decisions.

Numbers Of Interviewees Who Had Failed To Pursue Internal Review

Although the national rate of take-up of internal review is low (discussed further in chapter two), a much higher proportion of our interview sample had pursued internal review—just under half of them (44 per cent). This figure is also considerably higher than the take-up rate in either Southfield or Brisford. It reflects the fact that applicants who did pursue internal review were more likely to be residing at the address they had given as they were still 'live' in the application process. They were, accordingly, easier to make contact with. Our interview sample is skewed disproportionately towards having a fairly even balance of both reviewing and non-reviewing applicants. This has permitted us to glean insights both into the failure to challenge decisions, as well as the motivations and circumstances of those who did seek internal review.

In relation to assessments decisions in Southfield (ie decisions about whether the applicant is given long-term housing assistance), 17 of the 19 interviewees did not pursue internal review. In relation to allocations decisions (decisions about how to house the applicants), 8 of the 11 interviewees did not pursue statutory internal review after the pre-statutory review process. Overall, then, in Southfield, only 5 of the 30 interviewees had sought internal review.

In Brisford, of the 44 assessments interviewees, 19 had failed to pursue internal review. Of the 20 allocations interviewees, 9 had failed to pursue the statutory internal review beyond the pre-statutory review stage. Overall in Brisford 28 of the 64 interviewees had failed to pursue internal review.

These figures are summarised in the table below:

Table 1: Number of interviewees who failed to pursue internal review

	Total Assessments Interviews	Level of non-take up: Assessments	Total Allocations Interviews	Level of non-take up: Allocations	Total Interviewees	Combined level of non-take up
Southfield	19	17 (89%)	11	8 (73%)	30	25 (83%)
Brisford	44	19 (43%)	20	9 (45%)	64	28 (44%)
Combined	63	36 (57%)	31	17 (55%)	94	53 (56%)

Assessing The Interview Sample

In this section we describe our interview sample in the context of the total group of applicants who might have been interviewed during the fieldwork period – the sampling frame. This is done with two aims in mind. First, it is done in order to be informative and transparent about the research process. Second it is done in order to assess our interview sample in terms of its representativeness of the sampling frame. However, a precautionary word is required here about what we mean by 'representativeness'. This research constituted a qualitative study of homelessness decision-making and internal review in two sites, examining these processes from both the perspectives of the citizens and the bureaucracy. We did not seek, accordingly, to achieve quantitative representativeness. Not only did we restrict our fieldwork to two sites, but, as we saw above, homeless applicant interviewees – particularly those who have been denied assistance—are difficult to recruit. Homeless people who are unsuccessful in their applications for housing are perhaps one of the most difficult groups of interviewees to recruit as they move on rapidly. Instead, our aim was to build an interview sample of sufficient size and depth to provide a rich dataset about the pursuit of grievances against the welfare bureaucracy.

The interview data was analysed to a point of 'saturation'. Like Parker (1999) who used a simplified version of Glaser and Strauss's constant comparative method (Glaser & Strauss, 1967), our applicant interview data was interrogated until no new themes emerged. These themes are offered to the research and policy communities for further testing and exploration in future research regarding different administrative contexts. Of course, we cannot (and do not) claim that our findings about the reasons for failing to challenge decisions comprise an exhaustive account of the failure to pursue internal review generally, nor even in homelessness specifically (though we were encouraged by the fact that the six reasons identified for failing to pursue internal review emerged from both field sites). Nor can we weight the reasons in relation to each other in terms of their significance to the general failure to pursue review. However, in chapter five we will set out our findings about the reasons for failure to pursue internal review as having emerged from the experiences of our interviewees. We can thereby provide empirically grounded insights into the failure to challenge welfare decisions, setting out an agenda for future research and policy development.

Nevertheless, it is important to assess our interview sample in order to explore the extent to which it represents a cross-section of the sampling frame. Our recruitment methods required self-selection by homeless applicants. We did not, then, have control over which applicants were interviewed. It is possible that this process induced bias in the interview sample—that the self-selected interviewees represent only a skewed sub-group of the sampling frame.

Ideally in this section we would compare the profile of our entire interviewee sample against the profile of all those who received adverse decisions during the fieldwork period. However, approximately one third (n=32) of our interviews constituted what we have termed 'aggrieved successful' applicants—ie those who were successful in being offered accommodation but were dissatisfied with the offer of housing they received. The sampling frame for aggrieved successful interviewees consists of all those who were aggrieved about their offers of housing. It was clearly impossible for us to ascertain the details of such a sampling frame, as aggrieved successful applicants may not make themselves known to the local authority in question. Indeed, as we shall see in later chapters, our findings suggest that in both sites applicants fail to challenge offers of housing with which they were aggrieved. The nature of the population, then, is simply impossible to determine. Accordingly, in the section below we make comparisons between our 'unsuccessful' interviewees ('the sub-sample')—ie those who were denied the right to accommodation—and the corresponding sampling frame consisting of all 'unsuccessful' applicants during the fieldwork period. Although this is not a perfect comparison, it nevertheless assists us to gain a reasonable sense of the representativeness of the interview sample as a whole.

Gender

In terms of gender, we were able to obtain information about the primary applicant as indicated on the actual application form. In Brisford, the majority (56 per cent) of applicants within the sampling frame were female (n=488). There were a total of 391 male applicants (44 per cent). The gender profile of Brisford's interviewee sub-sample, however, is tipped the other way. Sixty-three per cent of our interviewees were male (n=27) and 37 per cent were female (n=16). In Southfield, 68 per cent of the sampling frame were male (n=549) and 32 per cent were female (n=337). This corresponds exactly to the interview sub-sample in Southfield. Sixty-eight per cent were male (n=13), and 32 per cent were female (n=6). Overall, the combined figures show a heavier proportion of male interviewees, though the difference is not significant. In both sets of figures, there was a greater number of men as opposed to women. As Table 2 below demonstrates, 53 per cent of the sampling frame were male (n=940), while 47 per cent were female (n=825). Of our interview sub-sample, 65 per cent were male (n=40) while 35 per cent were female (n=22).

Ethnicity

As regards ethnicity, 53 per cent of Brisford's sampling frame were 'white' (n=462). This includes those defined as white British/Irish/European. Black and minority ethnic ('BME') applicants (n=379) accounted for 43 per cent of the overall sampling frame. Data on the ethnic identity of 4 per cent of the sampling frame was missing. This profile similarly corresponds quite closely to our interview sub-sample. Fifty-three per cent of our interviewees were 'white' (n=23). BME applicants accounted for 47 per cent of interviewees (n=20). In Southfield, 62 per cent of the sampling frame were white (n=546), 30 per cent were BME (n=263), while the ethnicity of 9 per cent was unknown (n=77). Eighty-nine per cent (n=17) of our interviewees were white, while 11 per cent were BME (n=2). Table 2 below offers a comparison of the combined figures, showing a reasonably close correspondence between the sampling frame and the interview sample.

Table 2: Combined Analysis of Interview Sub-Sample in Terms of Gender and Ethnicity

	Combined Sampling Frames	Interview Sub-sample
Gender		
Male	940 (53%)	40 (65%)
Female	825 (47%)	22 (35%)
Ethnicity		
White	1008 (57%)	40 (65%)
BME	642 (36%)	22 (35%)

Initial decision-type

Another way of exploring the representativeness of the interview sample is to examine the subject matter of the negative decision being challenged. Unfortunately, we can only present here a partial picture. The information was available in relation to Brisford but not in relation to Southfield. Table 3 below demonstrates, however, that there is a reasonably close correspondence between the profile of the 43 Brisford interviewees and Brisford's sampling frame. There is a slight over-representation of applicants who

Table 3: Analysis of Brisford's Interview Sample in Terms of Initial Decision type
Initial Decision Type

	Sampling Frame	Interview Sub-sample
Not homeless	255 (29%)	5 (12%)
Not in priority need	351 (40%)	20 (49%)
Intentionally Homeless	100 (11%)	6 (15%)
Referred to another authority	70 (8%)	5 (12%)
Other	103 (12%)	5 (12%)

received a 'Not in priority need' decision, though, again, the difference is not significant. This may also account for the slight over-representation of male interviewees.

Nevertheless, the above analysis, although imperfect, offers considerable encouragement that our interviewees represent a reasonable cross-section of the sampling frame. Of course, our systematic assessment of the interview sample is limited by the available data about potential interviewees from the HPUs which took part in the research. Clearly, there are other factors which may be significant in assessing the representatives of the interview sample, some of which are difficult, if not impossible, to record or assess. One such factor which may be of particular pertinence relates to the vulnerability of the applicants within the sampling frame. It may be that individuals who for reasons of personal vulnerability are disinclined to challenge welfare decisions are also disinclined to self-select for interview. If only the 'less-vulnerable' or 'more-capable' individuals presented for interview, this would skew our sample. There is no systematic method for assessing the representativeness of our interview sample in terms of 'vulnerability'. However, we can explore the interview sample itself and determine whether it contains individuals who may be regarded as personally vulnerable. We may also consider whether it contains a diverse population in terms of individual vulnerability.

Personal vulnerability

In thinking about the vulnerability of the homeless applicant population generally, it is important to remember that this population is quite diverse. As we shall see in chapter two, the legal definition of 'homeless' is much broader than the notion of 'rooflessness'. Nationally, a very small proportion of homeless applicants—approximately 2 per cent in 1996 (O'Callaghan & Dominian, 1996)—are sleeping rough at the time of their homeless application. Most homeless applicants apply for assistance when residing in accommodation of some sort, though this accommodation may be temporary, precarious or unsuitable. Structural factors (such as unemployment, housing supply and housing affordability) seem to underpin the various 'pathways' into homelessness. However, a full understanding of the circumstances which give rise to individual homeless applications must also include consideration of personal risk factors and personal histories. As Anderson and Tulloch have noted:

> It is broadly accepted that, for individuals and households, homelessness arises through a complex combination of events and circumstances reflecting personal/individual life experiences, as well as broader social and economic factors. (2000: 4)

These personal/individual life experiences might include experience of local authority care, family breakdown, sexual or physical abuse, drug or alcohol use, experience of prison, mental health problems, and so on (Anderson & Tulloch, 2000; Ravenhill 2000). We should expect, therefore, to find individuals within the homeless applicant population who are socially excluded and vulnerable, and others who are less personally vulnerable but nevertheless find themselves (perhaps for economic reasons) to require the assistance of the local authority. Our interview sample contains individuals with various levels of 'personal vulnerability'. As a whole it represents a diverse group in this regard. This diversity can be illustrated by examining the contrasting circumstances of a few of our interviewees:

Interviewee B12 Interviewee B12 was a single man aged 25 years. At the time of interview he was sleeping in a car in the car park of a supermarket. He was unemployed. He had recently completed a 'detox' programme in a drugs rehabilitation unit, but at the time of interview was still taking drugs. He had spent time in prison. His period of homelessness had begun when a previous relationship had broken down. He had shared accommodation with his partner, but was excluded by his partner for unreasonable and threatening behaviour. He suffered from anxiety and depression and was described by his doctor as 'extremely vulnerable'.

Interviewee S2 Interviewee S2 was a single man aged 30 years. He was unemployed and in receipt of Incapacity Benefit. His housing history had been punctuated by a criminal record which stemmed back to when he was 13 years old. It began with shoplifting, and his most recent prison sentence occurred after he shot another man. Combined with this history, he had a history of using serious drugs, and had been through various detoxification programmes. At the time of our interview, he was again trying to kick his drug habit. He also had serious mental health problems, including panic attacks, which had punctuated his housing history. As he put it during his interview, 'all right, mentally I can be fucked up, but in my heart I know that I don't go out there intentionally to hurt anyone'. He had been in and out of council tenancies, and had made at least three homelessness applications in the previous couple of years. His file notes record that he had been evicted from his temporary accommodation after having been 'drugged up and apparently he likes smashing fire alarms'.

Interviewee B56 Interviewee B56 was a single man aged 38 years. He was unemployed and had a long history of rough sleeping. At the time of interview he was living temporarily in a hostel for homeless men. He was a drug user. He also suffered from mental health problems, having previously tried to commit suicide and having spent time in a psychiatric ward. During his interview he described some of his experiences of rough sleeping:

I was living rough around [Bronte Road] and all of that and you don't fancy, when you're living rough in cardboard boxes and soaking wet, you just don't get, I was soaking wet, didn't have a sleeping bag when I lived rough, and I only had one, the last night I found a sleeping bag, which was brilliant, you know what I mean, and I was back in here again, the other nights, I was sleeping in wrapped up cardboard boxes, when I woke up I was soaking wet and when you're soaking wet you don't fancy doing nothing, you know what I mean. You're starving hungry (...) turn around going round chasing round things, when you're in a place like this you can turn around and stay nice dry and warm, get up in a morning and sort out your life. When you're getting up in a cardboard, six o'clock in a morning, soaking wet, you just don't fancy doing nothing.

The three cases above represent some of the more vulnerable interviewees in our study. Other interviewees, however, had contrasting circumstances. Two examples are given below:

Interviewee B1 Interviewee B1 was a social worker for a local authority. He was married with children. His wife was a student. He was a tenant of a local authority property. However, his landlord discovered that, at the time of the creation of his tenancy, he had also been the tenant of another local authority but had not declared this. His landlord accordingly sought to have him evicted for having obtained his current tenancy through deception. When the court granted the eviction order, Interviewee B1 applied for housing assistance to Brisford's HPU.

Interviewee B40 Interviewee B40 was a woman of 60 years in receipt of a pension. She had recently retired from being a resident housekeeper. She moved in with her son temporarily on her retirement but could not remain there long-term. She had originally hoped to find other work but could not do so as she suffered from tinnitus and Raynard's disease. She applied, accordingly, to the HPU for housing. She noted in her application that she wanted a place of her own where she could read and sew.

Conclusions About the Interview Sample

In the above section we have tried to assess the representativeness of our interview sample to the sampling frame. Our statistical analysis on the basis of gender, ethnicity and initial decision type suggests that the interview sample does represent a good cross-section of the sampling frame. Additionally, the analysis of the sample shows considerable diversity within these parameters. In terms of personal vulnerability, a factor which may have skewed our interview sample, our qualitative data demonstrates that our sample contained people of diverse vulnerability and personal circumstances. On the whole, the interview sample constitutes quite a close match to the profile of the sampling frame and offers a solid foundation for our data analysis.

In the remainder of this chapter we set out the structure of the book as a whole, and set out the range of related research issues which will be explored in addition to the central aim of increasing our understanding of the (non-)emergence of disputes in welfare.

Chapter 2 offers some contextual details about the subject matter of our case studies. It introduces the reader to the basics of homelessness law to facilitate an understanding of the gist of the legal provisions being implemented by our case study authorities. The chapter also provides a social and political background to homelessness law as well as describing the introduction of internal review to the adjudicative process for homeless applicants. Some national survey data about the use of internal review is also presented.

Chapters 3 and 4 present our ethnographic studies of homelessness decision-making (at both initial and internal review stages) within our case study authorities. These chapters constitute valuable studies of welfare bureaucratic practices in their own right. However, their main purposes for this book is to contextualise our subsequent exploration of the pursuit and non-pursuit of internal review. In later chapters, where pertinent, we link our explanation of disputing behaviour to the citizen-bureaucracy relationship. Our descriptions of the social reality of decision-making within Southfield's and Brisford's HPUs are necessary, then, for a full appreciation of our interaction perspective on the (non-)emergence of disputes.

Chapter 5 explores the failure to pursue internal review. It presents our analysis of the interview data with applicants and ties this in with our prior descriptions of bureaucratic practices. This chapter sets out the various 'barriers' to the take up of internal review and thereby sets out a careful conceptual structure on this issue which we hope will be useful for future research.

Chapter 6 explores the converse situation – where applicants did pursue internal review. This chapter explores the motivations of applicants in pursuing their grievances, and their perceptions about the grounds for internal review: the specific criticisms which were levelled against initial adverse decisions. This data permits us to reflect on and critique the explanatory models of disputing behaviour which exist in the general socio-legal literature.

Chapter 7 looks at the role of lawyers in relation to internal review. The significance of lawyers and legal representation to the administrative justice system has long been a concern of socio-legal studies. We explore applicants' experiences of seeking legal assistance: their motivations, methods and perceptions of assistance. We also re-visit our ethnographic data about decision-making practices within Southfield and Brisford to comment on the impact of legal representation on the internal review process. Additionally, however, and significantly, we look at applicants' alternative coping strategies. Our survey data in chapter 2 suggests that the use of legal representation is atypical in relation to internal review. An exploration of what applicants do in order to better their situation, other than seek legal help, is perhaps a more pertinent question, then, for an analysis of citizen's engagement with the administrative justice system.

Chapter 8 contains the conclusions of the book. We consider our data in the round and summarise the main contributions of our findings. We also explore the policy implications of our findings in terms of increasing citizens' access to grievances mechanisms. Finally, we set our findings against the wider research task of exploring the (non-)emergence of disputes in welfare and propose an agenda for future research.

2

Homelessness Law and Internal Review in Context

In the previous chapter we set out the aims of our research and placed it within a broad context of socio-legal studies about the (non-)emergence of disputes, with particular reference to social welfare. Our aim in this chapter is to narrow the contextual focus and to describe the specific background to, and role of internal review in English homelessness law, the subject matter of our case studies. As part of this process we present data obtained from two national surveys of local authorities about internal review activity in relation to homelessness decision-making. Additionally, we provide a brief description of the main provisions of English homelessness law so that readers may grasp the legal scheme which was being administered by the two local authorities which took part in the research. First, however, we set out the social and political background to English homelessness law itself.

SOCIAL AND POLITICAL CONTEXT OF ENGLISH HOMELESSNESS LAW

In this section we describe the legislative history of the current homelessness law provisions in England and Wales. We also examine the broader political context which shapes and informs the contemporary implementation of the law by local authorities. We conclude by examining the particular history of internal review in the field of homelessness law.

History of Homelessness Law

In the 1960s and 1970s, a number of studies exposed the shortcomings of the safety net system for homeless people then in operation under the National Assistance Act 1948 (Greve, 1964; Greve et al, 1971; Bailey & Ruddock, 1972). The premise of the 1948 Act was that provision should be made for 'unforeseen and unforseeable misfortune' and not for 'negligent' or 'foolish' action, such as the foreseeable eviction (HC Debs, vol 448, cols 690-2, 5 March 1948). Families were separated, children taken into care, and provided accommodation was most often dormitory-style. Broadly, a consensus emerged that the National Assistance Act 1948, which had repealed the Poor Law in its opening sections, had retained much of the ethos of that old law as well as the accommodation used to house its subjects (Somerville, 1994). Public awareness of these issues was raised—in a way which seems remarkable today—by a television drama, *Cathy Come Home*, broadcast by the BBC in 1966 (although its significance has, perhaps, been overrated: Jacobs et al, 1999).

A constellation of various influences, such as pressure groups and politicians, led to the foundation and formulation of the modern homelessness legislation in the Housing (Homeless Persons) Act 1977 (Somerville, 1999). The 1977 Act reflected a balance between different interest groups (a joint charities group and other housing organisations, on the one hand, and local authorities, on the other) and, as a result, was highly contested during its passage through Parliament. It resulted in a complex, discretionary framework which survives today in slightly modified form. Major changes to the legislation were made in the Housing Act 1996, Part VII, but the key concepts together with their definitions remained almost as they were in the 1977 Act, with one or two alterations. Notably, the 1996 Act introduced a provision whereby the duty to house 'successful' homeless applicants is owed for an initial period of only two years, after which the needs of the applicant will be re-assessed. Previously under the 1977 Act no time period had been stated and local authorities generally allocated permanent accommodation.

Contemporary Political and Social Context of Homelessness Law

This reduction in the quality of assistance owed to 'successful' homelessness applicants can be understood as a reaction to a number of prevailing popular and political concerns regarding the impact of the homelessness legislation on the social housing sector. First, it was said that in certain areas only those accepted as homeless were likely to be allocated public housing (DoE, 1994: para 2.6). Consequently there was a concern that homeless people were 'jumping the queue' for housing—that there was a perverse incentive for people to have themselves declared homeless (para 2.8) as it provided a fast-track into housing (para 2.9).

Second, it was recognised that the homelessness legislation was at least partly responsible for a significant change in the make-up of the occupants of social housing stock. Although the pattern had been set before the mid-1970s, increasingly social housing was being occupied by households in the lower income deciles (Murie, 1997a). This meant that the social sector had become responsible for the provision of accommodation to increasingly marginalised populations in an increasingly residualised stock as a result of local authority tenants' right to buy their homes (Forrest & Murie, 1990). There were very clear links with the funding of social housing. Since the late

1970s, a chronic undersupply of new social housing combined with an underfunding of property maintenance were key contributing factors—no longer was social housing a choice for households; it had become the tenure for those who had no other choice.

Third, consequentially, this marginalisation within the sector was linked with understandings about its popularity (or lack of it), relationships with crime and anti-social behaviour, and problematic policing (Page, 1994; Murie, 1997b; Stenson & Watt, 1999). Contrary to the previously taken-for-granted view, there was a lack of demand for social housing in certain areas, largely (though not exclusively) in the North of England. This was in part a consequence of demographic change—the shift to the South of England—which in turn also meant that the old paradigm of undersupply was true in certain areas. Despite this spatial unevenness, social housing was regarded as inherently criminogenic and included spaces which were out of control (Cowan & Pantazis, 2001). The Housing Act 1996 responded to these concerns by giving local authority managers various powers to deal with criminality and anti-social behaviour (Hunter et al, 2001). Increasingly, local authorities have excluded social housing applicants with rent arrears and previous evidence of bad behaviour (Butler, 1998). Some local authorities have engaged in relationships with police in terms of information-swapping, leading to exclusion (see, for example, the scheme in South Tyneside MBC laid bare in reports of the Commission for Local Administration: 97/C/3827; 97C/2883). The subsequently emerging discourse of housing rights is explicitly related to the responsibilities of occupiers to their locality (DTLR, 2002: Law Commission, 2002: ch 13). Indeed, since fieldwork, the Homelessness Act 2002 was passed. Section 14 gives local authorities power to exclude those who have 'been guilty of unacceptable behaviour serious enough to make him unsuitable to be a tenant of the authority'.

Political Context of Implementation

These trends, therefore, can account for why homelessness was graded a *short-term* housing need in the 1996 Act giving rise to a limited duty to secure housing for an initial period of only two years. However, they also had an impact on the implementation of the entitlement provisions of the homelessness legislation. The increasing ethos of exclusions referred to above placed greater pressure on local authorities to deny certain applicants the legal status of homelessness (and so a re-route into public housing) (Carlen, 1994). Indeed, our case study of Southfield, as we shall see in the next chapter, illustrates these pressures particularly well. The background to the implementation of the homelessness legislation, then, is one in which the rights of the marginalised have themselves been narrowed and further doubt has been cast on the legitimacy of the status of homeless.

Allied to these trends, significant alterations have occurred to housing management practice(s). Partly these have been a response to these trends, but partly also there have been impacts from broader changes in public sector management—what Harlow and Rawlings term the 'blue rinse' (1997: ch 5). Broadly encompassing New Public Management ('NPM') approaches, social housing management has undergone radical transformations involving closer relationships with its 'consumers' and 'clients', outsourcing, benchmarking, as well as other management strategies such as audit and monitoring techniques (see Walker, 2000; Jacobs & Manzi, 2000). This has been a direct result of the focus on the three 'E's of the Conservative government's programme of compulsory competitive tendering (economy, efficiency, and effectiveness) and the four 'C's (challenge, compare, consult, and compete) of the New Labour best value programme (DETR, 2000). Despite the apparent lack of success of the CCT programme of housing management (in that few outside organisations won contracts to provide local authority housing services), the reorganisation of housing services implied by CCT had important effects, not least in inculcating NPM values in local authority housing departments. It is clear that throughout the sector, including Homeless Persons' Units, performance indicators have developed a powerful status in the assessment of housing departments' operations (see, for example, Jacobs & Manzi, 2000; Cowan & Marsh, 2001). Our case study of Brisford, which we explore in chapter four, offers a particularly clear illustration of the power of these monitoring standards on the routine operations of a Homeless Persons' Unit.

The Introduction Of Internal Review To Homelessness Law

Since the Franks report (1957), there has been a broad trend within the UK's welfare system towards informal mechanisms for seeking redress of grievances. The development of tribunals, the introduction of ombudsmen and complaints systems under the Citizen's Charter, together with more recent shifts in the civil court system towards the use of mediation and conciliation services, are manifestations of this trend. However, there are strong grounds for doubting whether we should account for the existence of internal review as part of this trend. The informal dispute resolution movement within administrative justice has been marked by the introduction of *additional* forms of dispute resolution. However, internal review is better conceived as a preliminary disputing stage, internal to an organisation, which mimics external review. The temptation to explain the rise of internal review as a planned feature of a coherent system of administrative justice should probably be resisted—certainly in relation to homelessness law. As we noted in chapter one, Sainsbury (2000) has made the persuasive point that the administrative justice system for social security is the product of piecemeal developments on the back of ad hoc political and practical pressures, rather than the outcome of a grand or principled design. On close inspection, the introduction of internal review to homelessness law seems to be no different. The genesis of the internal review procedure to homelessness law lies in a peculiar marriage of two very different policy concerns.

The first focused on the plight of the homeless applicant as the subject of the administrative process. A research study (Niner, 1989) had made a forceful statement that:

> [local] authorities should seek to redress the very weak position the homeless are forced into by the absence of appeal procedures, denial of choice in rehousing, single offer policies and so on. Well-publicised procedures for appeal ... seem an essential minimum basis on which to build better relationships with the client. (1989:103)

This suggestion was adopted in the 1991 Code of Guidance which 'recommended that authorities should have in place arrangements to review decisions on homelessness cases where an applicant wishes to appeal against the decision' (para 9.6). Although caution should be exercised in linking cause and effect around the rise in internal review mechanisms (Halliday, 2001), it seems likely that the Code of Guidance had an impact in that 58 per cent of local authorities developed written internal appeal procedures. This represented a doubling of the number of such mechanisms in existence since 1986 (Mullins et al, 1996: 38). There was, however, considerable variability of practice on internal appeals, some being extremely weak in terms of principles of administrative justice (Cowan with Fionda, 1998).

The second policy concern, however, focused on the plight of the High Court as the subject of an inflated judicial review workload. Considerable disquiet had been expressed by the judiciary about the volume of judicial review cases in homelessness. In a much-cited part of his judgment in the *Puhlhofer* case, Lord Brightman expressed concern at the

> prolific use of judicial review for the purpose of challenging the performance of local authorities of their [homelessness] functions. ... I think that great judicial restraint should be exercised in giving leave to proceed by judicial review ... [I]t is not, in my opinion, appropriate that the remedy of judicial review, which is a discretionary remedy, should be made use of to monitor the actions of local authorities under the Act save in the exceptional case. ([1986] 1 All ER 467, 474)

Subsequent research demonstrated, in fact, that the concern about the use of judicial review in homelessness cases was misplaced. Sunkin (1987) reported that there had been just 66 applications for leave in 1985. By 1992, the level of applications for leave to apply for judicial review had risen to around 400

(Bridges et al, 1995: 28-9). Expressed as a percentage, the proportion of unsuccessful applicants which used judicial review was less than three per cent (this does not include potential local connection or suitability cases). Further, there was evidence to suggest that some local authorities were using the leave stage to filter out applications, caving in just before the leave hearing (*ibid*, p 120). Nevertheless, despite this empirical data, the Government's 1994 Consultation Paper repeated concerns about the 'substantial number of cases in which there is an application for judicial review' and consulted on whether local authorities should be required to have their own 'appeals mechanisms for handling disputes' (DoE, 1994: para 16). The introduction of internal review which followed was part of a dual strategy to relieve the pressure on the High Court. The County Court was granted jurisdiction to hear appeals on points of law from aggrieved homeless applicants, with the aim of substantially reducing the judicial review workload. Significantly, homeless applicants must go through the internal review process before an appeal to the County Court is possible.

THE LEGAL PROVISIONS

Homelessness law is found in Part VII of the Housing Act 1996 (amendments made by the Homelessness Act 2002 are not dealt with here). Part VII is quite short, amounting to only 29 sections. However, these sections (and their predecessors) have given rise to so much litigation that the leading textbook on the subject has a twelve page closely typed table of cases (Arden & Hunter, 1997). The Code of Guidance issued by the Secretary of State to local authorities was at the time of fieldwork over 100 pages long and had eight annexes (DoE, 1996, as subsequently revised). There are also a number of Statutory Instruments. Homelessness law, despite inhabiting just a small corner of the statute books, has become very detailed and highly complex. The aim of this section, however, is to set out only the very basics of the legal provisions so that the technical legal detail in the empirical data becomes intelligible. Those with a deeper interest in homelessness law per se are referred to more detailed legal works (Arden & Hunter, 1997; Robson & Poustie, 1996).

In the rest of this book, we make a distinction between two functions of the HPU: (1) assessments decision-making, and (2) allocations decision-making. These correspond to two elements of homelessness law: (1) rules about entitlements to housing duties, and (2) the provisions about the nature of the housing duties owed to 'successful' applicants. These will be explored in turn before turning to the specific provisions about internal review

Entitlement: Assessments Decision-Making

The rules of entitlement (assessments decision-making) dictate which persons are entitled to the long-term housing duty. They have been referred to as an 'obstacle race' which applicants must successfully negotiate in order to win the right to housing (Robson & Watchman, 1981). Originally, there were four obstacles: homelessness, priority need, intentional homelessness, and local connection. The 1996 Act added a fifth, initial obstacle relating to 'eligibility'. These are summarised below:

Eligibility

In the context of homelessness law 'eligibility' has a particular meaning relating to immigration status. The concept did not appear in the 1977 Act and was introduced by the Asylum and Immigration Appeals Act 1993. Essentially, persons subject to immigration control are excluded altogether from assistance, unless re-included by regulations. Other persons from abroad (eg UK nationals who are not habitually resident in the UK) may be excluded by regulations. The regulations in place during the majority of the field work were contained in the Homelessness (England) Regulations 2000 (SI 2000 No 701).

Homelessness

A local housing authority must determine that an applicant is homeless before any duties can arise. The definition of homelessness has always been wider than mere rooflessness. It is defined by the 1996 Act, section 175 in three different ways:

1 A person is homeless if s/he has no accommodation anywhere in the world which s/he and her/his family unit have a legal right to occupy;
2 Even if a person has the necessary legal right s/he is homeless if s/he cannot secure entry to it (eg because of an illegal eviction by a landlord) or it consists of a moveable vehicle or vessel (eg a caravan or houseboat) and the person has nowhere which s/he is legally permitted to station it;
3 Even if a person has accommodation which s/he has the legal right to occupy it is not to be treated as accommodation unless it is accommodation which 'it would be reasonable for her/him to continue to occupy'. This brings in questions amongst others of the physical standard of accommodation. It is not reasonable for those fleeing domestic violence to continue to occupy accommodation: section 177(1).

Priority Need

Even if one is homeless, one must have a *priority* need to be owed a housing duty. The priority need categories are contained in section 189:

1 pregnant women
2 persons with dependent children
3 the vulnerable. This category is the most contested, since to qualify for housing single (childless) people must bring themselves within it. Section 189(1)(c) refers to 'a person who is vulnerable as a result of old age, mental illness or handicap or physical disability or other special reason'. A leading case on the meaning of vulnerability (*R v Waveney DC, ex p Bowers* [1983] QB 238) defines it as meaning 'less able to fend for oneself so that injury or detriment will result where a less vulnerable man will be able to cope without harmful effects'.
4 those who are homeless as a result of emergency such as fire, flood or other disaster

Intentional Homeless

A number of amendments were accepted to the 1977 Act due to concerns that the very tight Parliamentary timetable would prevent it from reaching the statute books at all. Of these perhaps the most significant was the concept of intentional homelessness, described even then as 'gobbledegook' (Loveland, 1995). Even for those applicants in priority need, the duties would be severely limited if the applicant had become homeless through his/her own fault. This concept of intentional homeless has perhaps generated the most litigation, and survives into the 1996 Act. By section 191(1) of the 1996 Act a person becomes homeless intentionally if s/he 'deliberately does or fails to do anything in consequence of which s/he ceases to occupy accommodation which is available for her/his occupation and which it would have been reasonable for her/him to continue to occupy'. Section 191(2) provides some form of defence, ie that an 'act or omission in good faith on the part of a person who was unaware of any relevant fact shall not be treated as deliberate'. The 1996 Act also added a new category of intentional homelessness (section 191(3)) which arises where a person enters into a collusive arrangement with another under which s/he is required to leave accommodation in order to obtain assistance. An example of this would arise where a landlord evicts a tenant at the tenant's behest when, if the arrangement had not been entered into, the landlord would have been happy for the tenant to remain. There was no evidence in either of the case studies that this provision had been applied to any applicants.

Local Connection

Where an applicant is eligible, homeless, in priority need and not homeless intentionally, the duty to house usually resides with the authority to whom the application has been made. Where, however, the applicant has no local connection with that authority and does have a local connection elsewhere, the housing duty may be transferred to the authority where there is such a connection, provided the applicant does not run the risk of domestic violence in that authority. Local connection is defined for these purposes by section 199 of the 1996 Act as arising where a person has a connection with the authority:

(a) because s/he is or in the past was, normally resident there, and that residence is or was of her/his own choice;
(b) because s/he is employed there;
(c) because of family associations, or
(d) because of special circumstances.

Housing Duties: Allocations Decision-Making

Successful Applicants

For those determined to be eligible, homeless, in priority need, and unintentionally homeless (referred to throughout this book as 'successful' applicants) the duty is to secure that 'suitable accommodation' is made available for a period of two years (section 193(3)). This usually entails the local authority offering its own accommodation to successful applicants, or arranging for another landlord to do so. However, this duty will cease to exist in the following circumstances:

(a) if the applicant refuses an offer of accommodation which the authority are satisfied is suitable (section 193(5));
(b) if the applicant refuses an offer of accommodation under Part VI of the 1996 Act (i.e. an offer of permanent housing from general Housing Register), which the authority are satisfied is suitable and which it was reasonable for him to accept (section 193(7)).

In either case the authority must inform the applicant of the possible consequences of refusal, and notify the applicant in the first instance that they regard the duty as having been discharged, and in the second that the accommodation was a suitable offer.

Unsuccessful Applicants

Where an applicant is in priority need but intentionally homeless the duty is also to offer advice and assistance, and in addition to secure accommodation for such period as the authority 'consider will give [the applicant] a reasonable opportunity of securing accommodation for his occupation' (section 190(2)). This duty is often interpreted by local authorities as requiring the provision of approximately four weeks' temporary accommodation.

Miscellaneous Duties

Advice and Assistance

If the applicant is eligible, homeless but not in priority need, the authority are only required to provide 'advice and such assistance as they consider appropriate in the circumstances in any attempts s/he may make to secure that accommodation becomes available' (section 192(2)). Such advice and assistance has been acknowledged by the Government to be 'variable', 'inconsistent' and sometimes of 'inadequate quality' (Standing Committee D, January 30, 2001, col 343, *per* Mr N. Raynsford, Minister of State for Environment, Transport and the Regions).

If an applicant is neither eligible nor homeless, the authority has no further duty towards him or her.

Temporary Accommodation

Temporary accommodation duties are sometimes also owed during the application process. If the authority has reason to believe that the applicant is homeless, eligible and in priority need, it must provide interim accommodation pending any decision (section 188).

Notification of Decisions

Local authorities have a duty to inform the applicant of its decision on the application for housing. The decision letter must give reasons for its decisions and set out the duties owed towards the applicant.

Internal Review

When an applicant is given an adverse initial decision, he/she must also be informed of the right to request an internal review and the time within which such a request must be made (section 184(5)). The notification requirement does not explicitly extend to cases where the internal review concerns the suitability of accommodation offered in discharge of the section 193 duty, although in practice most decision letters on this issue will include some form of notification.

Section 202(1) provides that an applicant has the right to request a review of:

(a) any decision regarding eligibility;
(b) any decision as to what duty (if any) is owed to a person found to be homeless or threatened with homelessness. This will encompass decisions as to priority need and intentionality. In *Warsame v Hounslow LBC* (1999) 32 HLR 335 the authority decided that it had no further duty towards the applicant because she had turned down a suitable waiting list offer. In this case it was held that the wording 'any decision as to what duty.... is owed' is wide enough to encompass a decision that a duty once owed, is owed no longer;
(c) various decisions relating to both whether a local connection referral can and will be made;
(d) decisions as to the suitability of any accommodation offered to an applicant in discharge of the duties to him or her.

Further details on the conduct of reviews are provided by the Allocation of Housing and Homelessness (Review Procedures and Amendment) Regulations 1999 (SI 1999 No 71). Once a request has been made, the authority must inform the applicant that s/he, or someone acting on his/her behalf, may make representations in writing in connection with the review and (if not already done) the procedure to be followed (reg 6). The regulations do not specify who must carry out the review, but regulation 2 provides that where the review is by an officer, then the officer must be someone not involved in the decision and who is senior to the original decision maker.

The request for a review must be made within 21 days of notification of the decision made under section 184. By regulation 9, notification of the review decision must be made within 8 weeks of the request for the review (10 weeks in local connection referral cases, 12 weeks where referred to referee), or such longer period as may be agreed in writing. There is then a further right to make representations:

> If the reviewer considers that there is a deficiency or irregularity in the original decision, or in the manner in which it was made, but is minded nonetheless to make a decision which is against the interests of the applicant on one or more issues, the reviewer shall notify the applicant –
> (a) that the reviewer is so minded and the reasons why; and
> (b) that the applicant, or someone acting on his behalf, may make representations to the reviewer orally or in writing or both orally and in writing (Reg 8(2))

Once the review has been completed a written decision with reasons must be given (section 203(3), (4)). Again it is treated as having been given if made available at the authority's office for a reasonable period (section 204(8)).

Housing Pending Review

Section 188(3) gives the authority a discretion whether to provide temporary accommodation pending the internal review. In some authorities, the discretion is only exercised in exceptional circumstances (*R v Camden LBC ex p Mohammed* (1997) 30 HLR 170, where such practice was upheld as lawful). In *Mohammed*, Latham J held that in exercising their discretion under s 188(3), a local authority has to balance the objective of maintaining fairness between homeless persons in circumstances where it has decided that no duty is owed to the applicant, and proper consideration of the possibility that the applicant might be right and that to deprive him of accommodation could result in the denial of entitlement. In carrying out this balancing exercise, certain matters will always require consideration, although other matters may also be relevant:

(a) the merits of the case and the extent to which it can properly be said that the decision was one which was either contrary to the apparent merits or was one which involved a very fine balance of judgement;
(b) whether consideration is required of new material, information or argument which could have a real effect on the decision under review;
(c) the personal circumstances of the applicant and the consequences of an adverse decision on the exercise of the discretion.

THE USE OF INTERNAL REVIEW

In this section we examine our existing knowledge of the practice of internal review in homelessness law. We set out our national survey findings about the uses of internal review in England and Wales.

Although the government collects statistics about the operations of Homeless Persons Units in England and Wales, it does not monitor use of the internal review process. To remedy this deficiency we conducted two national surveys: the first in January 1998 and the second in May 2001. Respondents were asked questions about the use of the internal review during the preceding six months. In the first questionnaire, the response rate achieved was 54 per cent (n=214). In the second questionnaire, the response rate achieved was 58 per cent (n=214).[1] Respondents to both surveys were

[1] This disparity is due to the ongoing reorganisation of local government in England and Wales.

geographically spread, had varying political control, and had different amounts of stock. A large number of authorities with no stock also responded (38 in 1998; 55 in 2001). The same number of London Boroughs (n=15) responded to each survey.

Volume of Internal Reviews

We asked respondents to indicate how many requests for internal reviews were received during a six month period preceding the survey. Figure 1 below sets out the data from the 2001 survey. Sixty per cent of respondents (n=121) indicated that they had five or fewer reviews (compared to 68 per cent, n=136, in the 1998 survey). Eleven per cent of local authorities (n=22) had received no requests for internal review whatsoever (compared to 20 per cent, n=42, in the 1998 survey). Sixteen per cent of respondents (n=33) had received 16 or more review requests (compared to 10 per cent, n=25, in the first survey). When these figures are placed against the volume of homelessness applications and refusals of assistance, the general take-up of rights to internal review seems very low. Generally, with over 200,000 unsuccessful homelessness applications per annum, combined with the possibility of the dissatisfaction of successful applicants (around 120,000 per annum) with their offer of accommodation, the level of reviewing activity seems much less than it might be.

Some caution, of course, must be exercised in drawing inferences from this data about the volume of review activity. How respondents answered this survey question will have been dependent on how they defined a

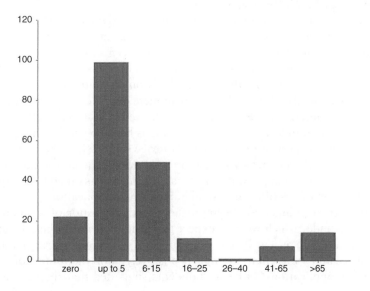

'request for internal review' (see Sainsbury and Eardley, 1991). In 1997, the Lord Chancellor's Department funded a project designed to consider both local authority and County Court activity in the Midlands region of England in homelessness cases (Atkinson et al, 1999). The qualitative data from this study demonstrated that while the statutory provisions may suggest a fairly simple linear process (adverse decision; request for review; internal review; review decision), the social reality of decision-making did not always, or even often, follow this pattern. A number of their study authorities operated an informal review process, particularly where fresh evidence was proffered by the applicant or their advisers. Indeed the study concluded that:

> there is some evidence that statutory reviews are perceived as a dysfunctional occurrence; the inevitable result of a breakdown in the 'normal', informal methods of decision making prevalent within the [Local Housing Authority] environment'.

Although the dataset underpinning this conclusion was small (observation and interviews with key personnel in eight local authorities) it urges caution in making conclusions about the level of review activity more broadly defined. Nevertheless, we may cautiously suggest that the level of challenge to initial decisions by way of requests for review is low. Most authorities have very little reviewing activity compared to the potential pool of review applicants. This finding is consistent with the position in Scotland (Halliday, 2001) and in relation to other areas of social welfare where the take-up of rights of redress is similarly low (Sainsbury & Eardley, 1991; Dalley & Berthoud, 1992; Genn 1994).

Two further points of interest emerge from our data about the incidence of internal reviews. First, although the take up of internal review is generally low, the volume of internal review requests seems to have risen recently. Between the first and second surveys, there has been a ratchet effect so that reviewing activity has slightly increased nationally (although only 20 per cent of respondents felt there had been an increase in activity in their area). Second, most internal review requests are received in London and the South-East of England. Indeed, all London Boroughs bar one which responded to our survey had experienced more than 41 reviews. Indeed, of the 14 authorities with more than 65 reviews, 12 were in London. The largest number of reviews within this sample was 261. This is of interest as other areas experience similar numbers of unsuccessful homelessness applications.

Both of these points raise the important research question of what are the conditions under which we may expect to see an increase in the take up of rights to internal review. There were suggestions from some respondents that advice and representation impacts positively upon the volume of internal review applications. Other respondents suggested that the increase in reviewing activity was due to the fact that they had made applicants aware, or more aware, of their rights to internal review. In relation to the concentration of internal review activity in London and the South-East, it might be suggested that the relative lack of alternative housing options for homelessness applicants would provide an increased impetus to challenge homelessness decisions. As we shall see in later chapters, our qualitative data demonstrates that each of these factors can indeed impact upon applicants' decisions about whether to pursue internal review. However, our findings also suggest that micro decisions about whether to pursue internal review can be complex and emerge from a constellation of various factors, including significantly, the individual's experience and interpretation of the homelessness application process and the support and advice they may (or may not) receive from family, friends, advisors, etc. The question, then, of what are the conditions under which we should expect an increase in the take up of rights to internal review becomes increasingly difficult to answer. Our research design and findings do not permit a macro analysis of trends of applicant behaviour which could adequately explain either the increase in internal review request nationally, or the concentration of review activity in London and the South-East. However, our qualitative data about the various 'barriers' to internal review should, we believe, provide a foundation from which this work might begin to be undertaken.

What are Reviews About?

Most review requests in the 2001 survey related to initial decisions about homelessness, priority need, intentional homelessness and suitability of accommodation. Seventy-four per cent of respondents had experience of review requests on intentionality; 44 per cent on priority need; 37 per cent on suitability; 36 per cent on homelessness. Between the two surveys, the most significant change was on the question of priority need. The number of local authorities reporting no reviews on priority need fell from 69 per cent in 1998 to 56 per cent in 2001. Internal reviews are rarely requested on initial decisions about eligibility and local connection (see also Halliday, 2001). Respectively, 81 per cent and 83 per cent of respondents had no experience of reviews on these issues (n=158 and 163).

Reviews on particular issues might depend on local decision-making practices. So, for example, one respondent said: 'Most of our adverse decisions are contested especially on intentionality. We make relatively few adverse decisions for PN cases—hence the relatively low number of reviews.'

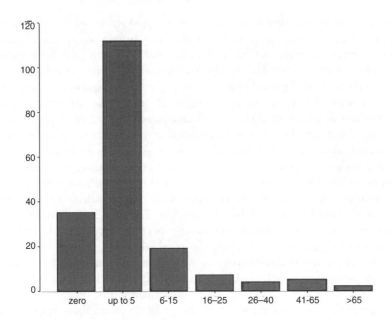

Success Rates

Figure 2 above shows the numbers of internal review requests which resulted in a successful outcome for the applicant. Similar to the numbers of review applications, success rates have slightly increased nationally between the surveys. Nineteen per cent of respondents (n=35) had no successful review applications (compared to 33 per cent, n=64, in the 1998 survey). Eighty per cent of respondents (n=147) had five or fewer successful reviews (compared to 89%, n=161, in the 1998 survey), and ten per cent of respondents (n=18) had 16 or more successful review applications (compared to 6%, n=11, in the 1998 survey).

   Once again, our quantitative data does not suggest an explanation for the increase in success rates. In open responses, a number of factors were suggested by respondents as being significant. These included: (a) member panels being more likely to overturn officer decisions; (b) concern that County Court judges were more likely to weigh in favour of applicants; (c) high quality of original decision-making; and (d) quality of representation. Our qualitative data provides some insights into the potential significance of representation, and the prospect of County Court litigation to the conduct of internal reviews. These themes are explored in later chapters.

   Another interesting point emerged from the open responses. Some respondents were critical of applicants who failed to present new information as part of the internal review request. Although these respondents recognised that such internal review applicants had a right to seek internal review, they nevertheless believed that new information was required in real terms to justify the request. This criticism reveals a conception of internal review which seems to be at odds with the aims of the scheme. We saw above that the range of homelessness decisions which may be reviewed is particularly broad. More importantly, however, applicants are not required to demonstrate 'good cause', or show that there has been a change of circumstances. The internal review is a 'second look' form of review (Sainsbury, 2000). At the mere request of the applicant, the local authority is obliged to reconsider its decision and check for mistakes. The scheme is designed to provide an accessible and cheap initial form of redress for the applicant, and a safety check for the local authority to prevent unnecessary County Court litigation. The conception of internal review evidenced in these responses to open questions and its implications for bureaucratic practice is explored further in relation to our two case studies.

Internal Review Procedures

Most reviews were conducted 'on the papers', with just 18 per cent of respondents saying that they always used oral processes. The majority of reviews were conducted by a single person. In the 2001 survey, 58 per cent of respondents conducted reviews by a single person (an increase of 7 per cent from the 1998 survey), almost always a senior officer. Some concerns were expressed by respondents, particularly in smaller districts, that the requirement to have a senior officer conduct the review was difficult to fulfil. There were also concerns that senior officers might not have the necessary expertise.

Where reviews were conducted by panels, these were more likely to be member panels. Fifty-four per cent of respondents who used a panel system were member-only panels (an increase of 8 per cent). Sometimes, member panels were used as a second tier review. Although there were some positive comments in open responses about member-only panels (particularly where members were guided by legal advice or had experience of the County Court appeals process), respondents were more often critical. Particular concerns were raised over the adequacy of training and knowledge of councillors, together with being 'sidetracked' by irrelevant information: '[members] often make decisions based on a sympathy vote, ignoring the legislation.' Where members had been removed from the process, some respondents felt liberated:

> Removing members from the process means that the review is conducted by a housing professional with reference to law, as opposed to personal/political feelings being allowed to come into play.

Third Party Advice/Assistance

Respondents were asked to estimate how often applicants were assisted by third parties in their internal reviews. Table 4 below demonstrates that levels of representation in internal review are reasonably low. Most respondents indicated that representation occurs in under one quarter of internal review cases.

Table 4: **Estimated Frequency of Representation (Lawyer and Non-Lawyer) in Internal Reviews**

	0–24%	25%–49%	50%–74%	75%–100%	No response
1998	38% (n=81)	9% (n=19)	7% (n=15)	11% (n=23)	36% (n=76)
2001	43% (n=93)	14% (n=31)	14% (n=31)	15% (n=33)	12% (n=26)

Representation from a lawyer is even less frequent, as Table 5 below demonstrates:

Table 5: **Estimated Frequency of Representation by Lawyer in Internal Reviews**

	0–24%	25%–49%	50%–74%	75%–100%	No response
1998	56% (n=119)	4% (n=8)	3% (n=6)	4% (n=8)	34% (n=73)
2001	68% (n=145)	7% (n=16)	8% (n=18)	5% (n=10)	12% (n=25)

Respondents were also invited to comment on the significance of third party advice and assistance to the conduct of internal reviews. Views were mixed. Good quality legal representation was said to be both useful to the review process and the reviewer. One respondent made clear that 'very few [applicants] present logical argument as to why they view the initial negative decision as flawed.' Particular praise was made of certain advisers (especially Shelter). Concern was expressed by some respondents about the lack of good quality advice available in their areas relative to neighbouring areas. However, other respondents were critical of, or sceptical about third party assistance. Some respondents suggested that applicants were encouraged to use the process by advisers only because of advisers' desire for legal aid funding. Other negative comments reflected upon (a) the limited knowledge of some lawyers (some of whom were reported as being unaware of the change in legislation), (b) the adversarial and occasionally aggressive approach of lawyers, (c) lawyers being overly concerned with technicalities rather than establishing the facts, and (d) solicitors' taking on 'no hope' cases.

County Court Appeals

In addition to the take-up rate of internal reviews being quite low, the drop-out rate *after* internal review seems to be quite high. Most respondents (75 per cent) had no experience of the County Court appeal process which unsuccessful review applicants are entitled to use. Six respondents had experience of between six and eighteen appeals. One local authority had 60 County Court appeals. This seems to confirm the findings of a smaller survey of Homeless Persons' Units by Atkinson et al (1999) (n=69) which also noted a high drop-out rate, and is consistent with findings in other areas of social welfare (Sainsbury & Eardley, 1991; Dalley & Berthoud, 1992).

CONCLUSION

In this chapter we have offered some basic contextual details concerning internal review and homelessness law in order to provide the reader with sufficient knowledge to understand and interpret in an informed way the empirical data which follows.

The history of homelessness law and its contemporary implementation by local authorities must be understood in the light of broader political contexts regarding social housing and public administration. The introduction of internal review to homelessness law must be understood more specifically in relation to concerns about the administration of justice in the High Court, and the welfare of the homeless applicants as the subjects of bureaucratic administration. The internal review process was intended to provide a local, immediate and simple form of grievance mechanism for homeless applicants—one which would detect and remedy deficiencies in initial decision-making and so reduce the extent to which the external review by courts was required. It seems reasonable to anticipate that within this scheme of grievance processes the take-up of internal review would be reasonably high, with a subsequent withering of cases proceeding to County Court and thence to the Court of Appeal. However, as we saw above, the take-up of rights to internal review on a national basis is actually quite low and comparable to the level of applications for leave to apply for judicial review prior to the 1996 Act. Further, the drop out rate after internal review and before County Court is very high. The combination of a low take-up rate and high drop-out rate significantly increases the empirical significance of internal review as a component of the overall machinery of administrative justice for homeless applicants. It also constitutes an unexpected policy dilemma and raises one of the central research questions of this book; namely why applicants fail to pursue their grievance rights. This and other research issues are explored in depth in later chapters. First, however, the decision-making practices of our case study local authorities are described in the chapters which follow.

3

Southfield Council

INTRODUCTION

Having described in the previous chapter the legal and political context of local authority homelessness decision-making and presented some national survey data about the use of internal review, we set out in this chapter to provide a more detailed picture about the operations in one of our field sites: Southfield Council ('Southfield'). Southfield is a large urban area in England. The Homeless Persons' Unit of Southfield Council is a large, busy and, as we shall see below, complex organisation.

The chapter has two broad aims. First, we provide an overview of the different teams which make up the Southfield's Homeless Persons' Unit ('HPU') and of the flow of the various stages which make up the overall homelessness application process. This allows us to understand the structure of the bureaucratic organisation which homeless applicants encounter when applying for housing. Our second aim, however, is to place the HPU under the microscope and to provide a deeper and richer description of its decision-making practices and culture. This data provides a more nuanced picture of how decisions are made, what influences the decision-making processes and the constraints within which the bureaucratic organisation must operate. The intricate picture we paint of Southfield is a valuable study of welfare decision-making in and of itself. More importantly, however, for the purposes of this book it is necessary in order to contextualise our analysis of applicants' reasons for failing to seek internal review of 'negative' decisions. One of the fundamental contentions of this book is that a proper understanding of citizens' pursuit of administrative grievances, and failure to pursue them, against official bureaucracies requires an examination of the relationship between the citizen and the bureaucracy which is played out in the application process. Our ethnographic descriptions of the welfare bureaucracies of Southfield and Brisford are, then, a necessary part of the process of understanding the non-emergence of disputes.

ASSESSMENTS DECISION-MAKING

In this section we explore the various processes whereby decisions about entitlement to housing under homelessness law are made: 'assessments' decision-making. The Homeless Persons' Unit of Southfield City Council is a complex and fragmented organisation. Assessments about entitlement to housing are made by four separate teams of officers. Applications from people with children are dealt with by the Families Team. Applications from single women are considered by the Women's Team. Applications from single men (or childless couples) are dealt with by either the Men's Residential Team or the Men's Casework Team.

The history of this fragmentation lies in Southfield's development of a 'singles homelessness strategy' approximately 15 years prior to fieldwork. Prior to this policy development, single homeless people were offered temporary accommodation in one of two run down Victorian hostels. These were replaced by two new residential units—one for men and the other for women. The staff from the old hostels were transferred over to the new residential units and the job of assessing homelessness applications from single people or childless couples was taken away from the centralised homeless person's units and given to the new residential units. The singles homelessness strategy also entailed an open and generous homelessness policy towards the single homeless—more generous than the provisions of homelessness law itself. Any single person (or childless couple), regardless of formal priority need status, could approach one of the residential units and receive assistance with housing. Homelessness law was thereby marginalised in the routine provision of services to single homeless people. More recently, however, this marginalisation was lessened to an extent in relation to single male applicants. Southfield created a Men's Casework Team in order to take on some of the more difficult cases within the Men's Residential workload, and to improve the legal quality of decision-making. A senior officer and five caseworkers from the Families Team were, accordingly, transferred to the Men's Residential Unit.

The functional fragmentation described above is matched by a 'cultural' differentiation between the teams. In the sections below, we describe the various processes of 'assessments' decision-making. The differences in decision-making culture can be understood within the context of the history of functional differentiation set out above. These themes will be explored in greater detail below. However, before we embark on this task, some explanation must be given of the methods we use to present the data about Southfield's decision-making practices (and, in due course in the following chapter, those of Brisford Council).

Contrasting Models of Decision-Making

In the sections below we describe and compare the decision-making cultures of the different teams within the homeless person's unit, looking initially at assessments decision-making within the Men's Residential Unit. This portrays both the complex social reality of homelessness decision-making within Southfield, and also assists with an explanation of the various reasons for applicants' failure to take up their right of internal review or their pursuit of that right. In contrasting the decision-making practices between the various teams of Southfield's homeless person's unit, we employ two related sets of ideal types as an heuristic device. These are idealised, descriptive accounts of how decision-makers arrive at decision-outcomes. Both sets comprise opposing end points of a continuum, and so represent opposite extremes. We would expect social reality, of course, to be located at some point between extremes and for there to be evidence of both styles of decision-making, though with one style being dominant. The first set of ideal types relates to the method of arriving at a decision-outcome. The second set concerns the nature of the relationship between the officer and the applicant. Table 6 below summarises the characteristics of each set.

In the first set, we contrast 'pre-emptive' decision-making with 'inquisitorial' decision-making. Pre-emptive decision-making involves the decision-maker coming to an immediate and preliminary assessment of the decision-outcome on the basis of a limited and pre-existing knowledge base (for example, databases about previous homelessness applications, previous tenancy files, applicant characteristics, etc) which are used to satisfy the criteria for the decision (for example, need, desert, tenantability, etc). The inquiry is then limited to the confirmation of the factors which inform the preliminary assessment of the decision-outcome. The decision-maker controls the interview and the flow of information gained from it in order to achieve this confirmation. Inquisitorial decision-making, in contrast, involves the decision-maker suspending judgement until all relevant information has been obtained. Although the decision-maker is the ultimate arbiter of what is 'relevant' (informed by criteria laid down in legislation and policies) he cedes substantial control of the interview and allows the applicant to tell her story in her own terms. The inquiry here is open and geared towards gathering as much information as is practicable to inform the decision about whether the decision-making criteria have been fulfilled.

Second, and related to the above, there are ideal types relating to the officer-applicant relationship. At one end of this continuum there is an authoritarian relationship between the bureaucrat and the applicant. Here, the bureaucrat controls the interactions between himself and the applicant. The bureaucrat maintains a strict divide between himself and the applicant whereby the applicant is pitted against the bureaucrat in representing and advancing her interests. At the other end of the continuum we find a co-operative relationship between officer and applicant. In this relationship, the investigation is a collaborative effort between the officer and applicant, though the responsibility for decision-making remains with the officer. The relationship is marked by openness and trust.

Table 6: Ideal Types of Bureaucratic Decision-Making

Pre-emptive Decision-making	Inquisitorial Decision-making
• Quick assessment	• Suspended judgement
• Limited knowledge base	• Wide knowledge base
• Investigate to confirm	• Investigate to find out
• Control of Interview	• Cede control of interview
Authoritarian Relationship	**Co-operative Relationship**
• Officer control of interactions	• Collaborative investigation
• Adversarial positioning	• Openness and Trust

Single Men And Childless Couples: Residential Team

The Physical Environment

The Residential Unit is a small, modern building situated about a mile away from Southfield's city centre. Most of the windows are protected by metal grilles. There is one entrance to the building through a locked security door which is opened by staff when someone presses the buzzer. In addition to being the place where homeless applications are made, the residential unit is also a 33 bedded hostel. The office accommodation is housed on the ground floor and the bedrooms are located on the first, second and third floors. On entering the residential unit, applicants are separated from the receptionist by a glass security window with metal strengthening, the security of which had been upgraded after a violent incident. The window is sealed and applicants speak to the receptionist, usually an administrative officer, through a microphone and an amplifier system. The acoustics are poor and applicants often find that they have to raise their voice to be heard by the receptionist. There are a number of interview rooms on the ground floor. These also have security screens between the applicant and the interviewer, with a window about two foot long and one foot wide through which officer-applicant interactions take place.

This physical environment reflects the team's belief that the type of applicant they now deal with tends to be more problematic than before, often exhibiting multiple problems.

The Staff

The residential unit is staffed 24 hours a day. There are 16 residential officers, two deputy team leaders, and one team leader. The residential officers perform a dual role. They are responsible for the management of the hostel on a day-to-day basis—'residential work'—but are also engaged in the receiving and determination of homelessness applications—'casework'. The residential officers work a complex shift system which is based upon an eight week cycle. This system means that casework and individual applications sometimes have to be shared between residential officers. The longevity of staff, on average, is about five years.

There is a tension experienced by the Residential Team between their residential work and casework responsibilities. There were concerns at management and officer level that residential officers are unable to do both parts of the job satisfactorily:

> they have that role of trying to deliver support to the residents here as well as try and administer that homelessness legislative framework, as well as working a shift system. And what I find is that's virtually impossible, something has to give. And over the years what's happened is people haven't been doing the investigations very properly. (**Senior Officer**)

This tension was exacerbated by the different demands of those applicants staying at the unit, together with the increasing numbers of applicants.

The Application Process

On arrival at the residential unit, all applicants are required to answer certain standard questions about themselves—their name, date of birth, last address and their reason for leaving it. Theoretically, every person who comes to the hostel is required to have a homelessness assessment conducted before they are provided with temporary accommodation, even if they are only seeking temporary accommodation. During the fieldwork period, it became apparent that some applicants did not know that they had made a homelessness application, an observation which was acknowledged by the Team Leader.

A number of standard checks about the applicant are made before the interview takes place. There are three main 'checks'. First, a search is made of the computerised database of previous homelessness applications to see if the applicant has applied before. Second, a check is made of the exclusions database—a list of individuals who have been highlighted by the Council as being unsuitable for future tenancies. Third, a check of the Housing Benefit's computerised database is made to confirm the applicant's address and details for housing benefit purposes.

The exclusions database is a crucial feature of Southfield's overall homelessness decision-making processes and requires some explanation. It is a database containing the details of past tenants where (a) there has been more than £100 rent arrears; (b) any neighbour nuisance issues exist; and (c) other concerns exist, such as damage to property. It is unclear exactly how many individuals are listed on the database. There were suggestions in our follow-up interviews that approximately 50 per cent of homeless applicants are listed. Another officer estimated that there are 29,000 entries and that it is larger in scale than the general housing register. The scale of the database is matched by its significance to homelessness decision-making and, as we shall see below, helps us account for the organisational paradox that, despite the ready availability of single persons' accommodation in Southfield, a sizeable proportion of single male applicants are nevertheless being rejected.

The purpose of the database is to prevent 'problematic' individuals from being rehoused by the council—or at least not until (where possible) they have addressed and resolved their problematic behaviour. It was an exercise in risk management, as a senior officer explained:

> It's a mechanism by which you can flag up people who have had problematic tendencies in the past so that you can have a possible indication of any life problems should they have a tenancy again... So there's a whole sort of number of things that we would look at associated to someone's past that might be warning signals for future things to watch for should they have a tenancy again... It's about how we manage tenancies and it's about what risk people might be and how we minimise that risk.

Decisions about whether an individual can address his problematic behaviour—to override the database—are made by a senior officer of the Homeless Person's Unit in conjunction with a senior officer of the unit which registered the applicant in the first place (for example, a district housing manager). So, for example, if applicants have rent arrears, they are generally required either to clear the arrears or to make an arrangement to do so before they can be rehoused—unless the level of arrears are considered to be prohibitively high.

However, some of the reasons for entry on the database relate to past behaviour which is more difficult to redeem—abandonment of tenancies, anti-social behaviour, drug-related behaviour, violence and so on. The difficulties associated with removal of an individual's name from the database and the consequences of inclusion on it for future housing, accounts for why some officers regarded it as a 'blacklist'. Problematically, it was widely recognised within the homeless person's unit that the quality of the data on the database was not wholly reliable, containing 'weird and wonderful entries' as one officer put it.

Although it is commonly accepted that a statutory duty to house an applicant under homelessness law formally 'trumped' their database entry, the checking of the database is nevertheless a routine part of an initial interview in the Men's Residential Unit (and, indeed, the Families Team). Within the employment relationship, officer failure to check the database for each applicant is a serious offence which has previously resulted in disciplinary action.

Another key feature of decision-making within the Men's Residential Unit is the completion of a declaration about certain previous offences. Unlike the preliminary checks, this declaration is completed as part of the initial interview, though its function is closely tied to that of the exclusions database. The declaration requires a applicant to self-declare whether they or a member of their 'moving group have been convicted of any serious offences that have not yet been spent'. The form gives a list of the offences that are taken into account, ranging from violent offences to sexual offences as well as including drugs offences, certain vehicle-related offences, burglary and kidnap.

An applicant who signs the declaration with 'yes' to any of these offences is then required to fill in a box headed 'Please state in your own words why you would no longer be a risk to your neighbour or community'. A file is prepared and sent for discussion at a multi-agency panel. This panel is made up of personnel from the Police, Probation, Social Services and Housing. It makes a decision about whether to register the applicant on the exclusions database based upon the perceived risk of re-offending. The declaration, then, is the twin of the exclusions database. In combination, these two tools comprise Southfield's most apparent risk management strategy.

Decision-Making Mode

The checking of the exclusions database and the other databases, combined with the completion of the declaration, operate to set up a presumption about the applicant's chances of success. Indeed, the Men's Residential Team's mode of conducting inquiries can be characterised as 'pre-emptive' in that the residential officers generally rely heavily on these 'checks' to construct a presumption about the housing application's outcome—akin to an adversarial burden of proof. Often, residential officers enter the inter-view room with a clear sense of whether assistance will be offered, or quickly come to that conclusion on completion of the declaration.

Dominant Discourses in Decision-Making Practices

This is not to say that these presumptions about character and past behav-iour are being applied to the categories of homelessness law in order to assess the applicant's chances of success. In relation to the Men's Residential Team, homelessness law is still marginalised in the overall assessments process. Southfield enjoys a surplus of single person's accommodation and so is in a position to exercise considerable 'generosity' towards single homeless men.

This surplus of housing stock dramatically decreases the significance of law to routine decision-making. Of the approximately 1,300 applications made in 1999–2000, 289 were awarded a discretionary duty (22 per cent), which was more than those who were owed a full duty (n = 218). Unlike homelessness decision-making examined in previous research (see, for example, Loveland, 1995; Cowan, 1997), Southfield is not forced to act as a reluctant gatekeeper because of a resource deficit, only allowing through those with legally defined need. Rather, it acts as a gatekeeper in terms of the *tenantability* of applicants. Formal decision-letters are, of course, issued. These are framed in terms of the law. And officers are aware of the legal categories, employing them in their decisions.

However, the *substance* of the Residential Team's decision-making is not about homelessness law, but rather about its 'discretionary housing scheme'. Under this scheme, applicants are offered long-term housing *despite* the fact that there is no legal obligation to do so. Indeed, the residential officers receive little training in homelessness law. Particularly in relation to single men, the presumption is that most applicants are not in priority need. However, in terms of the decision-making task of the residential officer, this lack of legal need is not of great significance. For some time in Southfield, the priority need status of single homeless men has not been pertinent to applicants' chances of housing. Instead, what really matters is whether the applicant fits Southfield's own criteria for discretionary housing—which revolves around past culpability as an indicator of future tenantability. This is why the preliminary checks of the exclusions database and the completion of the declaration are so crucial to the routine operations of the residential officer.

It is no surprise, then, that applicants' perceptions of the initial interview were that their chances of housing hinged upon their past behaviour and criminal history:

> they asked for a bit like [about my housing circumstances], but it was mainly offences and all that. ... Its like they have no time for me, sort of thing... I had an interview here that lasted all of five minutes, you know what I mean, and didn't ask me really anything about how I felt or anything like that, it was more like 'what have you been to jail for?' and all that. (**Interview S12**)

> she just told me [the decision] over the interview. She said 'Right, you've got violence in your record and we can't, can't house you.' (**Interview S2**)

Of course, we are not suggesting that the Residential Team never find applicants to be in priority need or intentionally homeless, or that homelessness law is of no significance whatsoever. Rather, we are suggesting that, generally speaking, homelessness law is marginalised in the assessment process—particularly, as we shall see below, in comparison to the other teams within the homeless person's unit—and that the discretionary housing decision is of greater practical significance to residential officers' daily routine decision-making. The core discourses of culpability and tenantability are picked up by applicants and, as we shall see below, helps explain why some of them feel that there is no point in pursuing internal review.

Decision-Letters

Decision-letters are formulaic and legalistic. They are written and signed by residential officers, about 10 per cent of which are subsequently checked by senior officers as part of a monitoring role. A stock formulation test is used in the vast majority of 'non-priority' letters, with no additional reasoning particular to the applicant provided:

> Having considered all of your circumstances, we have decided that you are not less able to fend for yourself as a homeless person, or in finding and keeping accommodation, so that you are not likely to suffer injury or detriment, in circumstances where a less vulnerable person would be able to cope without harmful effects. Your difficulties are not of an unusual degree of gravity, therefore, you do not have a priority need for housing.

It was clear that few if any applicants understood such decision-letters:

> Well, I read to there, reason for decision considered (mumbling) (...) as a homeless person. What do they mean? You see, I don't understand that, you are not less as a homeless person, able to fend for yourself as a homeless person? (**Interview S2**)

Instead, applicants make sense of Southfield's decisions by focusing on their personal interactions with officers and the messages conveyed expressly and impliedly in those encounters. As we noted above, this often leads to misunderstanding about the basis of the homelessness decision and acts as a barrier to the take-up of internal review. This is a theme to which we will return in greater detail in chapter five.

Some decision-letters are retained at the Residential Unit on the basis that there is no known address for the applicant. In these cases, it appears that applicants do not receive written notification of Southfield's decision, which includes information about the right to internal review. We observed also that some files had no decision-letter attached to them. One is therefore left with an uncomfortable feeling in such cases that, unless the applicant either re-presents or contacts the Residential Unit again, they might not discover the decision in their case, let alone know that they have a right to review it.

Single Men And Childless Couples: Casework Team

One of the peculiarities of Southfield's homeless person's unit is that homeless applications from single male applicants (or childless couples) are dealt with by two separate decision-making teams. As we saw above, the Casework Team was created in order to introduce a stronger legal element to homelessness decision-making. It was also created to assist the Residential Team with a high volume of cases.

Physical Environment

The Casework Team is situated in an adjunct building to Southfield's Town Hall. It is approximately a 25 minute walk from this building to the Residential Unit. There is insufficient space for the Casework Team to be housed in the Unit, so the Casework Team officers conduct interviews in the Residential Unit, but do their office work in their own building.

Staff

During fieldwork, there were six caseworkers in the Casework Team (four full time and two part time), one Deputy Team Leader, and one Team Leader.

Application Process

Unlike the residential officers, the Casework Team officers do not undertake any residential work. Their sole remit is to administer homelessness applications. In theory, the Casework Team are supposed to take on the 'difficult' applications. In practice, however, most applicants are interviewed on the basis of which officer was available to interview the next in line. So, although some cases are allocated to the Casework Team because of perceived complexity, most cases are allocated randomly between the Casework Team and the Residential Team.

Decision-Making Mode

Although the Casework Team's decision-making practices can be characterised as being pre-emptive (relying heavily on the use of the exclusions database), they are less so than those of the Residential Team. The Casework Team officers adopt a less authoritarian interviewing style. They explain what is being written and its meaning. They are also more aware of the legality of homelessness decision-making. As we noted above, that was the purpose of the Casework Team's creation. Further, their decisions have to be ratified by their senior officer (unlike the Residential Team where a small sample of decisions are scrutinised by a senior officer ex post facto). This monitoring technique offers greater potential for the significance of legality to the Casework Team's decisions.

Nevertheless, pre-emptive decision-making is still the dominant model of decision-making behaviour. Casework Team officers generally spoke in their focus group of the 'gut feelings' they have when interviewing applicants, which is generated by practical experience of interviewing applicants:

> You normally get a feel within the first interview of what the applicant's like and you do go off what they're saying. When they come to saying the reasons for their homelessness … I think we, well, obviously we've practiced. The fact that we've been in the job, you do get a feel of whether someone really does want that re-housing. You know, they'll come out with priority need, things like that, and it comes across whether they're a heavy drinker or a drug user. (**Casework Team Focus Group**)

Dominant Discourses in Decision-Making Practices

Similarly, the discourses of culpability and tenantability are apparent in their routine operations. Although formally at the end of each file questions are framed in terms of the requirements of the homelessness legislation, the enquiries seem to be aimed at a rather different question—would this applicant make a good tenant? Thus, the types of issues which are probed relate, for example, to previous offending histories and drug use. In short, although the Casework team can be placed in a less extreme position along the continuum, their routine decision-making practices can still be characterised as being pre-emptive, and their relationships with applicants as authoritarian.

Decision-Letters

Decision letters are prepared by caseworkers but signed by the Deputy Team Leader, a process which operated as a form of quality control of decision-making. They tended to be framed in similar terms to those of the Families Team below, being legalistic and formal in tone.

Single Women

The Physical Environment

Homelessness applications from single women are considered by the Women's Team. The Women's Team is similarly based in a Residential Unit. This Unit has a comparable number of bedrooms to the Men's Residential

Unit. There are also three interview rooms and a canteen. Unlike the Men's Residential Unit, however, the interview rooms do not contain a partition to separate the officer and applicant. Instead, they contain two easy chairs facing each other with no barriers between them. This open interviewing environment is characteristic of the co-operative approach adopted by the Women's Team to the processing of applications.

The Staff

The team has one Team Leader, two Deputy Team Leaders, and 17 officers. All staff are women. There is a considerable longevity amongst officers, some of whom have been there since the Residential Unit was set up, and who worked previously in the old Victorian hostel. Generally, the officers have a background in lodging and residential work, although staff have also been appointed from, for example, the prison service.

The Application Process

Unlike the position at the Men's Residential Unit, only the briefest information is taken from the applicant at reception and no forms are completed at this stage. If there is no officer available to see a new applicant, she will be told to wait in the canteen until one is available. Waiting time is generally short. Prior to the interview, computer checks do not generally take place. It is at the post-interview enquiry stage that the various computer checks are made on applicants, specifically looking for rent arrears, previous tenancies, and any history of anti-social behaviour. The initial interview itself is also short in comparison to other teams within Southfield's homeless person's units. However, in sharp contrast to decision-making in the Men's Residential Unit, the initial interview is only the first short step of a longer ongoing process of inquiry. Applicants were continuously observed during their stay in the Residential Unit, for example, for signs of use of drugs and alcohol or mental health issues. The content of the application form is continuously added to over time during the applicant's stay as the applicant provides additional information. Pertinent questions can be asked after the initial interview and the officers are thereby able to build up a 'more accurate picture'.

Decision-Making Mode

Underlying the inquiry process is a flexible attitude towards the legislation, described as 'leniency'. Officers indicated that they do not want to turn people away and let applicants make repeat applications 'until we get it right'. Flexibility or leniency means that, similar to the position in the Men's

Residential Unit, homelessness law is marginalised in the application process:

> sometimes we make judgments based on what we would view as a good quality of life... some of it comes from feminist politics as well. (**Women's Team Officer**)

As in the case of the Men's Residential Unit, this approach is enabled by the ready availability of single persons' accommodation in Southfield. However, there are very marked differences between the approaches of the Women's and Men's teams to the determination of applications. Whereas decision-making in the Men's Residential Unit can be characterised as being pre-emptive and authoritarian, decision-making in the Women's Unit should be characterised as being inquisitorial and co-operative, although the applicant might not be aware of this continuous process. This approach emerges from the team's identification with feminist politics and the ultimate goal of assisting women to meet their housing need. Indeed, even where the Women's Team refuse assistance, applicants are usually helped into other accommodation to solve their immediate homelessness issue. The ability to achieve this goal is curtailed by the familiar concerns of Southfield Council about tenantability, but the Women's Team's method of determining whether they can help is markedly different to that of the Men's teams, perhaps because they have a smaller caseload of less difficult groups. The longitudinal approach to decision-making allows the applicant to divulge information in a more naturalistic fashion, and the relationship between the applicant and the officer is marked by co-operation and the building of trust.

Dominant Discourses in Decision-Making Practices

Crucially, however, the longitudinal and co-operative decision-making mode offers the officers time to assist the applicant to address problems which may impinge on her tenantability. The goal of meeting the women's housing need entails a collaborative effort between officer and applicant at challenging and addressing the applicants' previous behaviour and current difficulties. If the applicant demonstrates over time that she has addressed previous problems, discretionary housing can be offered. If, however, she fails to do so, Southfield will not offer assistance itself, but will try to arrange assistance from outside the Council. The significance of the exclusions database as an indicator of potential tenantability problems is clear:

> if somebody was on the [exclusions database] and they was on it just for arrears say, we would look at well how much are the arrears and is the person willing to sort of try and resolve that... If it's not as straightforward as that,

which can often be the case if it's an applicant who has, is on the [exclusions database] due to antisocial behaviour, due to damage, really high arrears, if they're not willing to address it or engage with us about it, we would provide them with interim accommodation. I mean for example it might be here initially, and we would transfer them to interim accommodation for a more long-term period and try and monitor how they got on there. In those instances, the cases I can think of that fall into that category, we tend to end up not rehousing them because those applicants tend to be quite chaotic, and they might just leave the interim accommodation that we've provided for them and just go off and then we won't know about them until they come to us in crisis the next time. (**Women's Team Officer**)

The application process in the Women's Residential Unit and the building of a relationship between officer and applicant can, accordingly, be characterised as therapeutic, but also disciplining.

Decision-Letters

Decision-letters are formal and legalistic in tone. However, as in the Men's Residential Team, applicants are usually informed about the decision prior to receipt of a formal decision-letter. This is an aspect of the co-operative relationship whereby informing an applicant of a decision is part of the process of helping her address the difficulties which preclude assistance from the Council. The formal, legalistic language used in the decision-letter contrasts sharply with the informal, oral explanation given to the applicant. The applicant's understanding of her decision might, not unreasonably, be taken from this more intelligible version of the decision. Once again, a negative decision in this context usually means rejection under the discretionary housing scheme, rather than rejection under homelessness law. The reasons for rejection under the discretionary housing scheme relate to culpability and tenantability, even though rejection under homelessness law may relate to a lack of need.

Our interviews with applicants suggest that some applicants do not receive decision-letters. Indeed, none of our single female interviewees had received a decision letter. Some applicants are excluded from the Residential Unit before or during their application because of violent or threatening behaviour. In such cases, delivery of the decision letter is problematic:

They're issued with an eviction letter and quite often they don't, because of the way that they leave here, they don't leave a forwarding address and therefore we can't forward a decision letter. (**Women's Team Officer**)

Where decision-letters are not received, there is a suspicion that at least some of these applicants are not informed about their right to internal

review. Although officers indicated that they would verbally inform applicants about their right, our interviewees were unaware of the right. These
are themes to which we return later.

Families

The Physical Environment

The Families Team is housed within Southfield's main Council Building.
Applicants' initial contact with the Families Team is via the reception. The
reception is a large room with a line of chairs around its periphery. One
corner is screened off for use by the on-duty clerical officer. The reception is
monitored by closed circuit surveillance cameras. The interview rooms used
by the Families Team contain a round table in each. There are no partitions
separating caseworkers and applicants. All parties sit round the open table.

The Staff

The team is staffed by one principal officer, two senior officers and 10 caseworkers. In addition, there are four clerical officers who operate the reception and are managed by a clerical supervisor, as well as one part-time
finance officer.

The Application Process

Caseworkers see new applicants on a rota basis. Usually, the routine
computer checks are made of the applicant prior to the first interview, just
as in the Men's Residential Unit. The initial interviews are structured by the
process of completing a full housing application form. The first two pages
of the form record simple information about the applicant: name; presenting address; housing tenure of last address; details of landlord/mortgagor;
family composition, etc. The remaining pages are entitled 'Statement given
by applicant' and are left blank. The caseworker fills these in having asked
the applicant about why they require assistance and their recent housing
history. Additional forms or declarations are also completed at the initial
interview. First, the applicant selects three areas within the Southfield
district within which they are prepared to live. Second, the applicant signs
the declaration of previous offences.

One of the most time consuming aspects of the caseworker's initial
encounter with the homeless applicant is the provision of temporary accommodation pending the outcome of the application and (potentially) allocations processes. Homeless applicants often require emergency temporary
accommodation. However, during fieldwork there was a shortage of available

temporary accommodation for families. This meant that it was becoming harder (and more time consuming) to secure a temporary accommodation placement. Many of the caseworkers described the situation as one of 'crisis'.

Decision-Making Mode

Decision-making in the Families team should be characterised as pre-emptive. Like the Casework Team of the Men's Residential Unit caseworkers rely on their 'gut feelings' and their experience to inform them of the likely chances of an applicant's success—'professional intuition' (Halliday, 2000a). Similarly, the relationship between the caseworkers and the applicants is authoritarian. As we saw above, interviews and enquiries are conducted under pressure of time, naturally militating towards officer control of interactions with applicants. However, in general, the Families team is less pre-emptive and less authoritarian than the Casework Team of the Men's Residential Unit. Although officers rely on gut feelings and organisational suspicion, the combination of their welfarism and their commitment to legality (discussed below) inclines towards a greater openness and suspended judgement about potential decision-outcomes.

Dominant Discourses in Decision-Making Practices

The decision-making practices of the Families Team can be characterised by the twin discourses of welfarism and legality. Caseworkers regard themselves as welfare-oriented in their approach to homeless applicants. However, the sense of increased work pressure acts as a constraint on their sympathetic approach. Caseworkers have less time to spend with applicants, less time and patience to cope with difficult applicants, as well as less time and opportunity to find temporary accommodation with which applicants are content. The general pressure of time experienced by caseworkers is transposed onto some applicants' experiences of the application process, particularly in relation to having to choose areas for long-term housing. Interview S27 had applied to the Families team over 10 years previously, but found her experience of applying again during the fieldwork period rushed and confusing. In the following extract she describes her interview at the Families team and her confusion about choosing her housing areas:

Applicant: there are a lot of things that have changed and they have not said 'this is us now' or 'this is how things go' you know. I thought it was basically the same thing but there is one or two changes now and I weren't aware of it. Which I should have been because that is what they are there for, to make you aware of who they are, what they do, and how things go with them.

Interviewer: Did you feel that they explained stuff to you?

Applicant: No, not really, not basic, not really. Some things they did, some things... I think that they expect you to know. Sometimes people tend to think you are supposed to know and that you have got the knowledge to know. It was like a rush kind of thing as well...

The pressure on caseworkers' time also impacts on their ability to 'write up' cases. Many of the caseworkers take notes during initial interviews and then 'write up' later—sometimes in typescript. However, it is not always possible to do this written work immediately after the interview, as the focus group with officers suggested:

Caseworker 1: And, yeah, often these days it's just impossible because if you are interviewing one family after another and you know you've got another family to see straightaway, you haven't got time to, to, to get everything sorted out, you think "Oh put that to one side, go and see the next family", by the time you've, the following Monday you get round to writing it up, you hardly remember who they are. And we've got to base, base ...

Caseworker 4: Yeah, well, the names don't match do they, they're all superimposed.

Caseworker 1: Base the statement on the few, on the, what you've written down but, you know, you're pressurised 'cos you know you've got another family, one family after another to see, and I mean like five in a day is ... it's happening now, you know, and it's just too much. It's far too much.

Interviewer: So how do you handle that, when you've got a backlog of cases and you need to write them up?

Caseworker 1: (Sighs.)

Caseworker 4: Automatic pilot. Don't know. Yeah. Automatic pilot.

Casework by 'automatic pilot' represents, perhaps, an extreme version of a more common practice whereby the gaps in individual applications which are left open by a rushed bureaucratic process are filled by routine inferences and assumptions rather than by intimate and careful interaction with the applicant.

Although caseworkers generally feel a tension between the pressure of a heavy workload and the sympathy of their approach to casework, there is one aspect of casework where these two motivations combine to produce a common result—preliminary decision-making. Where caseworkers feel early in an application process (often at the initial interview) that a negative decision will ensue, they will often communicate this immediately to the applicant—before any formal decision is made by the senior officer. This can happen as part of the rushed process of resolving an application as quickly as possible where the final decision seems clear to the caseworker. However, preliminary decision-making can also happen in order to give the applicant every opportunity to respond to a preliminary negative decision— an instance of the fair hearing principle in practice:

> I do my best not to make somebody intentionally homeless, you know, you even try and come up with some argument, even if it's the slightest thing that you can, you can come up with so as not, not to make them intentionally homeless. So I do warn them in the initial interview, if there's anything that sounds like that, it's, it's going to look bad for them, that I'm not going to be able to get by, you know, the senior officers here, then certainly, you know, I'd be warning them immediately. (**Caseworker 5**)

Despite feeling overworked and overstressed, caseworkers nevertheless take pride in their skills as decision-makers. They trace this back to high quality legal training which they used to receive from barristers. Legal training from external personnel had stopped, and caseworkers are disparaging about the internal training they receive on an ad hoc basis. Nevertheless, they retain a pride in their skills which could be evidenced, for example, in how they compared themselves to their peers. They regard themselves as being more competent in homelessness decision-making than the workers in the Residential Units and are also critical of neighbouring Councils. (These views, incidentally, were shared by local solicitors who represented homeless applicants.)

> **Caseworker 3**: if you went to [Neighbouring] Borough Council, I think they're appalling. No they can get, yeah, they can get their decision date, in the average time they make a decision down to 3 or 4 days, because they tell most people to piss off at the counter.
>
> **Caseworker 4**: And they don't give them the appropriate [decision letter]
>
> **Caseworker 2**: No, they just send them all though, don't they.
>
> **Caseworker 4**: If you see the [decision letter] that they're given, "Not home-less", and it doesn't say anything, well, we have to give a detailed reason why they're not homeless or you know.

Caseworkers also reported that where an applicant was to be found intentionally homeless, they will often advise the applicant to seek legal advice about pursuing internal review. That is in keeping with their sense of welfarism in their general approach to homeless applicants. However, it is also suggestive of a confidence in their own decision-making skills whereby specialist expertise would be required to challenge their decisions. Indeed, caseworkers attribute the low level of internal reviews to the fact that, after a change in management, senior officers had ceased to make poor decisions.

The principal challenge to their commitment to legality comes from tenants who are evicted for anti-social behaviour. We have already seen in relation to 'singles' decision-making that concerns over anti-social applicants are felt most acutely at the stage of deciding whether to offer a discretionary housing service. Historically this has not been available to the Families Team (though at the time of fieldwork minor developments were occurring). Substantively, then, for the Families Team, Southfield's concerns with anti-social behaviour has a pertinence to the application of homelessness law. Officers perceive a pressure not to accept a duty to rehouse an applicant who has previously been evicted for anti-social behaviour. This pressure emanates from the housing management sections of the Council, and although such pressure may have been condoned under the previous manager, such cases can still be a locus of intra-organisational struggle:

> we try very hard not to let it have an impact on what you think your final decision's going to be. But it is quite difficult because there's a lot of political pressure, specially if the [anti-social behaviour] team being involved in a case to make a finding of intentionality.. Cos it's been such a high profile. You know the whole antisocial behaviour order strategy in [Southfield], the whole neighbour nuisance, the process has been very high profile. So I think there is an anxiety for staff that if they find that there's a full duty to someone and they end up having to rehouse them and we explain that to the [anti-social behaviour] team who've just spent the last 12 months collecting evidence and information, persuading witnesses, promising to try and keep the anonymity and safety of a witness who's gone through hell and then … so that's led to a successful eviction. And then we come along and say 'Sorry we're not going to find them intentionally homeless'… (**Senior Officer**)

A good example of this kind of pressure can be seen in the case of interviewee S19. Her family had been evicted for anti-social behaviour from a Council property and were notorious within the housing department. On the advice of Shelter, the interviewee's son applied in his own right for housing and included his parents and siblings on his application as his accompanying family. The homelessness case file contains a memorandum to the homelessness officer from the [anti-social behaviour team] officer:

> I think whenever [we] talk to Homelessness Officers about these matters the rubric is to say that we should provide the least service we can in the circumstances to comply with statutory obligations. In terms of the effect this business has had on the neighbours and the estate as a whole and our strategy to try and turn round what has been an estate in decline, I would say that the best outcome from the City's [anti-social behaviour] Strategy would be that we did not accommodate the family at all.

Decision-Letters

Decision-letters are legalistic and formal in tone. It is easy to understand why they might be confusing or intimidating for those who are inexpert in homelessness law. This is a theme to which we will return when considering the barriers to take up of the right to internal review.

Conclusions about Assessments Decision-Making: The Risk Authority

The above section has offered brief descriptions of the decision-making practices of the four teams which make up Southfield's homeless person's unit. It has sought to highlight the influences upon decision-making routines and to characterise them in terms of dominant discourses which were observed during fieldwork. This will help us describe and account for the reviewing behaviour of applicants (see further below). An overview of assessments decision-making is provided in Table 7 on p 59.

In light of our data, we have characterised Southfield in general as the 'risk authority'. We have done this on the basis that its homelessness decision-making practices give prominence to the risks posed by applicants. This designation allows us to contrast the prevailing discourse within its operations from that prevailing in Brisford (explored in chapter four). However, this should not be taken to infer that Southfield is averse to other influences such as audit (see our discussion of Brisford's decision-making). Rather, it is to suggest that Southfield, in contrast to Brisford, displays a particular preoccupation with the goal of weeding out those whom it knows or assumes to be too risky.

The risks with which Southfield are concerned revolve around what Cowan (1997) refers to as *tenantability*. Context is important to an analysis of the development of the content of risk regulation (Hood et al, 2001). In an economic climate in which social housing management has been chronically under-funded, when empty properties impose a financial cost on local authorities, and there is increasing competition for new tenants amongst housing providers, tenantability can become a central concern (Cowan et al, 1999: 412-5). Further, when tenants express considerable concern about anti-social behaviour, and central government rhetoric and policy (for example, Social Exclusion Unit, 1999; cf Damer, 1974) make links between empty housing and deviant behaviour, the incentive to tame the risks posed by *un*tenantability is explicit. Yet, at the same time, the elimination of such risks is elusive and stakeholder confidence in the bureaucratic ability to tame risk is at an all-time low (cf Taylor-Gooby et al, 1999). It is this insecurity which 'drives the insatiable quest for more and better knowledge of risk' (Ericson & Haggerty, 1997: 85) to improve future management.

Table 7: Overview of Assessments Decision-Making—Southfield Council

	Men's Residential	Men's Casework	Women's Team	Families' Team
Physical Environment	Exclusionary	Exclusionary	Open / welcoming	Open
Decision-Making Mode	Pre-emptive (1)	Pre-emptive (2)	Inquisitorial	Pre-emptive (3)
Officer – Applicant Relationship	Authoritarian (1)	Authoritarian (2)	Co-operative	Authoritarian (3)
Dominant Discourses	Tenantability / Culpability	Legality / Tenantability	Therapy / Tenantability	Legality / welfare
Communication of Decision	Immediate Oral / Written Decision	Written Decision	Incremental / Discursive	Natural Justice Dialogue / Written Decision

There is a further reason for the designation of Southfield as the 'risk authority'. Recent work in law and sociology which has explored the signifi-cance of risk to the organising of social relations in contemporary society suggests that a focus upon risk provides an important theoretical insight into our understanding of Southfield. As Garland explains, insecurity in social economic relations

> is the background circumstance that prompts our obsessive attempts to monitor risky individuals, to isolate dangerous populations, and to impose situational controls on otherwise open and fluid settings. (2001:194)

Risk provides a common platform for the crime control industry and the broader welfare state. Indeed, the broader welfare state takes on the goals and tasks of the crime control industry (Garland, 1996; Cowan & Pantazis, 2001). Risk assessment processes are, therefore, often explicitly focused on crime control issues as well as housing management costs.

A shift from focusing on housing need to risk is more than semantic. Risk implies a need to control negative outcomes and focuses on 'bads' rather than needs (Parton, 1996). As Ericson and Haggerty (1997: 42) put it, '[e]veryone is presumed guilty until the risk profile proves otherwise'. Risk involves implicit and explicit moral judgements (Ericson & Haggerty, 1997: 90). It is a new role for experts, with the obligation to take responsibility for their calculations, advice and risk management strategies (Rose, 1996: 349). The interlocking nature of risk and morality in contemporary social policy is played out in Southfield's decision-making. Southfield offers redemption through the discretionary offer. Here, the purpose of the assessments inter-view is to assess not housing need but whether the applicant is sufficiently susceptible to retraining, for example by maintaining payments of rent and previous arrears for a period. This was particularly evident in the work of the Women's Team.

Dean (1999: 177) suggests that risk is

> a set of different ways... of ordering reality, of rendering it into a calculable form. It is a way of representing events in a certain form so they might be made governable in particular ways, with particular techniques and for particular goals. It is a component of diverse forms of calculative rationality for governing the conduct of individuals, collectivities and populations.

This perspective diverts attention, then, to the ways in which risk becomes knowable, and calculable. In the modern welfare state, one way of assessing risk has been through the development of computer technology—indeed, Geary and Leith (2001) suggest 'that the technology behind the computeri-sation projects mould views of how welfare recipients should be processed'. As we have seen, in Southfield it is the existence of a multiplicity of inter-locking and overlapping databases which allow risk to be defined and assessed. At the same time, these databases exist to give Southfield a comfort blanket—essentially, they provide an insurance 'in order to "panoptically sort" individuals into pools of standard, sub-standard, and uninsurable risks' (Ericson et al, 2000: 534, citing Gandy, 1993). Indeed, 'the concept of risk is a construct of insurance technology' (Ericson & Haggerty, 1997: 39).

Insurantial techniques are both productive of risk and provide a protection against its inevitable breach. As Ewald (1991: 199) suggests,

> Nothing is a risk in itself; there is no risk in reality. But on the other hand, anything *can* be a risk; it all depends on how one analyzes the danger, considers the event. (original emphasis)

Ewald (1991: 207) also regards insurance, inter alia, as 'a moral technology'—in calculating risk, we 'master time,... discipline the future'. Although uncertainty remains, we are able to tame it by excluding certain people who have proved to be 'bad' risks before, policing another sub-category to ensure that they are willing to exercise self-responsibility by (for example) paying their rent/arrears on time, and keeping a watchful eye on those who are 'good' risks (because they are still potentially risky) (see Baker, 2000: 570).

Of course, the characterisation of Southfield as the 'risk authority' is not perfect. The information gleaned to help assess risk is limited and crude. One might expect assessments interviews to be somewhat lengthier than they are, and to be designed to produce further information about the subject. The practices described by Halliday (1998) as 'information bingeing' are often far from those observed in Southfield. Equally, the databases are known to have errors on them. This suggests to us that adherents to the risk society thesis must take account of the bureaucratic practices which enable risk to be managed. Bureaucracies may adhere to the concept of risk but, in everyday life, limit it to reflect the realities of day-to-day administration.

ALLOCATIONS DECISION-MAKING

In this section we explore the process of allocating long-term housing to 'successful' homeless applicants: those who have been deemed to be unintentionally homeless and in priority need.

The allocations process is split between 'singles' (including childless couples) and 'families'. The allocation of Southfield's housing stock is ordinarily conducted at a local area office level. However, the local area offices assign empty properties on a quota system to the allocations officers of the Singles and Families Teams.

Singles

Where a single person or childless couple are accepted for rehousing they are referred to the Resettlement Team who conduct 'take-on interviews', accompany the applicant to view the property which is eventually offered, and provide aftercare once the applicant has moved in. The actual allocation of long-term housing, however, is made by an allocations officer. These aspects of the allocations process will be looked at in turn.

Single Persons Resettlement Team

The Resettlement Team is a 15 person team. The team is managed by a Deputy Team Leader and a Team Leader. Overall responsibility for the team rests with a resettlement manager. The Resettlement Team is housed in the same office block as the Men's Residential Casework Team. The Resettlement Team are responsible for guiding applicants through the allocations process and assisting them in applying for grants for furniture, or providing applicants with a cooker and a bed, as well as providing support for applicants once they have moved in to their property. They also assist applicants in developing any relevant support service network. There is quite a degree of longevity amongst the Resettlement Team officers, although two members of staff had been replaced recently for personal reasons.

The Take-On Interview

The take-on interview is pivotal to the allocations process. The meeting takes place in the applicant's temporary accommodation and is scheduled to last an hour. The formal purpose of the interview is for the applicant to select the three areas of Southfield in which they wish to be housed, and for the officer to assess the applicant's support needs. However, officers use the opportunity to prime the applicant about the realities of the allocations process. The difference between the allocations process for homeless persons and other housing applicants is explained:

> you usually tell them what the main way of getting a property is if you're homeless in Southfield which is putting your name on the homeless list. It's not the only way but you usually incorporate that into the interview and make sure that they know that because it's a faster track system than going on a general list with the council... There's restrictions on the homeless list. So it's good in some ways, speed wise, but other ways it's restricted and we have to go through the restrictions with them, and one of the restrictions is the one offer only policy. So that's where if you get offered a property and they've got strong reasons for not taking it then we'd explain that they do have the right

of appeal against that but what happens if they won the appeal and what happens if they don't win the appeal. (**Resettlement Team Focus Group**)

Resettlement Team officers also seek to dampen applicants' expectations about the quality of prospective offers. Officer 3, for example, was observed explaining to an applicant that the flat which would be offered probably would not look very nice. She encouraged the applicant to picture the flat once it had been decorated. Other officers might ask clients about their expectations and then disabuse them:

> What I do is say, 'Let's make a wish list of what you would like in like a perfect world' you know, and they sort of laugh sometimes and say like a castle in the sky and all that, but make, or, you know, a great big house somewhere nice. But, so they put things down like a one bedroomed flat in these areas, what floor it's on, whether it's furnished or not, and what I say before that is, 'We'll make a wish list of what you'd really like and then we'll have a look at that and I'll tell you what's available out there in reality and we'll see if we can get, bearing in mind what your support needs are we'll see if, what, you know, if we can get something that's quite close to that, so. (**Resettlement Team Focus Group**)

The Allocations Officer

The support needs assessment and the applicant's choice of areas are passed on to the Allocations Officer. The Allocations Officer sends a standard letter to the applicant confirming the areas chosen for rehousing. The letter concludes with the following two paragraphs which further serve to dampen applicants' expectations:

> I would like to take this opportunity to remind you that you may be offered suitable accommodation in **any** of the areas listed above, and that the duty owed to you as an eligible person will cease at that stage. If there is a very good reason why this would cause you exceptional difficulty, please contact your Support Worker or an Allocations Officer **immediately** to discuss this.

> I also want to remind you that you will be assisted in securing only **one** offer of a property which the City council considers suitable to your needs. There is no guarantee about the **type** of property it will be. You may be offered a flat or maisonette **on any floor,** or any other non-family type accommodation, and the property **may** be either modernised or unmodernised. It may be accommodation which belongs **either** to the City Council, **or** to a Housing Association, **or** to a private landlord. The type of property you get will depend entirely upon what is available. Please be assured that any medical circumstances you have told us about which affect the housing you need will be taken into account in assessing the suitability of the accommodation.

Properties are allocated to single persons by the Allocations Officer in one of their areas of choice in strict date order. Applicants are informed about their offer by an offer letter. These offer letters explain again the 'one offer only' policy and inform the applicant about the 'refusals' process (discussed further below).

Viewing the Property

One of the practices under Southfield's Singles Homeless Strategy is to have accompanied viewings of offered properties. Resettlement Team officers are responsible for this. This service is highly influential in determining whether a client accepts the property. Indeed, as we argue further below, accompanied viewing is a key factor in the singles allocations process which, taken as a whole, militates against the take up of internal review. Resettlement Team officers recognised their persuasive role during accompanied viewings:

> the state of repair's not that good [in some properties] so you've got to look out for repairs… You're trying to sell it to them saying like, you know, as I said before, 'It'll be great with wall paper on and carpets and furniture and …' and then you go back to the sign up and usually you'll give 'em a little talk about what's gonna happen …

Officers were asked how they would sell the property to the client:

> I mean you might think it's a really good offer and they might be a bit iffy about it so, you know, you would show them some good points and a part, I mean the way I do it, part of what I do is I remind them again at that point about the one offer only and the appeal process and, because some people it's obvious that you like it, some people are a bit iffy, some people absolutely hate it when you walk in but they still end up probably taking it, but, I mean at some point before we go I'll say, "Well, I'm asking you now, do you want to take it cos we need to know, bearing in mind the one offer only policy and the things we've discussed while we've been in the property, do you want to take it? Yes or no?" (**Resettlement Team Officer 3**)

The Resettlement Team Officer's perception of the quality of the offer is clearly significant to the remaining part of the allocations process. If the officer believes that it is a 'good offer', the officer will try to persuade the applicant and remind him or her of the one offer policy. A property which is considered a bad offer, however, might lead the Resettlement Team officer to suggest that the Allocations Officer look at the property. Similarly, officers' views about the legitimacy of the clients' complaints are important in that, if they believe them to be reasonable, the officer would support the refusal (discussed further below). Officers felt able to discern between genuine and bogus complaints:

I'm not being cynical about people but, you know, sometimes they come up with the same excuses and then when you actually say, 'Well, no, you have to live there.' They say, 'Oh, all right then.' And they're not that bothered at all, but I mean, I mean you've got to tell, I don't know, you need the evidence really, and you're not saying these people are lying but it is used as like a lever to kind of get 'em out of that offer. (**Resettlement Team Focus Group**)

Applicant Decision

As indicated above, the applicant must make a decision about whether to accept an offer of housing. Applicants are given seven days within which to refuse the offer in writing. Such refusals are considered by the Refusals Panel (see below).

Families

Where an applicant with children is entitled to a full housing duty, the application is passed onto one of the allocations officers of the Families Team. The allocations officers match available properties against homeless applicants' three chosen areas. The allocations officers are faced with two, sometimes competing pressures: to house homeless applicants quickly, and to house them in property which is suitable to their needs:

> Basically the objective is to re-house families quickly, satisfactorily, so that they can establish themselves permanently in satisfactory accommodation... It's trying to get people re-housed quickly, but also into the type of property where they will be able to settle and we are actually very limited with the properties that we get. We have this sort of pressure on the one hand to re-house quickly, on the other hand to re-house satisfactorily. A lot of the time, properties simply aren't there that are going to help them to settle permanently. (**Allocations Officer**)

However, the allocations officers expressed a general scepticism about whether the allocations process was capable of achieving an acceptable balance between these two aims:

> There's a huge difference between simply administering the system and trying to tailor it to people's needs, because you can't let people queue. You really do have to try and re-house people as quickly as possible for all sorts of reasons. I mean in a sense it's sometimes best to just do it without even thinking 'will they like this property or won't they?' It becomes pointless anyway and you simply can't. (**Allocations Officer**)

One of the major frustrations for families allocations officers related to the way in which applicants made their choices about the areas in which they

LONDON metropolitan university
LIBRARY SERVICES

would like to settle. In most situations, applicants make these choices as part of their initial interview with a caseworker. A number of officers were critical of this method as they felt applicants were often not in the best position at that stage to make considered choices. This view was born out in interviews with applicants:

> I put, when I first went, I had some areas down and er, I put really far areas away for the simple reason my head was messed up, I was on anti-depressant tablets and I was just, my head was just not there. (**Interview S19**)

Applicants were allowed to change their areas of choice at any stage during the course of their application. However, the allocations officers found that applicants often did not appreciate this fact. This created problems at the housing offer stage:

> People sometimes wait until they've been made an offer to say I really don't want, I've decided I wanted to change that area for another one and you don't find out until you get to the refusal stage... Caseworkers are kind of so busy and so tied up in all their investigations and everything, that choosing the re-housing areas in a way is just a little bit of a job and it's done quickly. Sometimes on the day people present and they're least able to think clearly and they don't seem to come back and say I know I said that, but I've changed my mind. (**Allocations Officer**)

Another misconception amongst applicants concerning areas of choice was that they were ranking areas in an order of preference. This also led to difficulties at the housing offer stage. A final aspect of the housing offer stage about which the allocations officers were critical, concerned the lack of accompanied viewing of new offers. As we saw above, single people or childless couples were generally accompanied by a support worker to view the prospective new property. The allocations officers felt that this practice would help cut down on the number of refusals in relations to families. Indeed, we argue further below that the practice of accompanied viewing operates to curtail challenges to offers through the Refusals Panel.

The allocations officers, accordingly, identified a number of systemic problems with the allocations process which translated into problems for the Refusals Panel. However, as we shall see below, the Refusals Panel, although recognising the systemic problems at a theoretical level, was, paradoxically, inclined to lose sight of the systemic dimension of refusals in its routine decision-making and instead to individualise the problem in terms of applicants' disingenuousness and unrealistic expectations.

Conclusions About Allocations

A crucial difference between the allocations process for single people and the process for families is the existence of the Resettlement Team. There are two key aspects of the operations of the Resettlement Team which we suggest are of significance to the internal reviewing behaviour of applicants. First, the selection by applicants of the areas of Southfield is conducted in a specialised interview with the Resettlement Team officer. This allows for greater dialogue with the applicant about the choice being made and for greater consideration on the part of the applicant in making the selection. The same decision on the families side is made under pressure as part of the initial homelessness interview. Officers and applicants both identified during the course of fieldwork that this environment militates against making considered choices and stores up problems for the allocations process.

The second key factor emerging from the work of the Resettlement Team is its role in dampening the expectations of applicants about the quality of prospective accommodation and in persuading applicants to accept offers during accompanied viewing. Such persuasion and dampening of expectations operates to influence applicants' perceptions of the meaning of 'suitability'. This function is missing on the families side and, as we argue below, accounts for the considerably higher levels of 'refusals' being made by families.

INTERNAL REVIEW

There are two forms of internal review which operate in Southfield's Homeless Person's Unit. There is, of course, the statutory internal review process which is described below. However, in relation to allocations decision-making there is an additional formalised pre-statutory review process called 'refusals'. The refusals process pre-dates the requirements of statutory internal review introduced by the 1996 Act. When the internal review processes were introduced following the 1996 Act, they were superimposed on the existing refusals process which remained intact. Refusals for singles (and childless couples) and families are considered under separate processes.

Refusals: Singles

Letters of offers of housing explain that applicants can appeal against the offer if the applicant thinks it is not suitable. Applicants make this appeal by writing a letter. This letter is considered by the Refusals Panel which is made up of the Allocations Officer, the deputy team leader of the Resettlement Team and a policy officer.

The Role Of Resettlement Team Officers

Historically, the Resettlement Team officers could also attend Refusals Panel meetings in support of their applicants, particularly where the Resettlement Team officer felt that the applicant had a legitimate complaint but had not expressed its basis very well in the letter. This practice has become much less frequent. Resettlement Team officers do, however, participate in other ways. They sometimes assist applicants in writing their refusals letters. Similarly, they sometimes write separate letters of support to be considered by the Refusals Panel. This clearly depends upon whether the Resettlement Team officer believes that the refusal is legitimate:

> if you felt it was a reasonable offer, then you'd be hard pushed to defend the client any more, or help the client any more than helping them write the letter cos you inside yourself think it's a good offer and that they should accept it. So you can't really put, 'I fully support the client in refusing the offer' because you don't in that situation. (**Resettlement Team Officer 4**)

The Panel considers the information in the refusal letter first and then looks at the file notes made by the Resettlement Team officer. A Panel member described it as follows:

> We look at, 'is the property suitable?', 'is it what they've asked for?', 'does it follow the criteria that they've set?', 'is it in one of the areas that they've chosen and at the height that they've chosen?', 'does it follow any medical recommendations that there are?' If we're happy with all that, then really the only thing... we'd be accepting a refusal on would be property condition... So there's a bit of a balancing act, we try and take into account what the person's put in their refusal letter and look at that in terms of the prevailing property conditions in the area. But also [the Allocations Officer] will normally know the property or the types, the way properties are set up in that area.

The Role Of The Allocations Officer

The Panel rely heavily on the local knowledge of the Allocations Officer. Indeed, the Allocations Officer, who makes the original allocations decisions, seems to play a central role in Panel decision-making. Not only does this officer prepare the paperwork for the Panel Meetings, but he also takes a leading role in the consideration of cases. For example, in case RT13/1, only the Allocations Officer had read the refusal letter. He began the meeting by explaining the case as he saw it, making it clear that he believed this was a 'straightforward' refusal, and not legitimate. The letter had stated that the applicant was refusing the offer due to poor property condition. The Allocations Officer said that the real reason for refusal was because the client did not like the location—that the applicant wanted a two bedroom flat near the University so that he could have a study. No Resettlement Team officer had attended the property viewing with the client. The housing officer had told the Allocations Officer that the client had refused to re-decorate the property. Only then was the applicant's refusal letter given to the deputy team leader. The file was not consulted by the deputy team leader. The meeting lasted five minutes and the refusal was rejected.

It is important to stress that we are not suggesting that the Allocations Officer is the sole decision-maker and that the other Panel members have no input into the Panel's decisions. Rather we are suggesting that the Allocations Officer plays a key role in, and exercises considerable (though not complete) influence over, the decision-making process. This nevertheless poses a problem for the impartiality of the Panel on two grounds. First, it is the Allocations Officer's decisions which are being reviewed in the Panel meetings. Systemically, therefore, there is insufficient separation between the original decision-maker and the reviewing decision-maker. Second, more generally, the Allocations Officer himself exhibits considerable scepticism about the merit of applicants' cases. For example, during the observation period, he ridiculed clients who refused offers of accommodation by doing impersonations of them telephoning him in whining voices. When discussing this, he said

> I only have a short concentration span. They have five minutes to convince me, then I stop listening… If they phone or come here and turn on the water-works, that won't work, they have less chance of persuading me. I've seen it too many times.

At a personal level, therefore, it is questionable how impartial the Allocations Officer is capable of being.

Concern over the quality of Panel decision-making was expressed by the Team-Leader who conducts internal reviews of Panel decisions. His concern was that the decisions were made hastily, in one sitting, and that further relevant information is not requested, nor further enquiries made:

> a lot of the things that I've been getting through for reviews have been things that I think should have been sorted out at that refusal stage.

Communication of Panel Decision

The applicant is sent a letter informing her of the Panel's decision. Where the refusal has been rejected, the letter addresses the basis of complaint, and gives the applicant one week in which to accept the offer. At the bottom of the letter the applicant is notified of her statutory right to internal review.

The Team-Leader, however, was critical of the content of these decision letters as being inadequate, using 'hideous stock phrases' which give rise to the suspicion that evidence hasn't been properly considered.

Additionally, however, oral feedback about the decision is given to the client about the decision by the responsible Resettlement Team officer. This feedback is a further instance of how the mediating influence of the Resettlement Team officer is used to redirect challenges. First, it was clear from the focus group that at least one officer had no knowledge of the internal review process. Second, other officers' advice is as follows:

> we could say you might not want this property cos it's not, in not quite the right area and you've been refused on that grounds, but you could say, look, the best option would be take that property cos otherwise you're gonna lose your temporary accommodation and everything and everything's gonna get a lot, theoretically a lot worse. So you could suggest to them that they look at it as a two stage process, that they take up the tenancy of this one, they don't have to live there for ever, they could move into that one, live there for a while, after everything's settled down they could, you could advise them about what other applications they could make, say directly to housing associations or something where they've got more, because they've got a safe roof over their head they've got, they've more choice how they can limit the other applications (**Resettlement Team Officer 3**)

Refusals: Families

In the Families Team, the Refusals Panel is generally comprised of one or both of the two Families Team senior officers and a deputy team leader from the Allocations team. It meets once per week. The allocations officers also attend refusals meetings. Although the senior officers have the final say, allocations officers take an active role in discussing the cases prior to decision.

Officers who take part in the Refusals Panel have never received any training in how to make these decisions. This perhaps has permitted the development of an observable haphazard approach to decision-making and the evolution of a complex character of decision-making which is discussed below.

Battle-Weariness Of Officers

The frustration felt by allocations officers about applicants' areas of choice is shared by the Refusals Panel. The meetings which were observed during fieldwork were often marked by the visible frustration of the officers taking part, particularly the senior officers who bear the responsibility of making the decisions. For example, in case HF5/2 the applicant, who suffered from mental health problems, had refused her offer on the grounds that the area was too isolated and unfamiliar to her. An officer was critical of the letter, describing some of its content as 'stupid'. However, her greatest complaint related to the applicant's failure to change her areas of choice before the offer stage:

> Every week we sit here and every week the same thing happens! ... Why the piggin' hell didn't she tell us? They can change their areas of choice but they never do! (**Officer 1**)

The sense of frustration—a common alienating effect of welfare decision-making which is conducted under the pressure of limited time and resources (Lipsky, 1980)—lends itself to a haphazard mode of operation. For example, the refusal described above was upheld and the offer was withdrawn because the Panel felt there was a 'risk of self-harm'. The refusal letter had noted that the applicant had been suicidal in the past. The senior officer was critical of the failure of the applicant's mental health key-worker for not having properly explored the significance of the choice of areas with the applicant in consultation with the council. Nevertheless, the case was resolved by the Panel members themselves deciding which areas would be more suitable for her. The applicant had noted in her application that she did not want to be housed near her ex-partner's parents. It was not clear, however, where her ex-partner's parents lived. The senior officer telephoned the applicant to find out. She did not, however, discuss her areas of choice further with the applicant. It is not known how this applicant's housing situation was eventually resolved.

This incident illustrates the haphazard character of the Refusals Panel decision-making. The battle-weariness of officers who endure the frustration of the Refusals meeting on a weekly basis propels them, on occasion, towards the quick but shallow resolution of cases. Indeed, much of the decision-making takes place very quickly, in a matter of minutes. The frustration at the process inclines the Panel towards a broadly sceptical approach to decision-making whereby many applicants are regarded as being unrealistic in their expectations and so have no legitimate basis to their complaints. Many refusals are, therefore, characterised as expressing disappointment rather than as setting out a legitimate case about the suitability of the offer. This attitude can lessen the inclination to engage in further enquiry.

For example, in case HF14/1, the applicant had stated in her letter that the property offered was too far away from her children's schools. Her four children each went to different schools. The offer had been made within one of her chosen areas. The senior officer examined the location of the four schools and noted that it was impossible to be housed near to them all.

Accordingly, she decided that the offer would stand. There were a number of gaps in this applicant's story, however, which were worthy of investigation. For example, some of the schools may have been better served by public transport than others. Some of the children may have been more capable of independent travel than others. The applicant had not hinted at any of this in her letter, but it is possible that she was not skilled in representing the full account of her reasons for refusal. Nevertheless, without the benefit of further enquiry, the Panel concluded that there was no real substance to the refusal, commenting that the applicant needed to 'be realistic'.

It is important to stress that the cursory and sceptical approach evidenced above was not uniform throughout the many cases which were observed. In other cases further investigations of applicants' refusals had been conducted which offered a fuller understanding of the applicants reasons for rejecting the offer. The point being made in this section is that the quality of decision-making of the Refusals Panel is inconsistent—a point which is recognised by a number of officers. For example, a Senior Officer in the Allocations Team commented:

> I'm not happy with it now, as a team leader. ... I think the role of the person who is making the decision needs looking at and the kind of information they're requesting. ... And I think it's, in the last seven years they've moved much more towards making a decision on the day, on what they've got there, and, because a lot of the things that I've been getting through for reviews have been things that I think should have been sorted out at that refusal stage. And things that haven't been properly investigated, and have not then been properly explained why the decision's been made in the letter that's sent out saying that its offer to stand.

The Importance Of Resources

Refusals decision-making takes place within the context of there being considerable pressure to house homeless applicants quickly, and this is influential to decision-outcomes. It has already been noted that one of the mantras of the Families Team is that it is experiencing an 'accommodation crisis'. There is particular stress on the Council's scarce temporary accommodation resources. This means that the senior officers feel under some pressure to move 'successful' homeless applicants into longer term housing, thereby relieving some of the pressure on temporary accommodation resources. Senior officers, accordingly, regularly consider the impact of an acceptance on the flow of houses to 'successful' homeless applicants.

The crucial questions are (1) if the refusal is accepted, will the property still be available for allocation to another homeless family? (For example, where the offer of housing is Housing Association property, if the refusal is accepted, the Families Team will lose their chance to allocate the property to a homeless family unless they have another applicant queuing for that area); and (2) if the refusal is accepted, is another vacant property likely to become available for the applicant soon (the question then becomes, is the applicant queuing for a 'high turnover' area?). This is a pressure recognised by a Senior Officer in the Families Team:

> I think there is pressures when it is around suitability in [the Families Team] around keeping properties, holding up that allocations process, so possibly, and that possibly causing conflict with area offices either because properties in the homelessness pool for a long time are more likely to get vandalised, losing rent, adding to the void figure, and sometimes you end up giving them back to the housing office at the end of the refusals process if that refusal is agreed. So I think that is an external pressure in relation to suitability of offers.

It is important to stress that these considerations are not always decisive. There were a number of observed cases where, despite the fact that the Families Team would 'lose' the property, the refusal was accepted. However, these considerations are a regular feature of refusals decision-making and are clearly influential in some cases, though not determinative in all.

Communication of Panel Decision

Unlike the position in relation to the singles Refusals Panel, the decision was communicated only by letter. These letters are drafted and sent by one of the allocations officers. It gives the applicant a week in which to accept the offer and informs the applicant at the bottom of the letter of her statutory right to internal review.

Statutory Internal Review

Introduction

All applicants may seek an internal review of both assessments and Refusals Panel decisions. Southfield as a whole did not have a rigorous system for dealing with internal review requests. Instead, internal reviews were passed from one team leader onto another on an ad hoc basis. So, for example, the Team Leader of the Men's Residential Unit might be asked to review a decision of the Women's Residential Unit, and so on.

Statistics On Internal Review

Take Up Rate Internal reviews are very infrequent in all aspects of homelessness decision-making in Southfield. By comparison with Brisford Council (explored in the following chapter) internal review activity is very low indeed. During the fieldwork period June 2000—May 2001, 886 negative decisions were made by the Assessments Team. During the same period, there were only 24 internal reviews of those decisions - a take up rate of 2.7%. In relation to the Refusals Panel, it rejected 92 cases during the fieldwork period. During the same period there were 14 internal reviews - a take-up rate of 15.2%. The position, then, in Southfield as regards the proportion of applicants challenging adverse decisions falls within a general pattern identified in other jurisdictions, as well as in other areas of social welfare, of the take up of formal rights of redress being low (Sainsbury & Eardley, 1991; Dalley & Berthoud, 1992; Lloyd-Bostock & Mulcahy, 1994; Atkinson et al, 1999; Halliday, 2001).

Subject Matter of Internal Reviews Data is available about the subject matter of internal reviews for the fieldwork period. They reveal that intentional homelessness and the suitability of permanent offers were the aspects of the homelessness decision-making process which were the subject of the highest number of review requests. Of the combined total of thirty-eight internal reviews conducted, thirteen (34%) related to intentional homelessness, while 14 (37%) related to the suitability of accommodation offers. The complete figures are set out below:

Table 8: Subject Matter of Internal Reviews—Southfild Council

Type of Decision	Total number	% of all reviews
Suitability of Permanent Accommodation	14	37%
Intentionally Homeless	13	34%
Not Eligible	4	11%
Not Homeless	2	5%
Not in Priority Need	2	5%
Priority Need and Intentionality	1	3%
Local Connection	1	3%
Not Known	1	3%
Total	38	100%

Outcome of Internal Reviews Fifty per cent (n=12) of the internal reviews of Assessments decision-making resulted in the original decision being overturned. In relation to internal reviews of the Refusals Panel, however, only three of the 14 reviews were successful and resulted in a fresh offer of accommodation being granted.

Provision Of Information About Internal Review

Information about the right to internal review is routinely included at the end of negative decision-letters. There is a standard paragraph which sets out the applicant's right to an internal review. (A similar paragraph is included at the end of Refusals Panel decision-letters). It says the following:

> RIGHT TO REVIEW – HOUSING ACT 1996 S.202
>
> You have the right to request a review of any of the following aspects of the decision we have made about your applications: a) your eligibility, b) what duty is owed to you, c) referral to another authority, d) local connection, e) suitability of available accommodation. Either you, or someone acting on your behalf should put the reasons for your request in writing, including *any* information you think should be taken into account.
>
> **Any such request must be made within 21 days of receipt of this notice.** Full details of the Review Procedure are available on request from your Caseworker, who will be pleased to help you with any queries you may have.

Some officers of the Families Team also indicated that they would verbally communicate the existence of the right to review during some interviews, particularly where an applicant is to be deemed intentionally homeless. This is not, however, a uniform practice.

The Internal Review Process

During fieldwork we were not able to observe internal reviewing. Instead we interviewed Principal Officers engaged in the process. We also interviewed more junior officers about their experiences of internal review. However, our data on the social reality of internal reviewing is limited, particularly in comparison to our data regarding, for example, the refusals process. Further, due to the general lack of statutory internal reviews, it is difficult to draw firm conclusions about the social reality of internal review, as officers at best were speculating about isolated incidents within the generality of their working routines. The comments below, therefore, must be read with a certain amount of caution.

Internal reviews are conducted 'on the papers'. Applicants are required to make the request in writing. This is read in conjunction with the applicant's case file. The reviewing officer may discuss the case with the junior or senior officer as part of the process of understanding the history of the case. In some cases, the reviewing officer will request more information (for example, a medical assessment) to be obtained before making the review decision. In others, the case may be returned to the caseworker for further interviews with the applicant before a decision is made.

There was a different level of confidence about the quality of the internal review process between the reviewing officers. One Principal Officer for a Casework Team, for example, was sceptical about whether internal reviews were always of an acceptable standard. This was attributed in part to the general lack of procedures and training, and partly to the fact that there was limited time and resources which could be devoted to the process. It was also reported that there could be more structure to the internal review process:

> **Interviewer**: What's your role in the internal review process?
>
> **Principal Officer**: Um, well I don't think any of our roles are particularly clear really. I think probably we haven't got a structured approach to review. What's tended to happen since I've been a team leader… is that requests for reviews that come to the… Team have come to me… but then most of the ones for instance on suitability I've been passing over to [the Principal Officer of a different team]… I don't think we've got a proper approach to it. I don't think I have got a clear approach to it in my head… I don't feel that we do it in a systematic way, I'm sure that I approach reviews in a different way to [the Principal Officer of the different team]. And we haven't really got a form of words clearly in our heads either about how to phrase review responses.

Another Principal Officer, by way of contrast, seemed more confident about the quality of the review process which he undertook. This person was critical of the decision-making practices of the Refusal Panel which preceded his involvement in a case. Indeed, his account of his own internal reviewing can be contrasted with the data obtained about the Refusals Panel. The Principal Officer reported that he would generally conduct further enquiries. For example, if an offer of housing was refused because of its inadequate size, he would visit the property himself and measure the rooms. Similarly, he might request that an applicant provide more information to clarify the basis of her complaint:

> [In one case] the refusal was on the grounds that it was too small. It was a two bedroomed property and she has a very small baby. There was no way they were going to be able to do that one as overcrowded. And there was stuff about, she was claiming to feel afraid in the area but she couldn't give any specific reasons as to why she was feeling afraid so I said 'well you need to write and say, give her another opportunity to elaborate on what possible reasons there could be'… (**Principal Officer**)

However, the allocations officers rarely heard anything about the process or outcomes of internal reviews conducted by different Principal Officers. Caseworkers in the Families Team also felt that internal review had little impact on their work. The process was divorced from their working environment and they felt little connection to the process or outcome—even where it was one of their cases being reviewed:

> when somebody review, goes for a review it's out of my hands, to be honest, most of the time... it's totally out of my hands, I don't even get, it, because it, because the family has to get the solicitor involved and it goes to them writing a letter. That letter then goes to [the Principal Officer for Homeless Families]... so it's totally out of my hands. If anything, [the Principal Officer for Homeless Families] might come along and say "do you know such and such a family? Do you have the file?" but that's about it. There won't be anything more. (**Families Team, Caseworker 5**)

CONCLUSION

In this chapter, we have placed Southfield's organisation and decision-making practices under the microscope. We have characterised decision-making along a set of continuums which demonstrate the varieties of different operating beliefs and cultures within each part of the HPU. In our description, we have laid down a number of markers for subsequent chapters which impact upon the use or non-use of the refusals and internal review procedures—such as, non-receipt or lack of understanding of decision-letters, and consistent reinforcement of the one offer policy. In general, we have observed that Southfield's assessments practices fit, albeit incompletely, within a risk model of decision-making. Despite the availability of a large number of single person's accommodation, considerable numbers of single persons are, nevertheless, turned away by the HPU on the basis of being poor housing management risks.

We also examined in this chapter the various review procedures available to applicants. As we will see in the next chapter, the take-up of internal review is much lower in Southfield than Brisford, despite a similar number of rejections at the initial stage. This low take-up rate prohibited us from exploring the practice of statutory internal review, though we were able to present data about the pre-statutory review process relating to offers of housing.

In the next chapter we explore the practices of our second case study—Brisford—before going on to consider the questions of why applicants do and do not pursue internal review.

4

Brisford Council

Like Southfield, Brisford is situated in an urban area in England. The volume of applications to Brisford is high (though not as high as that of Southfield Council) and the Homeless Persons' Unit is, accordingly, a busy organisation. The HPU is a separate and single unit within the Housing Department. It is divided into two separate units: the Assessments Section and the Allocations Section. The Assessments Section determines what legal duties (if any) under homelessness law are owed to applicants. The Allocations Section fulfils the housing duties to homeless applicants. These two sections and their operations will be discussed in further detail below, drawing upon the schemas developed in relation to Southfield.

ASSESSMENTS DECISION-MAKING

Introduction

In contrast to the Homeless Persons' Unit ('HPU') of Southfield City Council, Brisford's HPU is a highly organised and homogenous organisation. Brisford is very conscious of its image within the local and public sector community, working to maintain this by way of intense self-monitoring of its operations. It likes to be seen as a local authority which is 'on the ball', as one officer noted. The HPU manager commented that 'Brisford's culture is to lead in many respects, in terms of standards and quality'. This monitoring culture and its impact on decision-making will be explored further below. However, for present purposes, it is sufficient to note that Brisford displays a level of organisational rationality and efficiency which stands in marked contrast to our findings in Southfield. Further, our data demonstrates that both homeless applicants and local solicitors also compared Brisford favourably with its neighbours in terms of its efficiency and customer service. First, however, some basic descriptions of the physical environment and the decision-making process are offered.

The Physical Environment

The reception area of the HPU is quite light and brightly painted. It contains a reception desk, a housing advice area and a series of open-plan interview cubicles. At the far end of the reception area there are a number of private interview rooms. The various desks operate as a barrier between public space and office space. The public space in the centre of the area contains rows of seats. There is a children's play area at the far end of the public space. Two televisions have been mounted on the walls—one in the main area and one in the children's area. The open plan interview cubicles are, in effect, a long desk divided into smaller units by partitions. They do not contain screens separating the applicants from officers. The desks, however, are sufficiently deep to operate as a minimal security shield for officers. The interview rooms contain a dividing table. Officers and applicants enter these private rooms from different doors. Two security personnel are permanently stationed in the reception area.

The Staff

The Assessments team is headed up by the Manager. There are three assessments teams, each containing six officers. Each team is managed by a Principal Assessments Officer. Additionally, during fieldwork a fourth Principal Assessments Officer was created to conduct internal reviews. His post is senior to the Assessments Officers but junior to the other Principal Assessment Officers. He is directly responsible, however, to the Manager. The reception is staffed by one receptionist. Finally, there is a team of four visiting officers who visit applicants' homes to confirm the applicant's account of their current living arrangements.

The Application Process

Applicants who wish to make a homelessness application must first report to the reception desk. The receptionist then either makes an appointment for the applicant to be seen later or, where required, immediately refers applicants to the on-duty homelessness officers. However, our observational data indicates that the receptionist also operates as a filter for homeless applications in that she gives initial advice to applicants about whether the HPU will be able assist them.

For example, in case BA1/1 a male and female with two children came to the reception desk indicating that they wished to apply for housing as homeless persons. The female claimed to be the victim of domestic violence. The receptionist indicated that the HPU could not help them because she did not have any evidence to corroborate the claim, which was necessary for

Brisford to be able to process the application. The receptionist privately indicated to our fieldworker that she was sceptical about the truth of the female's claim because of inconsistencies in her story. In this particular instance, the male insisted on speaking to the duty manager who confirmed the receptionist's advice. However, this filtering role of the receptionist does not always result in managerial involvement and may be significant to the reviewing behaviour of homeless applicants.

This is a point which was highlighted in one of our interviews with local solicitors. One of the local law centres noted that they had experience of applicants who had been advised by the receptionist that they were unlikely to be in priority need and so were referred to the Housing Advice Section for information about renting in the private sector or registering on the Council's general housing register. Similarly, there was evidence of filtering on the basis of an anticipated lack of local connection. Here, the reception-ist advises applicants who were thought not to have a local connection with Brisford to apply to other local authorities where a connection was presumed to exist. In all cases which are filtered out of the application process applicants are not formally assessed, do not receive decision letters and so are not informed of their right to internal review.

Most applicants who approach the reception, however, do see Assessments Officers and are formally assessed. Assessments Officers take turns to be on duty to see new applicants. The system is computerised so that details of new applications are displayed in the Assessments Officers' open plan office. One of the performance targets imposed by the Charter Mark regime is that new applicants must be seen within five minutes. The interview takes the form of the completion by the Assessments Officer of an application form. Temporary accommodation, where required, will be provided by the Accommodation Team.

Enquiries about an applicant's story often have to be made in order to determine what duties, if any, are owed under homelessness law. Some of these enquiries are conducted by Visiting Officers. For example, where an applicant is threatened with homelessness because a resident landlord or family member is asking the applicant to leave, a Visiting Officer often visits the property to confirm the applicant's account of events. Further investiga-tions will be conducted by the Assessments Officer. On completion of enquiries, the Assessments Officer writes a decision-letter in their own name. This, however, must be ratified and 'signed off' by the Principal Assessments Officer. Indeed, during the course of enquiries, the Principal Assessments Officer often discusses the progress of cases and offers advice about further required lines of enquiry.

Decision-Making Practices

Decision-Making Mode

The decision-making mode of Brisford should be characterised as pre-emptive. Generally speaking, Assessments Officers control interviews with applicants and the officer-applicant relationship is authoritarian in character. Officers often frame the interview exchange in terms of legal categories and language. For example, an officer might begin the interview by explaining that its purpose is to complete an assessment form under the Housing Act 1996 and require applicants to sign a declaration 'under the 1996 Act' that they will tell the truth.

Officers employ a limited pool of data to signify the 'facts' of a case and to exhaust their enquiries. The investigation process occurs under pressure to meet the target of determining applications within 33 working days. Interviews with local solicitors revealed their observations that there is a tendency—particularly in relation to decisions about priority need—for officers to approach new applications with pre-determined suppositions about entitlement, and for officers not to probe applicants too deeply for further information which would refute or at least question their initial suppositions.

However, the decision-making mode is less pre-emptive than that of Southfield's Families Team. For example, there was also evidence within Brisford of some officers being more open and less controlling in interview situations than others. Indeed, a more informal interviewing style can be contrasted. Here, the officers are less reliant on legal language to frame the interview exchange and the interaction between officer and applicant is more open, informal and balanced. Further, there was a general openness within Brisford's HPU to the reconsideration of cases, particularly after representations from solicitors or other legal advisers—a factor which emerged clearly from our interviews with local solicitors. The focus within the organisation on customer care and the welfarism of some Assessment Officers inclines officers (though not exclusively) towards a sense of accountability to applicants about how the application process unfolds and so mitigates the controlling tendencies of routine casework.

Dominant Discourses in Decision-Making Practices

There are three identifiable discourses within Brisford's decision-making practices—legality, efficiency, and customer care. These three discourses, and the relationship between them, will be explored in turn below.

Legality Brisford is a particularly 'legally conscientious' (Halliday, 2000a) HPU. Of course, competing concerns can override concerns with the legality of decisions. We already saw above, that the receptionist operates a filtering function. This, it is suggested, involves unlawful decision-making. Brisford's legal conscientiousness, it would seem, is weakest at this initial stage of the overall application process. Nevertheless, Brisford displays a strong commitment to the legality of decisions. The HPU generally ascribes importance to compliance with procedural and substantive legal requirements. It has already been noted that local solicitors found Brisford's HPU to be very co-operative, professional and open to criticism. The general view which emerged from these interviews was that Brisford engaged in the genuine reconsideration of cases on the basis of representations from advisers about the legality of decisions. Brisford was also compared very favourably with its neighbours in terms of its professionalism and the general quality of its decisions. Indeed, one adviser characterised Brisford rather colourfully as 'the Manchester United of HPUs'.

Our observational data also confirms Brisford's commitment to legality in routine casework. A simple comparison of the content of application files between Brisford and Southfield shows that, generally speaking, Brisford's enquiries are more extensive, detailed and more carefully recorded. Further, Brisford regularly disseminates new legal information concerning homelessness law. The role of the Principal Reviews Officer is key in this regard. He regularly checks the website of the (then) Department of Environment, Transport and the Regions for updates on homelessness case law and emails these to his colleagues. He also attends County Court hearings, feeding these experiences into the ad hoc informal training of Assessments Officers. Finally, he uses the internal review process itself to educate Assessments Officers about the legal requirements of homelessness law.

Some officers felt that the legal advice community within Brisford's area encouraged a professional concern with legality. Although we do not have quantitative data regarding the levels of legal representation, the general impression of officers was that there had been an increasing level of representation in homelessness applications in recent years. Further, there was a sense that the number of available solicitors' firms and advice agencies was considerable, combined with a view that the quality of advice and representation in many cases was high. Principal Assessments Officer 2, for example, compared her experiences of working in Brisford for the past three years to her prior experience of working in a neighbouring Council:

I always just get the impression that Brisford doesn't get away with very much in the sense that everything is challenged, whether it's saying that somebody can't have a daughter on an application or if it's just absolutely everything, and I didn't get that impression with [Neighbouring Council]... And you didn't feel like you had solicitors breathing down your back all the time. Whereas with here you do actually feel like the solicitors are on everything.

Like you make a decision on a case and they're straight there. And we've got quite a few, you know there's quite strong, quite good legal places—you know [Brisford Law Centre], [Solicitor Firm 1]—they're all quite good law centres I think basically, and they don't let us get away with very much. I think we very much stick to the legislation book

Efficiency Brisford's commitment to legality, however, is countered by its commitment to efficiency. By 'efficiency' we refer to the twin concerns of speed and cost. Brisford is particularly concerned with meeting the Best Value performance standards—in particular the determination of applications within 33 working days (BV67—see ODPM, 2000: ch 8). Assessments Officers are subject to other performance targets which have their source in the Charter Mark regime. These will be discussed further below in relation to the discourse of customer care. It is sufficient to note at this stage that within the overall monitoring culture of Brisford's HPU, the 33 day target is by far the most important. The monitoring culture within the HPU is particularly strong and evident. Assessments Officers are monitored by Principal Assessment Officers who are in turn monitored by the Manager. The meeting of targets is a strong pressure on the day-to-day work of the HPU:

> statistics is a very, very important pressure within [Brisford]. My line manager… is very, very into the figures. They must be accurate, we must be hitting this target. (**Principal Reviews Officer**)

Indeed, Assessments Officers' performance in relation to the time taken to determine applications is internally published, creating a kind of internal competition. Although there is no performance-related pay, most officers are conscious of how they are performing in relation to their peers. The pressure to meet the 33 day target is of sufficient concern to Assessments Officers that it sometimes impinges upon the quality of decisions. A number of officers were candid about feeling a pressure to 'cut corners'. This often means compromising on the depth or extent of the enquiries carried out.

Making decisions quickly not only assures Brisford of a good standing in relation to Best Value standards, but also has the additional benefit of promising economic savings—another strand of the efficiency discourse. The major financial cost to the HPU relates to temporary accommodation. Where a local authority has reason to believe that a homeless applicant may be homeless and in priority need, it is legally required to provide temporary accommodation pending a formal decision. Many of Brisford's homeless applicants are in this position. To make a decision quickly, therefore, is to minimise Brisford's costs in maintaining such applicants in temporary accommodation, particularly where the decision is to refuse assistance. However, there is another less direct sense of 'cost' which relates to long-term housing resources. Brisford suffers from a housing deficit. The available resources to meet its longer term housing duties are scarce. The fewer the number of applicants there are who require long-term housing, the easier and cheaper it is to fulfil these duties. This translates into a pressure only to grant long-term assistance to those who are legally entitled to it. Indeed, it is considered to be much more important to avoid 'false positives' than 'false negatives'. Failing to grant assistance to those who are entitled to it is less problematic than granting assistance to someone who is not entitled:

> **PAO2**: if officers are accepting a case that perhaps shouldn't have been accepted that would be my worry more than anything, the fact that, you know, making sure that people are doing enquiries...

> **Interviewer**: Why should people making an incorrect positive decision be more worrying to you than somebody who makes a negative decision?

> **PAO2**: Well ultimately, if somebody's made a positive decision it means that they're being rehoused into permanent housing stock doesn't it? So that's where the worry is, you know. We're protecting public funds and as I said the housing stock is very limited. That's the worry really, the fact that somebody might be offered permanent accommodation. By the time they're offered the permanent accommodation or by the time something's discovered that it's not correct, you know, or it might be fraudulent, it's too late, the person's been offered the tenancy.

In juggling the competing demands of legality and efficiency, the internal review scheme has an important role to play. It acts as a security blanket when legality is sacrificed to efficiency. The reason why the Principal Assessments Officer above felt that making an incorrect positive decision was less of a problem than making a false negative decision was that incorrect negative decisions can be picked up at the internal review stage. She noted:

> If [decisions] can be legally challenged and you discover that there's an error by the challenge perhaps, ultimately that can be rectified at the review stage. So you're not really losing out a huge deal.

This was a common view within the HPU and helps explain how Assessments Officers make practical decisions about the competing demands of legality and efficiency:

> **AO1**: [AO3] is absolutely correct, in terms of like we've been forced to make decisions quicker than what we might like to. We'd like to carry out further investigations in certain cases, but because of this pressure to meet these Best Value targets etc, the Principal's attitude normally is 'Well you can make a negative decision, they've always got the right for a review of their decision'.

Interviewer: Can you give an example of that?

AO2: Well if you're making a non priority decision on someone and you haven't investigated absolutely everything they might have—you know periods in and out of prison and you haven't confirmed that, or they may be referred to a consultant or something for extra treatment, but they haven't been for the appointment yet. So you're forced into a position of making a negative decision basically. And all that happens is that they'll go for the appointment, the consultant will write them a letter, they'll put in an [internal review request] and you have to change your decision. But rather than wait, you know, for that to happen, you're more or less forced to make that negative decision and sort of see the [internal review] as a fall back, 'Well they've always got a second bite' sort of thing.

As we shall see later on, however, this rationalist view of applicant behaviour is largely unwarranted. Consequently, the use of the internal review scheme as a security blanket for premature or otherwise problematic decision-making creates a problem for administrative justice.

A further note about the relationship between the efficiency discourse and a discourse of welfarism should be added at this point. At an Assessment Officer level it is possible to observe a discourse of welfarism whereby officers on the ground demonstrate a commitment to the welfare of homeless applicants and the provision of assistance to them. The perception of some officers is that Brisford has become too harsh in its approach to decision-making. Some suggested that the HPU has become less caring, more concerned with saving money and meeting quantifiable targets:

AO4: What we're talking about here is, to me it seems like it's a sneaking thing, it wasn't always like that, this kind of tightening off on decisions. You know and that's what it is, it seems to be a kind of, I feel like it is that they're trying to find ways of not assisting people, which isn't what you should be about to me. To me it should be the other way round.

AO5: But you've got to do it in the nicest possible way and as quickly as possible because statistically it looks good.

A tension thereby exists between many of the Assessments Officers and their Principals regarding substantive decision-making. The routine separation of Principals from direct interaction with applicants is crucial to this tension and to the dominance of efficiency over welfarism. The Principal Officers stress that their distance from face-to-face interaction permits them to be more 'objective' or 'professional' in their approach to decision-making and note that Assessment Officers can, at times, be blinded by sympathy. From the perspective of the Assessment Officers, however, the separation between Principal and applicant prevents Principals from exercising empathy:

I feel also there is a complete absence of any ability to empathise. Now I just find that astounding, you know... I just feel that that, with certain managers just, you know, it can crush you. Because you've been sitting with an individual for an hour and a half and you know where this person's at, you know what they're going through, ... For example.., managers—particular ones more than others, but it did seem to spread across the board—would refuse to provide temporary accommodation for someone if they thought that the medical condition might not give that person priority or vulnerability. So they would say 'Mm, depression, mm on medication. No, I think we'll wait till we get the medical back before we provide accommodation'. And you're sitting in the cubicle with someone who's giving you no eye contact, who's really low, you know, and you say 'Look, this man is really bad, he's on this medication, there's all this going on. I'm telling you he needs somewhere, he hasn't got anywhere to go', and they'd say 'I'm sorry, I'm not placing them until we get the medical'. Then we'd get the medical and it would be assessed as vulnerable with very high priority and you have to go and take it and say 'Look, don't tell me somebody who's suffering from depression isn't vulnerable'. There's lots of battles like that. (**Assessment Officer 4**)

However, despite the existence of this tension, the discourse of efficiency usually overwhelms the discourse of welfarism. This can be explained by, first, the separation of Principal Assessment Officers from routine interaction with applicants; and second, the bureaucratic structure of the organisation whereby assessments decisions must be checked and ratified by Principals. In combination these two factors facilitate the dominance of efficiency over welfarism or, to put it another way, the dominance of formal over substantive rationality.

Customer Care The final discourse present in Brisford's decision-making practices is that of customer care. As already noted above, Brisford was granted Charter Mark status which attests to its standards of customer care. The Charter Mark regime has its own set of performance targets which, although not as pressing as the 33 day time limit discussed above, are nevertheless regarded internally as important in judging the overall performance of individual officers and the HPU as a whole. The Charter Mark targets include answering telephones within 5 rings, responding to correspondence within 10 days, and seeing new applicants within 5 minutes. Officers are mindful of these targets, though, as noted above, some expressed scepticism about their value when compared with the importance of granting substantive assistance. In many ways Brisford is an exemplar of the Weberian formally rational bureaucracy.

Decision-Letters

Decision-letters are formal and legalistic in tone. They are also very lengthy, often extending to several pages. The local solicitors which we interviewed appreciated the quality and details of Brisford's decision-letters. Although standard paragraphs and phrasing is used, decision-letters are often explicit about the particular factors which have been considered in making the decision. Indeed, given the fact that legal representations are a common feature of the life of the HPU, letters are written with the potential threat of legal challenge in mind. Although decision-letters are addressed to the applicants, the real audience is the potential legal representative. Unsurprisingly, therefore the details and legal content of these letters are often confusing for applicants. (Indeed, they proved confusing to our fieldworker at the beginning of his research in Brisford.) Interview B14, for example, noted:

> they said that I am eligible for support, but I'm not homeless. So I suppose it's technically correct. A lot of people would get more than that... I don't know what they mean by I'm 'eligible for support' whether that means I'm on a waiting list and in five years I'll get a flat or whether it means that, you know I've been turned down, but I don't know.

The confusing nature of decision-letters, therefore, is a common finding with Southfield Council. However, the significant difference between Brisford and Southfield is that Brisford applicants, despite failing to understand the detail of the decision-letters, often learned about the right to review from the letters. As we shall see below, on the basis of our respective applicant interview data, there are some limited grounds for suggesting that Brisford has been more successful in effectively communicating the right to review by way of letters, even though the precise legal basis for refusals is often lost on the applicants.

Conclusions About Assessments Decision-making: The Audit Authority

In the above section we have provided descriptions of the homelessness application process in Brisford and of decision-making practices. We analysed the social reality of decision-making in terms of various (sometimes competing) discourses. The findings in Brisford can be set against those in Southfield Council. An overview of the two field sites is provided in Table 9 on p 89.

In the light of our data, we have characterised Brisford as the 'audit authority'. Prominence is given to the values of audit and inspection within the assessment decision-making process. Although audit has an intimate relationship with risk (Power, 1997), the risks are of a different order than are prominent in Southfield. In Brisford, audit is used to negotiate

Table 9: Overview of Assessments Decision-Making — Southfield & Brisford

	SOUTHFIELD				BRISFORD
	Men's Residential	Men's Casework	Women's Team	Families' Team	
Physical Environment	Exclusionary	Exclusionary	Open / Welcoming	Open	Open
Decision-making mode	Pre-emptive (1)	Pre-emptive (2)	Inquisitorial	Pre-emptive (3)	Pre-emptive (4)
Officer – applicant Relationship	Authoritarian (1)	Authoritarian (2)	Co-operative	Authoritarian (3)	Authoritarian (4)
Dominant Discourses	Tenantability / Culpability	Legality / Tenantability	Therapy / Tenantability	Legality / Welfare	Legality / Efficiency / Customer Care
Communication of Decision	Immediate oral / Written decision	Written Decision	Incremental / Discursive	Natural Justice Dialogue / Written Decision	Written Decision

institutional risk within a vertical hierarchy. The rise of audit has taken place since the 1980s against, and because of, a number of institutional shifts in the relationship between central and local government, characterised by Paul Hoggett (1996:20–4) as 'centralising decentralisation'.

Hood et al (1999: 93) have noted that, in terms of regulatory oversight, there has been a 'striking growth in both its scope and intensity' in local government. Increasing specification of permissible local authority action in regulatory instruments has been combined with an increasingly crowded regulatory space, filled with regulatory bodies overseeing the role and practice of local authorities (Loughlin, 1996; Vincent-Jones, 2000). A particularly important example of these techniques of government was the development of Compulsory Competitive Tendering, a rolling programme through which a variety of local authority organisational units, including housing management, were put out to tender. In housing management, in fact, just five per cent of these contracts were won externally, but the impact of CCT has been key to the developing managerialisation of housing management. As Walker (2000: 287) suggests, 'Externalisation has enhanced managerialism and established a business culture in social housing'.

CCT involved fairly crude 'command and control' mechanisms (Vincent-Jones, 1998). Its replacement by a 'Best Value Regime' has involved a more reflexive, but equally controlling, regulatory emphasis so that competition is 'now being encouraged in a more subtle and controlling manner' (Vincent-Jones, 2002: 42). Best value works through an 'inculcation of common calculative technologies, forms of evaluation, and norms and values' (Vincent-Jones, 2001).

A crucial aspect of both regimes has been the development and progression of a form of New Public Management. Rather than seeking to govern bureaucracies, the Thatcherite solution was to

> transform the very organisation of the governmental bureaucracy itself and, in so doing, to transform its ethos from one of bureaucracy to one of business, from one of planning to one of competition, from one dictated by the logics of the system to one dictated by the logics of the market and the demands of customers. (Rose, 1999: 150)

Whereas welfare expertise was constructed around an assumption that experts themselves would behave in an altruistic and public-spirited fashion—like knights—the new construction of public management assumes self-interest—knavish behaviour—as a key motivation and provides incentives such as performance related pay (Le Grand, 1997). What is interesting in this context is that, using Le Grand's terminology, Assessments Officers in Brisford sometimes operate as knights but this is swamped by hierarchical monitoring systems which, effectively, turn them into pawns, creating the frustration and powerlessness expressed above.

New Public Management prioritises performance measurement as a calculative technique, prioritising efficiency and economy over the less easily calculable notion of effectiveness (Harlow & Rawlings, 1997: 137). Performance measurement involves the development of auditable systems which are then used internally and externally to demonstrate the quality of service being provided (although, in fact, demonstrating only the quality of system in place: Power, 1997: 59). As Rose (1996: 351) suggests, 'government by audit transforms that which is to be governed'. So, for example, Brisford's status as a charter mark institution is based not on their performance but on the management systems in place to measure their performance against a set of hierarchically designed criteria.

Calculative practices are technologies of government, creating the calculating, responsible individual (Hacking, 1986; Miller, 2001). Rose and Miller point out that

> making people write things down and the nature of things people are made to write down, is itself a kind of government of them, urging them to think about and note certain aspects of their activities according to certain norms. (1995: 200)

This government at a distance is a crucial part of the operation at Brisford. The individual inscription of time taken on individual decisions—the prioritised Best Value Indicator—reflects an organisational efficiency goal impacting upon Brisford's local economy. The publication of individual Assessment Officers' performance against this goal creates a form of internal account and competition, in that individual performance can be measured against each other. These organisational goals are then prioritised over the individual officers' welfarism so that 'the ethos of the welfare state has been displaced by one of "performance government"' (Dean, 1999: 173). In this, we see a shift from public service ethos to one of private management (Rose, 1999: 150).

New Public Management techniques pose the question, who is government for? In other words, to whom are we accountable? In a service like Brisford's HPU, that question is answered in two different ways. First, the collation of statistics of performance enable them to be externally audited and compared against other HPUs as well as an internal audit of performance against each other. In these ways, they give an account to local taxpayers as well as central government. However, one of the tenets of the New Public Management programme is 'the enshrinement of the rights of consumers or users in the internal regulation of government departments' (Dean, 1999: 169). Applicants are no longer envisioned as applicants but as consumers of a service, a false logic which suggests that the applicant can exit from the service being offered. As we see in subsequent chapters of this book, the types of service assumed to be desired by 'customers', relating to efficiency in terms of performance against a series of timed acts (answering a telephone within a certain number of rings, for example), are not the only requirements of applicants. To anticipate the argument, they also want procedural and substantive fairness in decision-making.

Just as Southfield did not entirely fit a risk-model of decision-making, so Brisford does not entirely match an audit model, and so our final words about assessments decision-making are to note some details of the imperfect fit. For example, the discourse of consumerism poses 'the rhetorical question of who is understood to be "on top"' (O'Malley & Palmer, 1996: 141). The clear answer to this question is that Assessments Officers are on top, which is emphasised by the closed, authoritarian approach used in most interviews. There has been no transfer of power other than in the creation of a clean, pleasant office space. The discourse of legality, prominent in Brisford's internal and external monitoring regime, does not fit neatly with a measurement regime as such a discourse collides with that of efficiency, as has been discussed above. The regular collision between welfarist and economy discourses also imply an ongoing uneasy transition between welfare state and 'advanced liberal' government. The discourse of welfarism, thus, can be seen as a sign of resistance to, or tension within, the programmatic intentions of New Public Management as operationalised in Brisford.

ALLOCATIONS DECISION-MAKING

In this section we explore the activities of the two teams which provide accommodation to homeless applicants. The provision of temporary and permanent accommodation is hived off in Brisford to two separate teams. Neither accommodation team is located with the homelessness assessment team and there is limited interaction between the teams. The Temporary Accommodation Team responds to the initial needs of homeless applicants, providing accommodation pending completion of the homelessness assessment process. The accommodation offered to applicants pending an assessments decision is then carried over into the two year accommodation duty owed to 'successful' applicants. It is usually envisaged that homeless households will be made an offer of permanent accommodation from the housing register, under Part VI of the 1996 Act, before the end of their two year temporary accommodation period. This offer is handled by a different team—the Allocations Team—which additionally manages the housing register function. Offers made to homeless households through the housing register are, however, also regarded as being in satisfaction of homelessness duties. Thus, homeless applicants are given the opportunity, over and above other housing register applicants, to a statutory internal review under section 202, 1996 Act.

In order to simplify the structure of this section, the following approach has been adopted. First, the role of the temporary accommodation team will be discussed. Attention is given to how applicants are matched to temporary accommodation together with the pressures of doing the job. Second, there will be discussion of the processes used by the allocations section to match applicants to permanent accommodation. Third, we will focus on the question of applicant grievances against offers of accommodation. This third section only considers grievances about offers of permanent accommodation. Homeless applicants do not have any rights to internal review of the suitability of temporary accommodation granted pending an assessment decision, and Brisford do not operate a discretionary review system for such offers. Successful applicants do, however, have a right to review offers of housing in relation to the two year duty under the 1996 Act. For Brisford, the accommodation which is offered pending an assessments decision is carried over into the discharge of the two year duty. None of our interviewees, however, sought internal review about such offers of 'temporary' accommodation.

Temporary Accommodation Section

The Temporary Accommodation Section is made up of seven accommodation officers and an administrative support officer. A number of departures meant that the team was under-resourced for at least part of the fieldwork period when there was an established team of three officers. The shortfall was made up through the employment of agency staff. The team has gradually increased in size in recent years in part because of the large numbers of applicants placed in temporary accommodation. The team is managed by one principal officer, who also conducts some of the internal reviews on the question of suitability. During any period when the principal officer is absent, the team is managed by the Support Manager, a former accommodation officer. That person shares with the principal officer the responsibility for conducting internal reviews about the suitability of housing offers. Duties of the team include identifying temporary accommodation and dealing with queries from applicants either by telephone or in person.

Resources

A central pressure lies in the availability and quality of accommodation for homeless applicants. Whilst not described as a 'crisis' by officers, it is clear that this is a constant pressure on the team. Family hostel accommodation units were said to be particularly low, with only about three or four generally available. A considerable amount of available stock is outside Brisford's boundaries (up to 80 per cent). The scarcity of resources means that temporary accommodation is generally only granted when deemed absolutely necessary. Applicants are required to remain in their current accommodation for as long as possible. Even where this is not possible, some applicants are advised that, despite their needs, temporary accommodation may not be immediately available on the day. Private Sector Leased ('PSL') property is a particularly highly prized asset, given only to those applicants where there are special considerations.

Applicants are expected to share facilities in hostel accommodation, which makes up most of the available stock of temporary accommodation. There is one hostel, Boonah Hostel, which caters solely for single males. Boonah Hostel has a poor reputation within the council and apparently also amongst applicants. It was described as a former prison with an institutionalised feel to it, arranged on a block basis. The Temporary Accommodation Manager described the problems in this hostel:

> I think because it's a single men's hostel I think you've got lots of people, different age groups, from the very young to the very old, mental health problems, drug problems, people who are very vulnerable and with a single men's hostel, 146 bed spaces, it's very difficult to control, and you know, you get lots of problems just having single men, that large a group in one place.

These problems are not, however, communicated to applicants prior to allocation as accommodation officers do not want to run the risk of applicants refusing the accommodation. The descriptions of Boonah Hostel given by some of our interviewees who had lived there would seem to seem to support the legitimacy of the officers' fears:

> I've never seen anything like this before ... Since I moved here, five people have been in here who are dead because of drugs. (**Interviewee 38**)

> the only one I didn't like was [Boonah Hostel]. Oh God, that was dreadful... I spent Christmas there, oh God... it was terrible. (**Interviewee 60**)

Bed and breakfast accommodation is generally used as a last resort where nothing else is available. There is a policy priority within the HPU of reducing its bed and breakfast use to zero, although it wavers at around the 300 level. Applicants initially placed in bed and breakfast will be moved on at the earliest opportunity. Bed and breakfast expenditure is a large and problematic draw on the HPU's budget.

Allocation of Temporary Accommodation

If it is decided that temporary accommodation is required at the initial assessment interview, the Temporary Accommodation Team is notified through the HPU's internal computer system. An Accommodation Officer will then seek temporary accommodation. The numbers of applicants requiring attention can build up quickly and there is considerable pressure to ensure a throughput of applicants. Accommodation Officers have a performance monitoring target in relation to the waiting time of applicants. Available accommodation is allocated on a 'first come, first served' basis according to what is available:

> Basically, some people are very fortunate, it just so happens that on the day they come into the office we have all these nice PSL properties. (**Temporary Accommodation Support Manager**)

Friday afternoons are a particularly difficult time for the Temporary Accommodation Team as the usual sources of accommodation are often unavailable.

Assessment Officers in the HPU appear to appreciate the pressures of the Temporary Accommodation Team together with the quality of accommodation available. They have a number of strategies designed to assist certain applicants who, for one reason or another, they do not wish to be offered hostel accommodation. These strategies are examples of benign deterrence (cf Carlen, 1994) in that Assessment Officers seek the best temporary accommodation deal for their applicants by deterring them from accessing temporary accommodation at that stage. In case BTA6/2 an assessment officer sought to advise a 16 year old applicant to continue staying with a friend for another night. AO3BF1 explained to the applicant that, as it was late in the day, what would be on offer would be unsuitable. The applicant was perceived by this officer to be a 'worthy cause' as she had a part-time job and was attending college despite her personal circumstances. AO2BF1 was observed operating a similar strategy advising an applicant to come early to the accommodation section on another day to be allocated accommodation other than Boonah Hostel. However, subsequently this officer was observed informing a refugee, who had been supplied low grade accommodation by social services, that the HPU could only offer similar quality accommodation. The officer appeared more concerned that the applicant should 'do something for [him]self' than anything else. Thus, not all acts of deterrence might be described as benign.

Although some applicants received advice about how to improve their temporary accommodation allocation, others had developed their own strategies to the same effect. So, for example, Interview B57 was initially going to be offered temporary accommodation in a neighbouring area, which would have made it difficult for his children to continue at their current school:

> They, they were going to put me in [neighbouring area] and... I begged them, could I come back tomorrow and see if they've got anything else and I waited.

[I now have] a B & B annex. It's like a little flat, but there's no-one there and they come on Fridays and bring bread and milk and stuff... I mean I'm quite happy with the accommodation, if it weren't...not too far from school... we left at seven thirty this morning to get to school for nine.

Interview B55, on the other hand, complained about her allocation on her arrival at the accommodation because it was unsuitable for her as she was five months pregnant and because of its 'social services' feel. The hostel manager apparently telephoned the HPU:

well, I don't know, actually know what she done, but somehow she managed to get me, I think she contacted back .. the lady there that actually placed me there and said that the room wasn't ready, which was true because they hadn't got the wardrobes or whatever. ... This was all sort of done behind closed doors, so I wasn't actually supposed to know anything about this. The lady just said to me that there was an accommodation which they're going to offer me, which she feels would be more suited, cos I think she told them, you know, that it wasn't actually for me.

Allocations Team

The allocations team is responsible for allocating property from the housing register. There are 60 officers split into three teams covering different parts of Brisford. Each team has a manager, a policy and information officer and a senior manager. Performance is measured on a ratio of the number of offers made compared with acceptances.

Differences Between Homeless Applicants And Housing Register Applicants

Offers of housing are made to both homeless applicants and housing register applicants, although there are important differences between them in terms of process.

One Offer Policy Unlike housing register applicants, homeless applicants are subject to a one offer policy. Successful applicants are given one suitable offer of housing. If this is refused, Brisford regards itself as having discharged its duties to the applicant. No further assistance is given. Of course, applicants may challenge the suitability of an offer. As we will see further below, Brisford operates both a pre-statutory and a statutory internal review scheme to consider the suitability of accommodation offers. Although not all applicants appreciate this fact, they may challenge an offer of accommodation at the pre-statutory stage—the 'Refusals' stage—without jeopardising the offer. If Brisford decides that the offer is suitable, the applicant may still accept it. However, if the applicant wishes to continue to challenge the suitability of the offer at the statutory internal review stage they take a risk. Brisford does not hold the property for the applicant pending the statutory internal review process. Consequently, unless the applicant is successful at the internal review stage, there will be no more offers of housing. As we discuss in detail in chapter five, this operates as a form of *coerced choice* for some applicants.

Areas of Choice A second difference is that housing register applicants enjoy a greater number of areas of choice (corresponding to wards), whereas for homeless applicants Brisford has been split into nine areas from which they must specify three areas of choice. Although the reason for this latter split was historical, the larger catchment areas allows Brisford to make offers more quickly to the statutory homeless, thereby easing temporary accommodation expenditure. However, it also impacts upon the number of refusals of offers of accommodation from homeless applicants:

> the area is so vast that they have to choose. So they quite often don't understand that they might be offered something on the periphery of this area which they actually thought was over here. (**Allocations Officer 2**)

The pressure on accommodation in Brisford means that, unless there are special circumstances, single applicants are only allocated bedsit accommodation.

Provision of Information to the Allocations Team

A rehousing form is sent with the decision letter for successful homeless applicants to complete and return. The guidance accompanying the form advises applicants that they

> may increase the speed with which an offer is made... by choosing more than 3 areas. The chart below shows the chances of receiving a quicker than average offer for all the areas of Brisford.

Throughout the assessments process homeless applicants are also advised to opt for as many areas as possible in order to ensure that they will be allocated accommodation quickly. Officers in both the Temporary Accommodation Team and Allocations Team regularly give advice that applicants should choose as many areas as possible—indeed, there is a 'pressure selling' approach adopted by some officers in order to expedite the applicants' allocations.

A separate page of the form gives the applicant an opportunity to provide additional information as to their allocations needs. The information about area choice is then recorded by the Assessment Officer on the HPU's computer system. The additional information provided by the applicant may be summarised on the computer file but this does not always happen. Offers are made on the basis of what appears on the computer file, to which Allocations Officers have access, rather than on the paper file, to which Allocations Officers do not have easy access. It appears, then, that there is an information deficit at this stage of the process which causes applicants to refuse accommodation. Not unnaturally, applicants anticipate that information given at one stage of the process will be carried on to the next stage.

> I noticed on that particular form that was filled in that day, half of the questions that were asked, were not noted. There was no noting of certain things, which I found, because I, I, I was very particular about explaining the problems with my wife and why I shouldn't live anywhere near her… It just happens and, and there you are, Mr Innocent in a situation made by two people who haven't communicated through the department and they can't, you know what's going to happen if they uphold my offer. Their supervisors will go 'Well why did you offer it? Why didn't you check his notes' and so you know I just feel there's a miscommunication within all the departments that puts people in this situation. (**Interviewee B57**)

Matching Properties To Applicants

As regards matching properties to applicants, the Allocations Team is informed by its district offices or Registered Social Landlord partners when a property becomes available. The Allocations officer then seeks to make a match of an applicant with that property, often going through 15 to 20 applicants before finding a suitable match. It is of some interest that one officer's practice is to telephone 'marginal cases' to see if they might be interested in the property. Those applicants who are not available by telephone are by-passed. Applicants can then reject this informal offer without penalty. This process makes bureaucratic sense, even though it may be potentially problematic in law, in that it ensures a more accurate match of applicant to property and, thus, a lower chance of refusal which will then positively impact on the rental income (and performance indicators of housing management).

The Offer

When an offer is made to an applicant, the applicant is usually sent a letter informing him/her that s/he should pick up the keys to the property from the District office or the relevant Registered Social Landlord office so that the property can be viewed. If the property has been refused more than twice in the past, applicants are accompanied when they view the property.

In this section we divide our analysis into two parts. The first part considers the internal review of assessments decisions. In the second part, we discuss internal reviews of offers of accommodation—reviews of decisions of the Allocations Team.

Assessments Internal Review

Introduction

Internal reviews of assessments decision-making are largely carried out by the Principal Reviews Officer. This post was created during our fieldwork period and was a reaction to an increase in the number of internal review requests being received. The number of requests had jumped from 201 in 1997 to 302 in 1999. Additionally, however, the HPU was finding that the sophistication of review requests, largely prompted by an increase in legal representation, was also requiring greater time to be spent in conducting and communicating internal review decisions. Internal reviews were, accordingly, not being conducted within the 56 day statutory target period. Prior to the creation of the post of Principal Reviews Officer, internal reviews were conducted by the three Principal Assessments Officers and the Manager. The Principal Reviews Officer has now taken on most of the internal review caseload, though some cases are still allocated to Principal Assessment Officers.

The Housing Act 1996 imposes a 21 day time limit following the homelessness decision for the submission of internal review requests. Local authorities may, at their discretion, conduct an internal review where a request is received out of time, though they are entitled to refuse. In Brisford this translates into the practical discretion of the Principal Reviews Officer. However, as with the Assessments Officers, the Principal Reviews Officers is subject to performance targets. The manager has set him a target of completing internal reviews within 28 days—half the time of the 56 day Best Value target. The pressure of meeting targets impacts upon his discretion about whether to entertain internal review requests which are received out of time:

> normally when somebody makes a request for review and it's not done within twenty one days the law says we can have discretion of saying we're allowing it. At times I'm under so much constraints and pressures that I don't really wanna entertain any discretion. And that then affects my judgement, basically. I look at it and I say 'Well, you're late, you're late. I don't care what you

have to say' And I just say 'You're late. Go to court if you want to but we're not, I'm not entertaining it.' That is an added pressure on, it's not something I would have expected to come with the job.

Some Statistics On Internal Review

Take Up Rate Brisford recorded 2446 homeless applications during the fieldwork period of October 2000 – September 2001. During the same period, 279 internal review requests were made regarding assessments decisions. We were not, unfortunately, able to obtain a precise picture about how many of these applicants received 'negative' decisions. However, statistics are available for a comparable and proximate period. During the financial year, April 2000 – April 2001, 1425 negative decisions were made. We can estimate, therefore, that the take up rate for the internal review of assessments decisions is 19.6 per cent. In other words, approximately one applicant out every five who receives a refusal of assistance, challenges the decision by way of internal review. Although the take up of internal review is much higher than that in Southfield, and indeed higher than the national figure detailed in chapter two, it still falls within the general pattern noted in chapter two of the pursuit of grievances being low.

Subject Matter of Internal Review Cases An analysis of the statistics during the fieldwork period reveal that priority need is the aspect of the homelessness decision-making process which is by far the subject of the highest number of review requests (45 per cent) in Brisford. Decisions regarding intentionality comprised 20 per cent of internal review requests, with homelessness status constituting the subject matter of 15 per cent of requests. These complete figures are set out in Table 10 below:

Table 10: Subject Matter of Internal Review Requests: Brisford Oct 2000—Sept 2001

Type of Initial Adverse Decision	Number of Internal Review Requests
Ineligibility for Assistance	14 (5%)
Not Homeless	41 (15%)
Not in Priority Need	126 (45%)
Intentionally Homeless	55 (20%)
Local Connection Referral	30 (11%)
Other	13 (5%)
Total	279 (100%)

Time Taken to Do Internal Reviews The average length of time taken to determine internal reviews over the fieldwork period was 50 days. Whilst this suggests that the HPU was relatively efficient in deciding review cases, closer analysis on a month-by-month basis reveals that for several months the time taken to decide review cases was considerably outside the statutory time limit of 56 days. In particular, the average time taken to process review cases in October, November and December 2000 was 89, 98 and 97 days respectively. This began to decrease significantly, in overall terms, from January 2001. By this time it was taking an average of 41 days to assess internal reviews. This subsequently fell to a low of 21 days on average by August 2001. This decrease in the average time taken for internal review decisions corresponds to the appointment of the Principal Review Officer.

Outcome of Internal Reviews The most common outcome of an internal review request is for the original decision to be upheld. During the fieldwork period such was the outcome in 54 per cent of cases (n = 150). By way of contrast, in 19 per cent of cases (n = 54), the original decision was overturned. In 12 per cent of cases (n = 33) the original decision was withdrawn on the basis that further investigations were required. Ten per cent of internal review requests were not considered because they were received after the 21 day time limit.

Table 11: Assessments Internal Reviews by Outcome — Brisford Council

Original Decision Upheld	150 (54%)
Original Decision Overturned	54 (19%)
Further Investigations Required	33 (12%)
Received too late	29 (10%)
Other	3 (1%)
Missing	10 (4%)
Total	279 (100 %)

It might be said, accordingly, that about one third of internal review applicants receive a 'positive' outcome if one aggregates the percentage of overturned decisions and those referred for further investigation. Of course, it not clear whether, after further enquiries, the original decision is overturned or upheld. However, in the cases where the original decision is withdrawn for further enquiries, Brisford at least recognises a deficiency in its original decision and seeks to rectify it.

Two notes of caution, however, must be made at this point. First, there is some quantitative evidence that the proportion of cases where the original decision is overturned was decreasing towards the end of the fieldwork period, with a corresponding increase in the proportion of cases being withdrawn for further enquiries. The dataset is, unfortunately, too limited to conclude that the trend was settled, but a note of caution is at least merited. If this trend continued, then it may be that the proportion of applicants who end up ultimately with a positive housing application may be less (on the presumption that at least some withdrawn decisions return with negative decisions after further enquiries). Second, and relatedly, our qualitative data suggests that not all cases which are withdrawn, and so coded 'FIR', actually entail the making of further enquiries. In addition to situations where the Principal Reviews Officer feels that the enquiry process was deficient, this course of action is also taken where he believes that the articulation of the initial decision is vulnerable to legal attack should the matter proceed to County Court. In this sense the deficiency which is remedied through the withdrawal of the initial decision does not relate to the substance of the decision-making process, but rather relates to the form in which the initial decision is presented to a potential legal audience. In this latter scenario, the decision-outcome remains the same, though the articulation of the decision has been made 'judge-proof'.

Provision Of Information About Internal Review

Information about the right to an internal review is included with every decision-letter—even where Brisford is accepting a duty to provide assistance. The information is contained within a separate 'information pack' which includes a copy of the appeals procedures, a review request form for completion, together with advice about local solicitors firms and advice agencies which may be able to offer assistance in submitting the review request. Assessment Officers also sometimes tell applicants about the existence of internal review during interviews prior to the homelessness decision and advise them to seek legal representation. At times officers also give advice about applicants' chances of success at internal review—particularly when asked directly about this:

> AO3 Well say someone's a sort of homeless gentleman, he might have sort of a mild form of asthma and it's been dealt with by medication, he's never been hospitalised. Some cases like that I think I have gone sort of 'Well you know, you could do but is it worth it?' but I've given advice and assistance under the legislation to do that. But you know I just think again it's being honest about people's, 'You could do it, but ...'

> AO1 I've said it in terms of like section 198 referrals, like if the person wants to be rehoused in Brisford, I know they've got no local connection whatsoever and there's no local connection for special reasons, I'll explain to them 'You can request a review of our decision to refer you to another Council, but the likelihood of that review succeeding is slim, next to none'.

Assessments Officers give this kind of advice out of a sense of fairness to the applicant, of not wanting to unnecessarily raise the hopes of the applicant. As we will see in chapter five, this information can prevent applicants from pursuing review.

The Internal Review Process

Most officers within the HPU are of the view that the creation of the Principal Reviews Officer's post has increased the consistency of decision-making at internal review level. The perception previously was that some officers were stricter than others, and the statistics bear this view out. The Principal Reviews Officer is also regarded with respect by his colleagues in relation to his decision-making abilities and professionalism. However, the pressures of the efficiency discourse influence the way he carries out his routine casework. In order to be able to meet targets he is selective about the depth and extent of his reviews. In relation to the cases of some officers he is very thorough and reviews the whole file, considering both the substantive and procedural aspects of the decision and the wording of the decision letter. Where, however, he has particular confidence in the skills of an Assessment Officer he reviews the case less thoroughly:

> when [Assessments Officer 1] does a decision you know he's probably done about twenty pages of the decision letter himself, and he probably would have covered almost everything. So what I tend to do is not work on what he's done, but work on the decision letter itself. So I just pick up the decision letter and I go through it: 'Yeah, he considered that, yep, yep, yep. Okay. This is what he told this person,' and then I say, 'Well, basically.., I've read this man's letter and I'm happy with it.' And [Assessments Officer 1] is very articulate, he might have a large case load but he does CID type investigations on every single case. And that is good. I mean, I appreciate that and it helps me as well.

The Principal Reviews Officer has been quite successful in meeting his targets. However, he was candid about having to compromise the quality of his review work where cases were nearing the Best Value target:

> what I do is I print off a report at the beginning of every week to tell me how many cases are close to completion within my target days. If I see there's something that's close to the target day I'm more mindful of getting it out, otherwise [the Manager] will come through that door and say 'Why is that one over 56 days?' and the decision at that stage might not be iron cast, it might not be something that's solid, but just so I meet the target and I make the figures required, I would just rather push it out, and the quality's not as good as it would be if I was given time to do it in my own time and space. So those are unnecessary pressures, I think. But touch wood, we don't really get

that many of those. I normally tend to do my cases within the first four weeks.

The vast majority of reviews are conducted on the papers. Applicants are offered the option of making oral presentations, though only a handful had done so to by the end of fieldwork. Brisford is not under a legal obligation to provide temporary accommodation pending an internal review determination. They may do so at their discretion. However, this happens only infrequently. Temporary accommodation is generally declined on grounds of economy. The failure to provide temporary accommodation in these circumstances was a universal criticism in our interviews with solicitors and advice agencies.

Allocations Internal Reviews

Like Southfield, Brisford has two forms of internal review in relation to allocations decisions. It employs a pre-statutory refusals system for permanent offers from the Allocations Team. Applicants have a right to an internal review of the suitability of an offer even if their Refusal is not accepted. This section considers both the refusals system and statutory internal review.

Refusals System

The bulk of complaints about the suitability of offers of accommodation are heard at the Refusals stage. Although no statistics about Refusals are collected, the common perception of officers was that there was a high drop-out rate after the Refusals system. Indeed, as we have seen, the take-up rate for statutory internal reviews of offers of accommodation is particularly low when compared to assessments decisions.

Provision of Information about Refusals Formal offers of permanent housing from the Allocations Team are made by letter. The offer letter includes information concerning the process of accepting the property together with a form to be completed should the applicant wish to refuse. The information about refusing an offer is as follows:

> The council has a policy of making just one suitable offer. If you consider your offer unsuitable, you should complete this form and hand it in on the same day when you return the keys to this office... If you have difficulty in writing or understanding English, please ask for help at the district housing office.

An A4 page is available on the appeal form for applicant to write their reasons for refusing the property. The final page gives space for applicants to provide further medical information. The guidance to applicants does not give any details about the right to the statutory internal review if the offer is deemed suitable at the Refusals stage. Rather, it simply says the following:

> 6. *What happens if I refuse a suitable offer?*
>
> If you are homeless, you will receive a discharge of duty letter telling you that you will receive no further housing offers. Any temporary housing provided for you by the Council will be cancelled...

The bureaucratic process, then, is specifically designed to facilitate the pursuit of grievances at the Refusals stage. Applicants are required to make a decision after viewing a property, and if that decision is to refuse, they are required to communicate this to Brisford at the point of returning the keys. At that stage, applicants are usually required to complete the refusals page providing details of why they are refusing the accommodation. As we will see below, the Refusals process is a streamlined grievance mechanism which is driven by Brisford's economic need to fill vacant properties and to move homeless applicants out of temporary accommodation.

Refusals Decision-Making   When a refusal is received by the District Office, it is sent through to the Allocations Team which makes a decision on that refusal. The applicant is then informed within four days as to whether or not his/her refusal has been upheld. In the case of homeless applicants, the four day period is significant. If the refusal is not accepted, the offer is kept open to give them a further opportunity to take the property. The reason for the swift turnaround of refusals is the need to ensure maximum recovery of revenue:

> Every week somebody's not living in the flat, we're losing a week's rent. (**Allocations Manager 1**)

The refusals process is dealt with by the Allocations Managers, each refusal generally being considered by two managers. The managers consider the applicant's reasons for refusal, the details of the property offered, and any casenotes available. On an apparently ad hoc basis, some allocations managers might also telephone the district office for verification of certain details about the property. Then a decision is made about

> whether the offer was a reasonable one within what we knew about the applicant and what they said they wanted and what we know about the property. (**Allocations Manager 2**)

Where 'social factors' are raised in a refusal (such as proximity of the property to a child's school or hospital for outpatient treatment), a further question considered is the likelihood of another property closer to the school or hospital becoming available. Decision-making was described as:

common sense. It either fits their needs or it doesn't ... or new information's come in that changes what their needs and preferences are. (**Allocations Manager 1**)

Medical factors and their impact upon the refusals process are problematic for a number of reasons. In follow-up interviews, the managers highlighted the problem of some refusals decisions being made without knowledge of medical factors relating to suitability which had been raised by the applicant. The managers make their decisions on the basis of information contained on computer files. The paper file is held in another part of the building. However, although applicants in the early stages of their application for housing may try and alert the HPU to medical factors which they feel should be fed into the allocations process, this information is not always put into the computer system. Such failures in information processing can lead to inappropriate allocations.

However, even where the managers are aware of possible pertinent medical factors, different practices exist in handling such cases. The pressure to make the refusals decision within four days is always present. This tight timeframe effectively means that applicants do not have time to get a report from their doctors about their medical conditions. Some managers accept the validity of certain refusals on the basis of an 'unproven' medical condition, subject to a later assessment by Brisford's own medical officer. Others make a point of requesting Brisford's medical officer to make an urgent assessment so that a more informed decision can be made within the four day time limit.

The pressure which the four day time limit places on the quality of medical investigations can be illustrated by the case of Interview B54. This couple were offered a property on the eighth floor of a housing block managed by a housing association. They viewed the property while accompanied by a housing officer. The male partner was on crutches and the female partner, who suffered from claustrophobia, was seven or eight months pregnant. After the viewing, the officer made it clear to the couple that he would fax Brisford to say that the property was unsuitable as 'you don't do lifts and you can't walk up stairs':

> So anyway, they faxed a letter through, and then they wrote back and said they wanted some doctor's... records or notes. My doctor unfortunately went away. I notified them ... saying he wouldn't be back until the twenty-eighth of March. Then on about the twenty-sixth of March, they wrote back and said the appeal had been denied because they hadn't heard from the doctor.

Equally, Interview B55 refused an offer on the ground that she was claustrophobic. Her refusal was rejected on the ground that there was no medical evidence of this condition. She was aggrieved by this:

They said to me, 'On the appeal, the medical side of it had to be assessed by a medical officer'. So what I then done, when I got the appeal back is I then said, 'Well, I've only just received the medical form. You can't sort of tell me that my appeal's been turned down and you haven't seen the medical evidence that you asked for'.

It seems clear that the four day time limit severely compromised the depth of investigations which could be carried out. We can see that in some cases applicants are given the benefit of the doubt in the absence of full medical enquiries, but that in others a decision is made on the basis of as much medical opinion that can be obtained within the time permitted. This equivocation is also reflected in decisions about more 'social' factors. In cases where the applicant feels that there is a risk of violence from someone living in the proximity of the offered property, the applicant is generally given the benefit of the doubt in the absence of full investigations. As Allocations Manager 1 noted: 'They can make up anything ... [though] it at least means they can't use it again.'

The short time limits for refusals mean that few applicants have third party support in conducting their refusal. Indeed, it was said that the only advisers who might become involved in the refusals process are key workers, generally with the single homeless, who might write a letter of support for the applicant.

Statutory Internal Review

If the Refusal is rejected, applicants are at this stage given information about their right to the statutory internal review. However, as we noted above, the level of internal review activity concerning offers of housing is much less than that concerned with assessments decisions.

Some Statistics On Internal Review   During the fieldwork period 71 internal review requests were received (see Table 12, p 108). Forty-one of these cases related to offers of permanent accommodation and 30 related to offers of temporary accommodation. Internal reviews of allocations decisions were generally resolved more quickly than reviews of assessments decisions. The average number of days taken to determine internal review requests was 25. A slightly higher proportion of cases were unsuccessful. During the fieldwork period, in 47 of the 71 cases (66 per cent), the offer was deemed to be suitable. In 23 cases (34 per cent) the offer was determined to be unsuitable. Only one review request was received beyond the time limit.

As we can see, the nature of the allocations process precludes any equivalent of 'FIR' (further investigations required). Offers of housing are either withdrawn or upheld. Interestingly, relative to assessments decision-making

Table 12: Allocations Internal Reviews by Outcome — Brisford Council

Original Offer Upheld	Original Offer Withdrawn	Received Too Late	Total
47 (66%)	23 (34%)	1 (1%)	71 (100 %)

a comparable proportion of internal review applicants receive a positive outcome—approximately one in three.

The Internal Review Process Internal reviews are conducted by the Temporary Accommodation Manager, the Support Manager or the Principal Allocations Officer. The Support Manager, a former Temporary Accommodation Officer, manages a vast array of different parts of the service, including the reception and security teams. Her involvement in the internal review process appears to have arisen because she manages the Temporary Accommodation Team in the Manager's absence. None of the reviewing officers have been given any training into how to conduct reviews—they learned on the job:

> So it was quite daunting … but obviously after you've been doing it for a while it becomes okay, you know what to look for. (**Support Manager**)

Whilst refusals decision-making is made under strict time pressures to ensure low void turnaround times, thus restricting applicant's ability to obtain advice and any further assessments, internal reviews decision-making operates over a more extended period. Indeed, officers conducting the reviews are likely to extend the time scales if further information is required as part of a defensive strategy

> it wouldn't look good on us if we go to court and, you know, we've not given them the extra time to provide the information we've requested. (**Principal Allocations Officer**)

As a general rule, once an application for an internal review is received it is allocated to one of the three reviewing officers in an ad hoc way. Each officers' practice is then to write to the applicant or their adviser to request that any further information be provided within 14 days. At that initial stage, the officer generally makes a prima facie observation of the strength of the case 'look[ing] at issues that I might need to pin point and look at, and just formulate a kind of idea, background in my mind basically' (Principal Allocations Officer). Applicants and advisers are also invited to make oral representations. Other types of enquiries would be made depending on the facts of the case. The Principal Allocations Officer used the following example to illustrate the types of necessary enquiries:

> I dealt with a review where we offered someone temporary accommodation at a bed and breakfast, he refused it on the grounds that his daughter was

assaulted in the school, they provided some articles which seemed to support that, but what I had to look at was is there, has the incident occurred since then, so that meant ringing the school, trying to find out information, ringing the police and seeing if there's been any further incidences since the incident last year. Was she the main focus of the attack or was it just a juvenile sort of ruck which got out of hand, was there another bus route that she could travel to, you know, to get to the school, you know, that sort of thing I had to consider. Although they provide that information you might have to do your own, and you'd have to do your own investigative work to sort of come to a conclusion as well.

It seems that particular store is placed by the provision of new information, and its verification, although certain new information may be regarded sceptically. It was said that most reviews involve medical evidence which had not originally been submitted during the assessment interview:

> It's mainly phobia of lifts, fear of heights, and those are the ones which, you know, have never been revealed before, even though we've gone through the assessment interview, we particularly ask the client, 'Is there any member of your household or family suffer from a mental of physical problem?' the answer's no, but then when they get an offer of the fifteenth floor of a tower block, then suddenly they've got a fear of lifts, a fear of heights (**Principal Allocations Officer**)

By contrast to the decision-making at the refusals stage, internal reviews decision-making, much like with assessments decisions, takes place 'in the shadow of the law' (Cooper, 1995):

> No matter how trivial we may think it is we need to take everything into account and we need to make sure that on our review letter that is pointed out, every single point they've made that we addressed it. (**Support Manager**)

The officers would spend up to two days formulating their letter in each case. The reviewing officers reported that most applicants have legal involvement with their case (anecdotally, it was suggested to be around 90 per cent) and that the benefit of legal advice was that :

> they know all the legal jargon and they know the Act, and a normal lay person probably don't understand anything. (**Support Manager**)

Temporary accommodation is not always provided during the internal review, although none of our applicant interviewees were evicted from their temporary accommodation before completion of the internal review. The client must make out a case as to why an extension is necessary.

CONCLUSION

In this chapter, we have examined Brisford's HPU, demonstrating its differences with Southfield. Whereas Southfield's HPU seemed chaotic and difficult to understand, Brisford's HPU has been described in terms of its high level of bureaucratic rationality. We described Southfield as a 'risk authority', whereas Brisford has been described as an 'audit authority', which pays particular attention to discourses of efficiency and accountability. At the same time, we have also noted that there were competing discourses of legality and welfarism within parts of the HPU. We have highlighted areas of unlawful decision-making (the receptionist) and factors which may result in the use or non-use of the internal review process (Assessments' Officers explanations to applicants about the likelihood of their success). The significance of bureaucratic practice to applicants' failure to pursue internal review is explored in detail in chapter seven.

We have also described the systems available for challenging adverse decisions, either on the basis of a negative assessment or the provision of unsuitable accommodation. Although different types of personnel and systems operate, there are some unifying factors. Economy is clearly uppermost and this is combined with efficiency output requirements to make a decision on the case within certain time limits. These factors impact upon the processes undertaken, combined with external factors such as the 'audience' of the review, a point to which we return in subsequent chapters.

5

Understanding the Failure to Pursue Internal Review

INTRODUCTION

In this chapter we consider our data about the non-emergence of disputes—where applicants failed to pursue internal review or dropped out of the process prematurely. Our interview data was interrogated until no new themes emerged. Although we make no claim about the exhaustiveness of the list of reasons detailed in this chapter which account for the failure to take-up internal review (even in respect to homelessness law in particular), we were nevertheless encouraged by the fact that the same set of reasons emerged from both fieldwork sites. Indeed, the applicant data from both sites are presented here together as a composite list.

Although the principal data in this chapter was obtained through interviews with applicants, we would stress that a full understanding of most (though not all) of the reasons for failure to take up the right to internal review must be situated in a parallel understanding of the social reality of bureaucratic decision-making. An examination of the relationship between the citizen and the bureaucrat(s) in the application process is essential to a deeper understanding of the low take-up of rights to review. It is a key factor which has been missing from previous research. Not only does this 'interaction perspective' give us a richer account of the failure to take up review, it can also feed directly into the policy agenda of increasing citizens' access to the machinery of administrative justice. In the sections which follow, we set out the reasons for failure to pursue review gleaned from our data and relate those reasons (where applicable) to the applicants' interactions with, and experiences of, the councils' bureaucracies.

There may, of course, also be factors particular to the applicant which assist us in understanding the failure of take up of internal review. Accordingly, we also seek to identify aspects of applicants' personal circumstances which have contributed to decisions about whether or not to pursue internal review. By setting out a schema of the 'personal' *and* 'bureaucratic' factors which together account for individuals' decisions about whether to take up internal review, we aim both to describe *and* contextualise these particular barriers to the pursuit of grievances.

One final point requires to be made about the reasons for failing to pursue internal review described below. We set out a list of the reasons as individual factors or circumstances which hinder the take up of internal review. This is necessary for analytic purposes. However, it is important to stress these factors often *combine* to form barriers to internal review. Some of the factors are more likely to operate on their own, but most of our interviewees demonstrated that their failure to seek internal review was accounted for by a combination of factors.

IGNORANCE OF THE RIGHT TO INTERNAL REVIEW

The first reason for failing to pursue internal review is applicants' lack of awareness of the right to do so. At first blush, this may seem obvious and unsurprising. It was, for example, a finding in the early research on local authority complaints procedures that they were poorly publicised and there was general unawareness of their existence (Lewis et al, 1987). However, our finding ceases to be unsurprising when we examine the homelessness case files in both of our case study local authorities and discover that information about the right to internal review is routinely included in every decision-letter. It should be noted that there are reasons to suspect that Brisford's method of communicating the existence of the right to review in written form may be more successful than that of Southfield, though given the small size of our sample in both sites, we cannot conclude this. However, a brief comparison between the two sites at least raises that suspicion: in Brisford, 37 out of our 43 assessments interviews were aware of the right to review. At least 17 of these applicants had learned of the right to review through the decision-letter alone. This stands in contrast to Southfield where the vast majority of our assessments interviewees were unaware of the right to review. Nevertheless, ignorance of the right to internal review occurred amongst both sets of interviewees. Our data suggests that there are three explanatory factors which helps us account for this situation.

Applicant Does Not Receive The Decision-Letter

There are some situations where the applicant does not receive the decision-letter and so is not formally informed about the right to review. In Southfield, for example, this may occur where a decision is made by the Families Team at the initial interview to refuse assistance and the applicant terminates the interview before the officer prints out a letter. In other parts of Southfield's HPU, some applicants lose touch with the bureaucracy and do not ever receive a written decision-letter. This may be because they are excluded as a result of threatening behaviour; or it may be because the applicant is only seeking overnight accommodation, has no interest in the outcome of the homelessness application, and moves on afterwards irrespective of the decision.

In relation to both Southfield and Brisford, it is impossible to gauge the extent of the problem of applicants failing to receive decision-letters. The experience of Interview B3, however, does illustrate the importance of verbal communication of the right to review. When he failed to receive a formal decision-letter, he contacted the HPU and was told about the decision verbally. No information, however, was communicated about the right to internal review. Other interviewees in Brisford indicated that they had learned about the right to internal review during the course of their interview with the Assessments Officers. Indeed, it seems to be a routine practice of some Assessments Officers in both sites to do this, but is by no means the practice of all.

The situations where applicants do not receive a written decision (and, consequently, written information about the right to internal review) are probably the exception rather than the rule in both sites. Of much greater interest and concern is the question of why homeless applicants are unaware of their right despite having received the information about it.

Applicant Receives, But Does Not Read Decision-Letter

Some applicants do not read their decision-letters, or at least do not read the whole of it. The formal decision-letter from a Homeless Persons' Unit may be but one of many formal letters which homelessness applicants receive about their housing and other welfare needs. For some applicants, it is easy to be overwhelmed by the extent of formal correspondence from various welfare bureaucracies, and to ignore its content. Interview S10, for example, was uncertain about whether she had received her decision-letter, and was certainly unaware of its content:

> **Interviewer:** Did they give you any reason why they weren't gonna re-house you?
>
> **Applicant:** No.
>
> ...
>
> **Interviewer:** Right, did they send you a letter to tell you this as well, that they weren't gonna re-house you?
>
> **Applicant:** Yeah, probably did, yeah.
>
> **Interviewer:** Right, I've got a copy of the letter they should have sent. Can you remember getting that one?

Applicant: No, no I don't remember 'em sending this, unless they've gimme it, you see they gimme a lot of letters when I was [in the temporary accommodation], do you know what I mean?

Interviewer: Right, so they might have given it to you there then?

Applicant: Yeah, probably did.

Interviewer: But they didn't explain to you what it meant or anything?

Applicant: No, I can't remember getting it, (she reads the letter to herself) ... What's it mean, that they won't re-house me?

Other applicants rely on what there were told in their interviews and so pay little attention to decision-letters or actively discard it because they are angry at their refusal of assistance which was communicated at interview. Interview B27 is an example of an applicant who relied on the face-to-face exchange with the Assessments Officer to understand Brisford's decision. This illustrates the importance of verbal as opposed to written communication to many applicants:

Interviewer: were you actually aware of the fact that you were entitled to appeal?

Applicant: No... Nobody tells you anything.

Interviewer: Had you been informed verbally when you had your interview or ...

Applicant: No.

Interviewer: ... or anything like that?

Applicant: No.

Interviewer: But it came with the letter?

Applicant: But, because if she had said to me 'Now you'll be getting a letter which you can appeal against any decision made but you've got to do it within 21 days, bla, bla, bla, this and that', I would have paid really extra attention, read it all and appealed straight away or whenever. So because this came and I thought, oh this is all (...) again, and just went, like exactly what I'm doing now and just couldn't be bothered with it.

Applicant Reads, But Does Not Understand Decision-Letter

Some applicants fail to understand the terms of a decision-letter despite reading it. This failure to understand can be accounted for at three levels.

General Confusion

Some applicants are simply confused. Interview B56, for example, was unaware that a decision had been made on his homelessness application. Indeed, he was unaware of even having made a homelessness application per se. He was a particularly vulnerable individual with a history of rough sleeping, drug abuse and mental illness. He was deemed to be not in priority need. However, he did not understand that his application for housing was being assessed under homelessness law. He thought that he had simply applied to the general housing waiting list and that his application could not be processed until he obtained his birth certificate and a doctor's letter for identification purposes. For this applicant, the legal and organisational differences between applying for assistance under the general housing register and under homelessness law were of no significance. He failed to understand the terms of his decision-letter and had failed to appreciate that there was a right to internal review.

For other applicants, their engagement with broader parts of the welfare system is overwhelming and they lose sight of the particularity of the homelessness application process relative to, for example, the housing benefit application process, the asylum application process, and so on. In this situation, being able to divorce one bureaucratic process from another can become difficult. Instead, the many welfare bureaucracies they deal with appear as constituent parts of a greater whole, and so the applicant fails to recognise the particular significance of a decision-letter from the council's Homeless Persons' Unit.

Such was the case with Interview S17. He was an asylum seeker. His plight was perhaps worsened by the fact that English was not his first language even though a translator assisted him. He displayed considerable confusion about his situation—even to the extent that he seemed to be unaware of having made a homelessness application. In his mind, he had simply made an asylum application. This had been refused and he was appealing against that decision at the time of interview. Of course, in a sense the interviewee was correct to regard the asylum application as being central to his welfare. He had been refused housing because his asylum application had been rejected. Further, the social services department had undertaken to pay his rent pending his asylum appeal. There was, perhaps, nothing to be gained by seeking internal review. However, the point of importance here is that this was not the reason that he failed to seek internal review. It was his ignorance rather than his understanding of his rights which led to his inaction.

Specific Confusion

However, even where homeless applicants are neither generally confused, nor subject to complex and confusing circumstances, they can still be uncertain about the content of a decision-letter. In relation to Southfield, a number of interviewees expressed difficulty in understanding the terms of decision-letters. Decision-letters (with the exceptions of offers of housing) were generally legalistic and formal in tone. It is easy to understand why they might be confusing or intimidating for those who are inexpert in homelessness law. Consider, for example, the standard format for a refusal of housing on the grounds of intentional homelessness. The letter would start as follows:

Dear [Applicant]

Re: THE HOUSING ACT 1996 PART VII (Homelessness) SECTION 184

Your request for assistance under the above Act has been considered. Following careful and extensive enquiries based upon the information you have given us, I am writing to inform you of our decision.

1. You are an eligible person
2. You are homeless
3. You are in priority need
4. You are homeless or threatened with homelessness, but we find you to be homeless intentionally

It seems paradoxical that a rejection letter should begin with a statement that the applicant is eligible. Indeed, this proved to be a source of confusion for some of our interviewees. Interview S2, for example, said:

I thought that meant that they would [house me]. It says 'You are eligible, you are homeless.'

Southfield's decision-letters comply broadly with the legal requirements of giving a formal explanation of the reasons for a rejection—though letters from the Residential Units are generally more formulaic and less detailed than those from the Families Team.

Generally speaking, as we can see, the letter is structured to reflect the separate stages of entitlement contained in the legislation. Further, at the end of the letter the applicant is formally informed of the right to internal review. Our data indicates that this mode of communication was successful in informing some applicants of their right to internal review. However, for many others the decision-letter proved to be uncommunicative. They failed to appreciate the existence of the right to internal review, despite having read the letter.

Instead, such applicants are more likely to gain their understanding of the nature of the decision and the reason for that decision from the personal interactions with the caseworker which precede the formal decision-letter. For these applicants, the formal decision-letter is a secondary and ineffective mode of communication, and so the information about right to review is missed or not comprehended. Indeed, particularly in relation to Southfield's Residential Units, a number of applicants believed that they were being refused assistance because of their past criminal or otherwise problematic conduct—a message which had been communicated during face-to-face interactions but which was not the formal base for the homelessness decision itself. We saw in chapter three that some of our interviewees' recollections of the application process were dominated by memories of questioning about criminal convictions, and that they took from this that their criminal records were the reasons for refusal of housing. These messages, gleaned through the face-to-face interactions with Assessments Officers, are more immediate and intelligible. They effectively trump the formal reasoning contained in the decision-letter.

Brisford's decision-letters are at least as complex and legalistic as those of Southfield, if not more so. However, by contrast to our Southfield interview data, there was no real evidence of this acting as a barrier to applicants learning about the existence of the right itself. Solicitors and other legal advisers within the Brisford area noted that, in their experience, most applicants did appear to have grasped that some kind of review or 'appeal' was possible, although they generally did not understand what was involved in an internal review or how it operated. This supports the suspicion mentioned above that Brisford's form of communication of the right to review is more effective.

English As A Second Language

Our applicant interview data does demonstrate that language problems operate to prevent applicants learning about the right to review in Brisford. Decision-letters and the accompanying information about the right to review are written in English only. Brisford's homeless applicant population, however, is multi-ethnic and for many English is not their first language. The fact that complex and legalised content was communicated in a foreign language confused some applicants. For Interview B32 the decision-letter was unintelligible without translation (by his cousin's wife, who translated all documents for him). Circumstance meant that translation of his decision-letter was not possible:

Interviewer: Right. Does he understand what was explained in this letter?

Applicant via translator: No, no, because I did not understand, my cousin's wife, I couldn't show the letter to my cousin's wife to see what it contained on that letter, what's on that letter, what, what that letter says.

Interviewer: Right. Can you ask him why he did not show it to his cousin's wife?

Applicant via translator: They weren't here during the holidays, they work away so I couldn't visit them.

INTERNAL REVIEW SCEPTICISM

One of the themes which has been highlighted in previous research about failure to pursue internal review or appeal relates to citizens' scepticism about the integrity of such processes. This theme also emerged from our study and constitutes our second explanatory reason for the failure to pursue internal review. However, the pertinent and interesting question in this regard, we would suggest, is *why* scepticism exists—an issue which has not been explored sufficiently in previous research. We found three reasons to explain internal review scepticism.

Lack of Independence

The first, and perhaps most obvious reason for internal review scepticism is the fact that the review process is *internal* and so not independent. This echoes the findings of previous studies (Sainsbury & Eardley, 1991; Huby & Dix, 1992; Genn, 1994). Sainsbury (1994a; 1999) has made some useful analytical distinctions between independence and impartiality. Whereas independence employs the understanding that 'no person should be a judge in their own cause', he argues that impartiality implies an absence of bias. Whereas independence is a process issue, impartiality is not an attribute that can be guaranteed by the structure of an appeals system. Rather, impartiality must be practised by decision-makers themselves.

At an empirical level, however, our data suggests that at least some welfare applicants fail to draw these distinctions, instead conflating independence and impartiality. A few of our interviewees displayed such scepticism towards the integrity of the internal review process, doubting, in effect, whether the local authority was prepared to overturn its own decisions. For example, in relation to Southfield, Interview S12 commented:

Interviewer: Do you intend to ask about getting an internal review?

Applicant: I don't think that it would make any difference. They are just going to come up with the same thing aren't they? I am not priority... its going to make them look pretty stupid if they turn around and say 'well they are priority now'. You know what I mean?

Similarly, in relation to Brisford, Interview B18 commented, reflecting a more general scepticism about appeal processes:

I never consider an appeal. If I can't get it done straight away then I don't, because there's no, cos if, I know that I'm verbose enough, I'm intelligent enough to get things done and if they can't deal with it right there and then, there's no point in dealing with an appeal, because they've made up their minds.

However, although a few interviewees doubted the impartiality of the local authority in conducting an internal review, a far greater number were unconcerned about this as the following extract from Interview B51 illustrates:

Interviewer: how do you think the council should go about appealing your case?

Applicant: I think that anything that [the Assessments Officer] has to say or has had to say in the past, should be scrubbed, should be scrubbed completely because it's a load of nonsense, which as I've just proved there from the letter, and I've got letters there from me doctor and everything else, and I've got letters from the solicitor and what not, I don't think he should be allowed to say anything, because I think that he's been very biased in his outlook, and anything that he writes or anything that he's got to say should be just slung out, and I think they should look at it independently.

Interviewer: When you say that, what do you mean by 'independently'?

Applicant: It should be a new case worker who can get the evidence that's given in front of him and judge it fairly without all this hassle that I've been having in the past, and to me that's the only way, that's the only way that any satisfaction will come from both sides, from their side and mine.

It seems, then, that understanding scepticism about internal review is more complicated than simply noting its lack of independence. Our data suggests that an examination of trust in the applicant-bureaucracy relationship also assists in gaining a full understanding of internal review scepticism.

Lack of Trust

Our data suggests that applicants' experiences with the bureaucracy during the initial application process, and the nature of that initial relationship, are significant to the existence of scepticism about the integrity of internal review. Internal review scepticism seems to focus more on the organisation and its integrity than on the features of the process itself. The suggestion here is fairly simple: initial experiences of applying for welfare assistance and receiving a decision will be influential in informing the applicant's perceptions of the integrity of the welfare agency. Where the individual's experience is one of a perceived breach of trust, this is conducive to scepticism about the value of pursuing an internal review.

Sociology of Trust

There is now a considerable sociological literature about trust. During the past 20 years or so a large and rich field has developed which may now be termed the sociology of trust. Our interest in the sociology of trust is grounded in our applicant interview data about the applicants' interactions with the respective welfare bureaucracies and the significance of trust in the applicant–bureaucracy relationship. Accordingly, our discussion of trust operates at the micro level and emanates from the experiences of our interviewees. Our aim here is also restricted to describing the function of trust in relation to applicants' failure to challenge adverse decisions. Much (though not all) of the sociological literature on trust operates at quite an abstract and macro level—particularly in relation to the 'risk society' thesis (see for example, Luhmann, 1988; Giddens 1990; Beck 1999)—though the function of trust has also been explored in relation to specific fields ranging, for example, from economics (Fukuyama, 1995) to welfare policy (Taylor-Gooby, 2000) to lawyer-client relationships (Webb and Nicholson, 1999). The concept of 'trust' itself has been the subject of much analysis. Seligman (1997), for example, draws his conception of trust particularly tightly, suggesting that trust exists in social interaction when systemically defined role expectations are not viable:

> Trust is some sort of belief in the goodwill of the other, given the opaqueness of other's intentions and calculations. The opaqueness... rests precisely on that aspect of alter's behaviour that is beyond the calculable attributes of role fulfilment; if it were otherwise, alter's actions would not be unknown but assessable within the framework of the defining system of role expectations and hence reflect confidence and not trust. (1997: 43)

Luhmann (1988), also makes a distinction between 'trust' and 'confidence' but in a different way. For him, trust is indivisibly bound up with risk. Trust exists where the individual makes an active choice between alternatives. Confidence, by way of contrast, involves expectations about contingent events without an act of choice. Sztompka (1999) makes a similar distinction:

> [Trust] differs from hope and confidence in that it falls within the discourse of agency: actively anticipating and facing an unknown future (1999: 25)

Giddens (1990), on the other hand, takes a broader view and sees trust as a particular type of confidence rather than as something distinct from it:

> Trust may be defined as confidence in the reliability of a person or system, regarding a given set of outcomes or events, where that confidence expresses a faith in the probity or love of another, or in the correctness of abstract principles. (1990:34)

Although we make no attempt to engage critically in further conceptual analysis of trust, the level and variety of the existing analysis within the sociology of trust urges us to be clear about what we mean when we talk of the 'trust' inherent in the citizen-bureaucracy relationship. To do this, we must look to our empirical data. The cases of Interviews B27 and B34 are helpful in this regard. Interview B27 (a husband and wife) were private tenants facing eviction from their home. They applied for housing, but were given the decision that they were not homeless. During interview, they expressed dissatisfaction with the application process. They were required to attend at the HPU's offices several times to produce documentation which confirmed their circumstances. They were also left waiting for long periods of time (Sarat (1990) argues that waiting time reflects whose time is valued and whose is valueless). They felt that the HPU officers did not believe their account of events. In the extract below, they give their impression of their treatment:

> **Interviewer**: How did you actually find the interview itself, I mean in terms of all the various things that were being asked of you?
>
> **Applicant 1**: It was just a formality. I just felt that they're not really interested. It's just, this is what they do every day and they're like a machine asking the same questions, they couldn't care less about you, they don't even look at you, and they just muck you around... She went away with about... three or four papers and it took her three quarters of an hour. This is just so that you will be upset by the time she comes back...
>
> **Applicant 2**: I have a feeling they're just some sort of tactics they teach them to do, I think it's sort of like putting people through a sieve and see who's genuine and who isn't. I mean you understand psychology for instance. I'm a tailor myself. I do see people every day, people come and buy for fitting. You know you try to suss out whether they're genuinely coming in to do something, to buy or waste time or just, and that for the genuine person is very annoying, you see because exactly like what happening you know when I took the papers second time...

Later, the husband described this second visit to the HPU. They were left waiting for a long time, despite having arranged an appointment to have their papers copied. He explains his frustration and disappointment at his treatment:

Applicant 2: She came back and I said 'I'm sorry, but do you know that you've kept me here for over an hour'—just for the sake of photocopying a few things. I could have photocopied it and handed it, but I wanted her to see the original because maybe they don't believe that's the birth certificate. And that's the only thing I was there for... I said 'Because my wife was on a day off, I left my business behind to come here', and I said 'at the end of the day I am your business'... I said 'This hurts [to] come here, trusting you to do something for [us], I am your business' and she didn't understand it. She was angry... And I said 'Anyway I'm not gonna waste my time arguing.' I said 'If you don't understand that, you wouldn't understand anything'... I never went back.

Interview B34, on the other hand, was a single man residing at a large hostel which specialised in providing accommodation for single men with drug and alcohol dependency and other socio-medical problems. He suffered from Parkinson's disease and depression and was a recovering alcoholic. He had received a couple of offers of permanent accommodation but he had either refused them and/or not turned up to view them. The HPU made a third offer in the same block of flats as a previous offer. In the extract below, he described his feelings on receiving this final offer:

Interviewer: How did you feel when you got this letter?

Applicant: I was mad.

Interviewer: What did you? Did you do anything?

Applicant: I wanted to do something... I seen this woman in [the hostel]... I said 'If he was here I'd stuff it down his throat, that letter', I said. It fuckin' upset me, you know, I said 'I'll kill him, I'm going down to see him.' (Laughing) The woman said 'Please don't, let me see about it first...' I was mad. And they said to me, 'Leave it'... They copied, they photocopied it, right. I don't know what happened, I don't know what they done then like.

Interviewer: So the lady [in the hostel] did something for you?

Applicant: I don't know. I don't know who to trust, you see. Like they say, but I don't know if these people are having me on as well, I don't know, but I'm still gonna see about this letter, I keep meaning to see about it.

These two cases illustrate the importance of trust to applicants' negotiation of the welfare system. We suggest that there are three senses in which our interviewees 'trusted' the welfare bureaucracy.

Trust That Needs Will Be Met

The primary sense in which applicants trust the welfare bureaucracy is to have their welfare needs met. As Interview B27 noted above, they had gone to the HPU trusting that Brisford would 'do something' for them. Of course, it might be argued that welfare applicants are not really exercising 'choice' in approaching the welfare agency for assistance. Surely, it might be argued, the act of seeking help (particularly if they are homeless people) is an act of last resort? If one subscribes to the distinction between 'trust' and 'confidence', one may be sceptical about the appropriateness of the usage of the term 'trust' here. We would suggest, however, that the act of welfare application is indeed a positive act of choice. Homeless applicants are not without agency and do make active decisions about where to go (for example, going to the HPU is an act of choice against, for example, continuing to sleep on the streets or in overcrowded accommodation). Equally, most are capable of developing strategies beyond their homelessness application to cope with their housing situation.

One's options may seem limited (welfare application *versus* self-help and the risk of further degradation), but welfare applicants exercise their agency which brings with it, as we shall see below, further risks. In any event, notwithstanding this view, the more important point is that whether or not one feels uneasy about the use of the term 'trust', our findings about the impact of a refusal of assistance on the existence of internal review scepticism remain clear. The disappointment of expectation can cause a loss of faith in the integrity of the welfare agency which can lead to internal review scepticism and the failure to take up one's right to review.

Trust In The Expertise Of The Bureaucrats

Although our interviewees entertained a core expectation that their needs would be met, they were less clear about precisely what assistance would be given and about how the process for meeting their needs would operate. This requires a second form of trust—trust in the expertise of the welfare bureaucrats to carry out the process properly which, in turn, will lead to delivery of the substantive benefit. The welfare system is an 'expert system' in Giddens' terms (1990). It is opaque and confusing for applicants. Rules of entitlement, the nature of entitlement, even the bureaucratic process itself, are all matters of complexity and, hence, uncertainty for most welfare applicants. Trust is necessary to counteract this uncertainty. As Sztompka notes:

> The complexity of institutions, organisations, and technological systems, and the increasing global scope of their operations, make them impenetrable to ordinary people, but also often to the professional experts. Who commands a full understanding of global financial flows, stock-exchange fluctuations, computer networks, telecommunications, transportation, or of administrative, managerial, governmental, or military machineries and international bureaucracies? More often than ever before we have to act in the

dark, as if facing a huge black box, on the proper functioning of which our needs and interests increasingly depend. Trust becomes an indispensable strategy to deal with the opaqueness of our social environment. Without trust we would be paralysed and unable to act. (1999:13)

Trust In The Respectfulness Of Bureaucrats

Additionally, applicants may have trust in the welfare bureaucrats to carry out the bureaucratic process in a way which is respectful to the applicant. This relates to the vulnerability of many welfare applicants—both substantively and in relation to the welfare system. In approaching the bureaucracy, applicants are placing their welfare into the hands of the agency. The process often requires the disclosure of personal information, in addition to the demands of presenting oneself at allocated times and generally co-operating with the demands of the bureaucratic process. Above all, it sometimes involves the recognition of one's relative powerlessness within the welfare system and the re-emphasis of vulnerability (cf Bumiller, 1988). This raises the importance of respectfulness (and, indeed, efficiency) on the part of front-line officers. The importance of being treated with respect and dignity was a theme which emerged clearly from our data. Some interviewees were surprised when their *felt* need was marginalised in interviews. So, for example, Interview S12 said

> they asked for a bit like [about my housing circumstances], but it was mainly offences and all that. ... Its like they have no time for me, sort of thing. That's the way I feel about it. Its like, he looked at me report, 'he's done this, he's alright, put him in [hostel accommodation].' You know what I mean. That's the way it comes across to me. I had an interview here that lasted all of 5 minutes, you know what I mean and didn't ask me really anything about how I felt or anything like that, it was more like 'what have you been to jail for?' and all that.

Other interviews framed such feelings in terms of not being treated as a person. Interview S2 had been in and out of drug rehabilitation programmes, hospital and prisons for a number of years. He was a 'serious offender' with violence in his record, and had an entry on the exclusions database. He was given a negative decision during his initial interview. Although he did not exercise his right to review because he believed (wrongly, as it happened) that he would be offered housing, his trust in the bureaucracy was undermined by what he believed to be discrimination:

> I don't know if I received [the decision-letter] but she just told me that over the interview. She said 'Right, you've got violence in your record and we can't, can't house you.' And I just thought, well, that's wrong. ... I just felt I was just being

discriminated against because I'd not done nothing, I'd not committed no crime since I'd been out … all I was running up against was … policies of like ignorance, just saying like, you know, because of what I've done in the past.

Later on, he made the point that the bureaucracy treated people insensitively—as he put it 'you're not a human being'. He went on:

> It's like dead insensitive, the way they treat you, as if you're just a statistic, you're not a human being, you're just … I don't know, it's like they're probably more worried about their job and the paper work that they've got to do, rather than understanding the people that they're dealing with. There's no understanding of the people that they're dealing with, they just understand statistics of law, things like that, policy of what their company says, you know what I mean, it's nowt to do with understanding the people, and you know, really helping the person. I realised that when I went through the process of it. Nothing to do with that at all. I think it's all about money to them and keeping a business running, more than anything.

Interview B58 similarly expressed disappointment at the bureaucrats' greater concern with organisational priorities than with his needs:

> the thing is, there is very little humanity because they looks like someone, pressurised I mean, by someone. There is some kind of pressure from above. They have to do certain things. You are not important bit. The owner, people at the top, the key worker are the important thing. It's like the corporation, the bureaucracy, it's important. You're there, you are not really, you are the least important, which should be the other way round.

The welfare applicant is generally the weaker party in the applicant-bureaucracy power relationship. Applicants have to make themselves subject to the discretion of the agency and must conform to its bureaucratic demands. As Sarat notes:

> Waiting is, for them, the experience of being 'spatialized', of having someone else's place triumph over their time. Waiting is the physical embodiment of their own weakness. Their experience with the welfare system is, moreover, often one of speaking into a void, of speech without response. What they have to say seems to be ignored or is, at best, impatiently tolerated by caseworkers and other officials. (1990:360-1)

The making of a welfare application, then, can be an act which renders the already-vulnerable more vulnerable still and one which necessitates trust.

The Breach Of Trust

We suggest that the trust inherent in the welfare applicant-bureaucracy relationship is characteristic of the general function of trust in modern society.

Our thesis is that uncertainty and vulnerability are the key elements within our interviewees which give rise to trust (see also Heimer, undated). Trust is a mechanism which allows welfare applicants to manage their uncertainty about how the system operates, as well as their sense of vulnerability and relative powerlessness within the system. Trust is, to a greater or lesser extent, a necessary feature of welfare applicants' initial interactions with welfare bureaucracies. Welfare applicants enter the welfare system trusting the front-line officers to be focused on them and their needs, often expecting the provision of substantive assistance.

However, trust can be breached. It should be clear by now that the role of individual welfare bureaucrats can be important here. Giddens has suggested that:

> Attitudes of trust, or lack of trust, toward specific abstract systems are liable to be strongly influenced by experiences at access points (1990: 90)

By 'access points' he means:

> points of connection between lay individuals or collectivities and the representatives of abstract systems. They are places of vulnerability for abstract systems, but also junctions at which trust can be maintained or built up. (1990: 88)

Individual front-line welfare bureaucrats operate as 'access points' to the welfare (expert) system. Poor customer relations may cause a breach of trust. We saw above that Interviews B58 and S2 complained because they felt that the front-line officers were more responsive to the demands of the internal bureaucratic hierarchy than to their particular needs. (Conversely, of course, good customer relations may engender trust. For example, trust in expertise, as Rose (1993) has observed, may be engendered by the 'experts' themselves.)

More significant, perhaps, for the breach of applicants' trust, however, is a refusal of assistance. Our data indicates that many applicants have very unrealistic expectations about both entitlement to housing, and the quality of that housing assistance. Many applicants believe that the local authority should and will house them simply because of their need. Others are more confident still about being allocated a self-contained property. The reality, of course, can be very different. As we saw in chapter two, the law only grants the right to housing to those who successfully negotiate the 'obstacle race'. A high proportion of applicants are refused assistance every year, and the availability and/or quality of long-term housing resources are very scarce in some areas, meaning that many applicants receive offers which are below the standard of their expectations. Where housing resources are not scarce (as in Southfield) the refusal of assistance can be particularly bewildering. Interview S12 noted:

there's places empty everywhere you look ... and they are saying they haven't got the spaces.

The failure of the local authority to meet the felt need of applicants can cause a sense of breach of trust. Indeed, the potential tension between good customer relations and the denial of assistance creates something of a paradox for the function of trust in influencing applicants' decisions about whether or not to seek internal review. A discourse of customer care (particularly evident in Brisford) encourages initial trust on the part of the applicant. However, a refusal of assistance encourages distrust which militates against the pursuit of internal review. The function of trust in such circumstances, therefore, is to give with one hand but then to take away with the other.

The sense of one's trust having been breached fuels internal review scepticism. In the section below we explore in greater detail the different manifestations of internal review scepticism.

Lack Of Faith In Specific Internal Review Process

The lack of faith which follows on from a breach of trust is often focused specifically on the internal review process offered by the HPU which caused the disappointment in the first place. Interview S6, for example, was refused assistance on the grounds that he was not in priority need. He described his decision-letter in the following terms:

> **Applicant:** The way I've read it, the way my understanding is of it, is .. they can't do anything for me, and ... I'm safe enough to fend for meself on the streets... In other words, I'm all right on the streets, 'here's a sleeping bag, on your way', that's the way I read that letter... I don't think anybody should get a letter like that. That's not acceptable to anybody. It's not doing no good for 'em and if anything, it's sending them back to square one. You just may as well have not been there in the first place... I was gonna bin that the day I got it, then I thought, no, I'll keep hold of that. I don't know why I kept hold of it. It's worth showing to people, I think, you know what I mean? You just don't expect to get a letter like that from a housing place, do you know what I mean? It's just ridiculous, it's ridiculous.

This applicant's experience was clearly one of disappointment and surprise at his treatment by Southfield. He understood from his decision-letter that he had a right to internal review of his refusal of assistance but had decided not to pursue it:

> **Applicant:** I didn't think I had that much of a chance really... cos the answer they give me in the letter, it doesn't look like they're gonna do much for me at appeal. They might, they'll have to go through the motions of it, obviously, if

you ask for one, but I don't think, feel I'd get very far... If they were going to accept me they would have accepted me first time.

General Lack Of Faith In The Welfare 'System'

A lack of faith in the integrity of an internal review process may also be just one manifestation of a more general scepticism about the likelihood of receiving assistance from the welfare system as a whole. This is an important point. In this latter situation a refusal of housing triggers a loss of faith in receiving assistance from 'the system'. This is particularly pertinent to applicants who feel marginalised in society and have had previous experiences of being let down by the welfare system. For example, Interview B16 was a single man with a history of rough sleeping and alcohol abuse. He had spent time in prison and had applied to the HPU several times previously. Most recently he had been referred to the HPU by a 'detox unit'. Brisford's HPU made the decision that he was not in priority need. In interview, he explained his disappointment at the decision which he described as a 'false promise':

> **Applicant:** they should have helped me out, should have helped me out a lot more then than I felt I should have been helped, I, I, in other words it was just like I wasn't satisfied with the whole, with the whole situation and I thought maybe something else could have been done...
>
> **Interviewer:** What were your expectations?
>
> **Applicant:** My expectations were at least, well, you know, half a chance of getting permanent accommodation, just half a chance, that would be something for me to like, you know, to bite onto like, you know what I mean, like get me going like.

Interview B16 failed to appeal because he felt there was no point. However, his scepticism was focused on his poor prospects of ever receiving help from the welfare system, and not on the internal review process per se:

> **Interviewer:** Did you consider challenging their decision at all?
>
> **Applicant:** (laughs) No, no, I didn't... I should, I should have, I should have, yeah, maybe I should have tried a little bit, you know, I should have tried, you know, challenge them a little bit then, you know, rather than give up like, but you know at the end of the day like, you know, I've just had so many knockbacks like off local authorities and you feel like just, you know, you just don't wanna carry, you know, what's the point?..
>
> **Interviewer:** Did you know that you have the right to challenge their decision?
>
> **Applicant:** I know I have, yeah. Absolutely know that, yeah. But what it is

like, I mean, it's like all, it's sort of, you know, if you challenge the right to somebody, like what I mean, like it comes from the top of the shop, as they say, then that top of the shop might just knock me back down, knock me back down [to] the bottom of the ladder again, and you're not gonna get nowhere, like. I mean, it is a pretty impossible situation sometimes, actually to get accommodation.

Such loss of faith may be a temporary phenomenon. Indeed, the fact that Interview B16 applied to Brisford in the first place and the fact that he expressed disappointment illustrates that, *despite* previous negative experiences, he had sufficient faith in the system to try again. However, the further refusal of assistance triggered a loss of faith sufficient to prevent him seeking internal review. This particular barrier to the take up of internal review has clear links with 'applicant fatigue' which is discussed further below.

There is a further dimension to this important point about disillusionment with the welfare system. Many of our interviewees in both locations, but particularly in Brisford, linked their dissatisfaction with their individual decision to a perception of specific social policy goals. They believed that their application for housing was rejected because social housing and other welfare benefits were largely going to asylum-seekers and other immigrants to the UK. (A less widespread belief was that welfare, and particularly social housing, was largely being allocated to single mothers). The loss of faith in the welfare system draws upon a socially and politically constructed narrative which suggests that incoming migrants are being prioritised in the welfare system ahead of, or instead of, their own claims. Such a narrative is, of course, substantively incorrect. Since 1993 asylum seekers and other persons from abroad have been excluded from making applications for council housing (see Cowan, 1999: chapter 10). Yet it has a long history (see Dummett & Nicol, 1990; Cohen, 2001) and is particularly powerfully expressed by many of those in our sample. The narrative is, however, constructed as 'truth' by our interviewees either because it is a taken-for granted assumption, or is founded upon observation of others who have been more successful than them in the application process, or after what some described as 'personal research'.

One thing I know is that, well, I've seen many people you know, maybe like asylum seekers and they have a place to stay and things like that, from all around the world, you know, they get help, you know what I mean? It's only that we unfortunate people, single, homeless … they're the people that they cannot help. (**Interview B35**)

Some guy has just come from Afghanistan, some part of the hand has been damaged in the war, some part, they just give him one bedroomed flat. He is a teenager, nineteen, something like that. (**Interview B38**)

LONDON metropolitan university
LIBRARY SERVICES

This link between the micro-decision of the applicant and macro welfare policies, like the less focused loss of faith in the welfare system already described, signals a shift in blame-attribution. Rather than blaming the council per se or the individual caseworker, interviewees attributed blame to the broader welfare system.

Negative Advice Of HPU Officers

The third factor which must be considered in relation to applicants' lack of faith in internal review relates to the advice of Assessment Officers. In Brisford, for example, we saw in chapter four that some Assessments Officers advise applicants in some situations that they have very little or no chance of 'success' at internal review. Such discussions may be driven by the desire to be honest with applicants and not to raise hopes unjustifiably. Such sympathy and honesty, however, can be influential in fuelling internal review scepticism as the following extract from Interview B49 demonstrates:

> I read, yeah I read this. (Long pause) Yes, I remember now what I did here. I said to the guy here, 'Can I see someone else about this if I didn't like the decision?' you know. So my, the guy who was elected to deal with my case explained to me in a nutshell …unless if I am in one of these categories, it's pointless to make an appeal or anything like that, you know… I was feeling so, you know, so low, you know, and when he said [that] to me I just gave up, you know.

Scepticism About External Review/Appeal Processes

The above section has drawn on our data to demonstrate the effect of a felt breach of trust on interviewees' scepticism about the integrity of internal review processes. Nevertheless, we would suggest that a perceived breach of trust can also be conducive to scepticism about the impartiality of *external* grievance processes. A great deal of research has shown that welfare applicants often fail to recognise the independent status of external fora such as tribunals (see, for example, Genn & Genn, 1989; Sainsbury et al, 1995; Harris & Eden, 2000). In the perception of many applicants, the independent tribunal is simply an extension of the welfare agency (see also Sarat, 1990). Although they do not couch their findings in terms of trust, Harris and Eden's (2000) study of school exclusions demonstrates how the breach of trust at an agency level can militate against the exercise of appeal rights to an external and independent body because of a failure on the part of potential appellants to recognise the independent status of the tribunal.

A final and important point requires to be made in conclusion of this section. Our aim here has been to describe this particular barrier to the take-up of internal review which emerged from our interview data. Where possible and pertinent, we have linked our micro findings about trust and scepticism to a broader literature on trust in the social sciences. However, we would stress that we are not suggesting that all applicants who have a sense of their trust having been breached or who experience disappointment fail to pursue internal review. Not all applicants who express scepticism about the integrity of internal review fail to pursue their rights. This would be to overstate the point. Some applicants who were sceptical nevertheless did make an application and, indeed, exercised their right to review. Our point here is, rather, that although internal review scepticism may not always be sufficient to prevent the pursuit of internal review, it certainly is for some applicants, either independently or in combination with other 'barriers' to review.

RULE-BOUND IMAGE OF THE DECISION-MAKING PROCESS

Introduction

The image held by applicants of the nature of law or, more particularly, of the nature of bureaucratic legal decision-making, can also help to account for the failure to exercise the right to review. The study of legal consciousness may assist us in explaining the behaviour of ordinary citizens in everyday life and understand why they manage their problems in particular ways (Sarat, 1990; Merry, 1990; Ewick & Silbey, 1992; Sarat & Kearns, 1993; Neilson, 2000). It may also help us understand the behaviour of local authority actors (Cooper, 1995). Our focus here, however, is on the decision of applicants about whether or not to seek internal review. The case of Interview S26 illustrates how one particular legal consciousness narrative—whereby the decision-making process is perceived as a discretionless application of clear, fixed rules to simple facts—may prevent the take up of internal review.

Interview S26 was a single mother living in an isolated location who asserted that she was being harassed by local youths to the extent that she could not carry on living in her house—that she was 'homeless' as it was not reasonable for her to continue to live there. The Families Team of Southfield Council, however, disagreed, deciding that she was *not* homeless and could not be offered any help. This decision was made quickly. She was informed verbally at the end of her interview, and was sent a formal letter two working days later. The interviewee understood that her failure to provide official corroborative support for her plight had led to Southfield's failure to believe her. Interestingly, however, she still retained a view of Southfield as having followed correct procedures and working within the constraints of 'the rules'. She deduced, accordingly, that there was no point in lodging an internal appeal:

Interviewer: What are your plans now?

Applicant: Sit here, what can I do? I can't walk out, I've got nowhere to take my kids.

Interviewer: So you said you were trying to get Social Services to help?

Applicant: I've got Social Services in, they were coming to see me. (...) They won't even pay the deposit for me, I've asked them to pay the deposit, so I can get out of here and get a private property.

Interviewer: Have you asked anyone about any advice about what to do next?

Applicant: I don't know what to do next. I am stuck.

Interviewer: Do you know anyone that might be able to give you some advice on what your options are?

Applicant: No. The [Homeless Persons Unit] know what they're talking about, they go by the book don't they?

Interviewer: Do you know that you can appeal a decision that has been made?

Applicant: Yes, but what's the point because they explained it quite clearly... I've got no more to tell them. Everything I've told them is its true, and they don't believe me so what can I do?

This interviewee's perception of caseworkers' decision-making was that Southfield 'go by the book'. This is an exaggerated image of bureaucratic formal rationality whereby the officers apply clear and fixed legal rules in a simple and neutral fashion. Under this image of legal decision-making there is no discretion. The role of the applicant is to give the bureaucrat all the facts of her situation. The corresponding role of the bureaucrats is simply to apply the legal rules in a mechanistic fashion to those facts. There is, accordingly, no point in appealing because the same answer is bound to be produced again, almost like a computer producing the same calculation time after time. The reality, however, was very different. The legal test which Southfield's Assessments Officer above was required to apply was whether or not it was 'reasonable' for Interview S26 to continue to occupy her home. This is a highly discretionary concept in itself. However, the process by which the homelessness officer arrived at the conclusion about reasonableness—the enquiries which she made and the conclusions she drew from them—is also a matter which could be examined in internal review. This too is a highly discretionary matter.

Blamelessness of Bureaucrats

A common theme amongst those who share this particular legal conscious-ness is that the bureaucrat has done his/her best, and cannot be blamed for the adverse decision. This depersonalisation of decision-making explains away, or diverts attention from, both the caseworker and the interviewees' own impotence (Bumiller, 1988; Quinn, 2000). Interviewees, then, are not so much 'lumping it' as reframing the decision. As Quinn observes in the context of her research subjects who did not take workplace harassment personally:

> lumping it evokes the impression of an emergent grievance recognized and then abandoned. In contrast, while the pain might be recognized, not taking it personal is a reframing of the incident that denies this very fact ... While related to lumping it, this tactic represents what is more accurately under-stood as a pregrievance, the harm that can never quite be named. (2000: 1171–2).

Interview B29, for example, had applied to be housed in Brisford, but was referred under the local connection provisions to a neighbouring council to be housed there. She was unhappy at this decision but did not challenge it. She knew that she could request an internal review but felt that Brisford had conducted the decision process properly and had applied the rules correctly to her situation (though she had in fact misunderstood the reason for her decision). An extract from her interview illustrates the propensity to deper-sonalise the decision and so to relieve the bureaucrat of any blame:

Interviewer: How would you describe the application process?

Applicant: It was ok, I mean I don't blame them, they are right because I was leaving [Neighbouring Area], I don't blame them at all, because the baby's father is in private rent, I know what they mean, they meant, but I don't blame them, it's not their fault.

Interviewer: Right, so it's not their fault?

Applicant: No, no, no.

Interviewer: OK, in overall terms how fairly do you think you were treated at Brisford?

Applicant: Not bad, it's good, it was ok.

Interviewer: Do you think they made the right decision?

Applicant: Sometime I think they made the wrong decision but sometime I think oh [there's] nothing I can do and they are ok and they are right because they've got reason why to send me back there...

Interviewer: Right, ok, when you got the letter from Brisford did you consider challenging their decision?

Applicant: No I was trying to call my caseworker but I said what's the point. It's not her fault, she did her best, so there is no point for me to call her.

Whilst recognising that an adverse decision has been made—one that fails to meet their needs, applicants nevertheless are often sympathetic towards Assessments Officers and grateful for their 'help'. Their frustration and disappointment can instead be focused on the rules or the management:

> I've got no problem with them people, or them people out there. It's not them that makes the rules up. It's like the police, the people on the beat are told what to do… You're going back about five levels. Like this is the ground floor and the person on the tenth floor is sitting up there with his feet on a chair, with a coffee and a secretary sucking his knob or something and the person on the ground floor is getting the bollocks. (**Interview B10**)

Situating Legal Consciousness Within Bureaucratic Practices

The legal consciousness of Interviewee B29 (and others like her) should be situated in an understanding of the social reality of homelessness decision-making. Neilson (2000) situates legal consciousness along the parameters of race, gender and class. She argues that legal consciousness emerges through individuals linking their current experiences and attitudes to law to their previous personal experiences. Such nuanced understanding of legal consciousness was obtained from qualitative interviewing where subjects were able to articulate and explore their reaction to a single issue—offensive public speech in the street. By controlling for a single issue Neilson was able to pick out the race, gender and class differentiations in legal consciousness.

Our aim in this section, however, is to suggest that legal consciousness may be situated within the particularity of the citizen-bureaucrat relationship around the application for welfare. This interaction effectively is constitutive of a consciousness within the citizen of the legality inherent in their relationship (Yngvesson, 1988). The signals imparted during this interaction constrain the interviewees' choices (Ewick & Silbey, 1998: 88–90). The interviewee 'is lulled into an acceptance of dependency that inhibits resistance …' (Bumiller, 1988: 78). The law—interpreted as fixed, immutable, unchallengeable rules—is reified, produced by this particular interaction (cf Ewick & Silbey, 1998: 81).

We suggest that an examination of the bureaucratic practices of our two case study local authorities may shed light on what we call a 'formal rationality' legal consciousness narrative which emerged from some of our interview data. This approach lacks the subject-focus of Neilson's work, or the 'everyday life' quality of part of the literature (Merry, 1990; Sarat & Kearns, 1993; Ewick & Silbey, 1998). Instead of situating legal consciousness along the parameters of race, gender or class, linking legal consciousness to previous personal histories, we suggest that the substance of bureaucratic practices, which is played out in the citizen-bureaucrat relationship, may be influential in informing the legal consciousness of applicants around the specific issue of the value of pursuing internal review. Our focus, then, is narrow. Although legal consciousness is 'continually produced and worked on' (Ewick & Silbey, 1998: 43), and although individuals may retain a range of competing legal consciousness narratives in relation to different aspects of their lives (Cooper, 1995), or at different stages of a problem or experience (Merry, 1990), we seek only to consider the potential for the homelessness application process to instil a formal rationality narrative in the consciousnesses of applicants which may militate against the pursuit of internal review.

It is important to stress, moreover, that our approach lacks the methodological validity of much of the legal consciousness literature. Our project was not set up as a study of legal consciousness per se, and so we were unable to explore our interviewees' legal consciousness in any depth to gain a deeper and more situated understanding of its genesis. This one particular image of bureaucratic decision-making discussed above emerged from our data as explaining some applicants' failure to pursue internal review. However, we were unable to probe deeper in any systematic way. Instead, we *suggest* potential links between bureaucratic practices and the legal consciousness of our interviewees. In the sections which follow, we highlight certain characteristics of the bureaucratic operations of our case study local authorities which we suggest may be significant in informing the development of a formal rationality legal consciousness narrative. We do not propose that the bureaucratic practices we highlight below are *necessarily* determinative of a formal rationality legal consciousness narrative. Rather, we draw inferences from our observational data about the *potential* for bureaucratic practices to influence the development of a formal rationality legal consciousness narrative, or, at least, to fail to challenge it. These inferences are methodologically unsubstantiated in our own study, though we suggest that they raise important research questions which would give rise to further fruitful research.

Professional Pride

If we examine Southfield's decision-making practices, for example, we can see that there are a number of factors which may contribute to, or at least bolster, a formal rationality legal consciousness narrative. First, the officers of the Families Team have confidence in their skills as decision-makers.

They take professional pride in their knowledge of the law, contrasting their abilities with those of neighbouring councils and former managers. This attitude, though perhaps laudable and positive from some perspectives, limits the opportunities for stressing the discretionary nature of their tasks to applicants, particularly when cases are being dealt with under pressure of time. Similar attitudes are equally evident throughout Brisford's HPU in tune with the professionalisation ethic of audit.

Deflection of Conflict

Second, the formally rational image of law is used to deflect conflict in interview situations. In both fieldwork sites it was common practice to communicate at least some detail of the decision before the issue of the formal decision-letter. Framing prospective refusals in terms of legal rules and their rational application masks the use of discretion and so depersonalises the decision. Such an image acts as a palliative to the angry applicant and manages conflict within the interview room.

Oral Justification For Decisions

The way in which different kinds of decisions are presented to applicants in face-to-face interactions may also be significant in informing (or at least not challenging) this particular legal consciousness narrative. Such a restricted image of the decision-making process may be particularly powerful where, as we found in Southfield, an applicant believes that his individual culpability is the basis of his rejection. As we saw in chapter three, in Southfield's Residential Units culpability and tenantability are dominant discourses within decision-making practices. Applicants take this message away from face-to-face interactions with Assessments Officers. Applicants are more inclined, we suggest, to regard internal review as a pointless exercise where they believe that their rejection is premised upon the existence of a criminal record, for example, about which nothing can be done. Whereas the concept of 'need' is discretionary and more open to argument, an historical event like a criminal record cannot be changed. The culpability and tenantability discourses within Southfield easily lend themselves to a formally rational image of the decision-making process.

Written Presentation Of Letters

Decision-letters are also important in conveying a non-discretionary image of decision-making. In Southfield, for example, it is important to contrast the decision-letters of assessments officers and the decision-letters of allocations officers (where the legal test for the council is whether the offer of accommodation is 'suitable' for the applicant). The *pro forma* paragraph which tells the applicant of her right to internal review of a caseworkers' decision, and is included at the bottom of every decision letter, is as follows:

RIGHT TO REVIEW—HOUSING ACT 1996 S.202

You have the right to request a review of any of the following aspects of the decision we have made about your applications: a) your eligibility, b) what duty is owed to you, c) referral to another authority, d) local connection, e) suitability of available accommodation. Either you, or someone acting on your behalf should put the reasons for your request in writing, including *any* information you think should be taken into account.

Any such request must be made within 21 days of receipt of this notice. Full details of the Review Procedure are available on request from your Caseworker, who will be pleased to help you with any queries you may have.

The parallel information in relation to allocations officers' decisions is contained in the middle of the offer letter and is as follows:

If you disagree with the City Council's view that this is a suitable offer and that it is reasonable for you to accept it, you should tell us why in writing immediately. Please ensure that you give full details as to exactly why you disagree: your refusal will then be considered and you will be notified in writing of the City Councils' decision. If you require further information please contact an Allocations Officer—Homeless Families Unit.

We can see that the suitability of offers of housing are described as being simply the 'view' of the council. Applicants are invited to 'disagree' with such views. Appropriately, the council stresses here the discretionary nature of the allocations process and invites the applicant to challenge the exercise of discretion where she believes it has been inappropriately exercised. By contrast, the caseworkers' decision-letter is much more formal in tone and gives no hint of the discretionary nature of the decision. Applicants are simply informed of a 'right to review' of the council's 'decision'. Similarly, the rejection letter of the refusals panel (where an applicant challenges the offer of housing) is very formal and legalistic. It contains a final paragraph very similar in content to the caseworkers' rejection letter.

Plurality Of Legal Consciousness Narratives

It is important to stress that what we term the 'formal rationality legal consciousness narrative' is but one of many legal consciousness narratives (Ewick & Silbey, 1998) which can be found in our data, or which have been documented elsewhere (see, for example, Sarat, 1990, Cooper 1995). Another legal consciousness narrative, for example, sees law as a 'game' to be played, in which citizens work 'with the law' (Ewick & Silbey, 1998: ch 5). Here law is used instrumentally to meet other ends, and has little intrinsic connection with justice. Conversely, as Levene and Mellema (2001: 17) observe in their important discussion of Ewick and Silbey's book, *The Common Place of Law: Stories from Everyday Life*, legal consciousness studies can have a tendency to place law first over and above the life experiences of marginalisation:

> While [truly marginalized persons'] life experiences are utterly circumscribed by the legal system, their behavior and language should sometimes lead us to question whether the law is truly central to their decision making, to their perceptions of themselves and their relationships, and to their understanding of available choices.

There was evidence in our data of internal review being used instrumentally despite, or because of, scepticism about the integrity of the process. The aims of this research, however, prohibit a full exploration of the various narratives of legal consciousness, or their centrality, found in our data. The point of this section, rather, is to demonstrate how one particular legal consciousness narrative can operate (though it may not always do so) to prevent the take up of the right to internal review.

APPLICANT FATIGUE

We have called this fourth barrier to the take up of internal review 'applicant fatigue'. By this we refer both to grievance apathy *and* appeal fatigue. 'Grievance apathy' is a phrase coined by Felstiner, Abel and Sarat (1980-81) in their seminal article which urged the examination of the emergence and non-emergence of legal disputes. They used this term in relation to the failure to pursue legal remedies to injurious events (or what Genn has termed 'justiciable events' (Genn, 1999)). 'Appeal fatigue', on the other hand, is discussed in much of the literature on the pursuit of citizens' grievances in relation to the situation where complainants rarely persevere beyond the first point of complaint (Sainsbury & Eardley, 1991; Dalley & Berthoud, 1992; Lloyd-Bostock & Mulcahy, 1994; Atkinson et al, 1999). Grievance apathy is a policy concern which is logically anterior to appeal fatigue. The two phenomena can be (and have been) explored separately. However, we believe there is greater explanatory power in discussing them as twin aspects of the same barrier to the pursuit of grievance rights—applicant fatigue.

By 'applicant fatigue' we refer to the situation where applicants fail to take up, or see through their rights to internal review because of fatigue. This fatigue can be caused by having already gone through a pre-statutory review process (as in the Refusals process) and so could be described as 'appeal fatigue'. However, fatigue can also be (and is perhaps more likely to be) the product of previous or concurrent events in their lives, often related to the circumstances which surround their homelessness. These events have sapped their energy to pursue a challenge to the welfare bureaucracy. In this sense, it is artificial to separate out grievance apathy from appeal fatigue. Both are products of the difficult lives which many welfare applicants have to lead and the consequent drain on their energies and abilities to struggle for their welfare benefits when adverse decisions are made. A focus only on the narrow circumstances of the application process itself would miss this wider context.

Interview B44 illustrates applicant fatigue particularly well. He was a victim of domestic violence. His fatigue was a result of having to negotiate the consequences of domestic violence with a number of welfare agencies. His claim for housing was just one aspect of the re-adjustments required of him following the history of violence. He was deemed to be not in priority need. He was surprised and disappointed by this decision. He was also aware of his right to internal review but did not exercise it:

> **Applicant**: I'm so fed up with it, I'm really fed up with it, I'm not gonna appeal, I just can't go through it again, it's too much it takes too much out of me, physically, emotionally and mentally and I'm not going to appeal. I just can't go through it all again, the whole appeal system... The letter they sent me on the back of it says you can appeal, but I'm not going to cos I've really had enough, can't go through it all again it's just too much, again it's just too much putting down again everything again on paper, why you think you need housing, you know, and you think 'No. I've been through so much I'm not gonna start dragging myself through this again'.

> **Interviewer**: I mean do you not think that your case is such that you have a valid enough case and therefore ...

> **Applicant:** ... No I don't, I really don't. I think they've just knocked it out of me so much, sort of knock backs that I just can't be bothered really, I'm just fed up with it, it's just too much to keep dragging on and on. I just can't... At the moment I'm just so, I'm just trying to slowly get together my life, at the moment and it's not, it's a priority of mine, but I'm still having counselling and things for the violence that I suffered, I can't take on loads of other things and thinking about loads of other things, 'specially housing at the moment.

Interview B44's fatigue was associated with a particular traumatic history in his recent past—domestic violence. However, applicant fatigue can simply be a product of the more general difficulty of simply being homeless. Interview S28 is a case in point. He had been refused assistance from Southfield on the ground that he had become homeless intentionally. He explained why he didn't pursue internal review:

> The timing of it was very bad, I can't think of a better way to say it. As in if you are just going into homelessness, you are so insecure, that is the last time you are able to make constructive decisions and whatever and that is the time they want you to think, yeah? And that's what it is about their process which annoys me a lot because they wanted me to make decisions, or wanted me to make decisions when mentally, I wouldn't have said I was mentally up to it at the time, I was mentally tired, I was physically tired, I was sleeping very rough, I was tired, I was very tired and they are expecting you at this time to be making decisions and things like everything is okay… so the timing of it I thought was very bad and that was a major thing, I was really just that mentally tired, I didn't have the strength to do it. I basically just gave up.

Applicant fatigue, however, can also be the result of having to pursue one's claim to housing through several stages. We refer here to the Refusals process—the pre-statutory review process concerning the suitability of accommodation offers. Perhaps the clearest case of this kind of applicant fatigue was Interview B55. She refused Brisford's offer of accommodation as unsuitable on the basis of her medical conditions (claustrophobia and stress). Her refusal was rejected. She then entered into a series of conversations offering further medical evidence, but did not formally seek internal review. Brisford held its line that the accommodation was suitable for her. Eventually, she gave up and accepted the property:

> I just got to the point where I realised that what I was actually saying, or what I was portraying as, as good reasons, to them meant nothing. That is how I felt, right at the end that's how I felt, that what I was expressing to them meant nothing. … If you're expressing your feelings to somebody, this was the thing with me, I was expressing myself, telling them personal things about myself, and it was all just being brushed under the carpet and brushed just to one side. Like, you know, I'm telling them things about my life, that I don't sit down and sort of discuss on a, on a sort of daily basis and it was just being walked over and, you know, taken like, like nothing really. You know and that made me, that made, that was hurtful to me and I think, you know, I just felt to myself, 'Well I, you know, I tried and what I feel has been personal good reasons, to them they weren't', so it didn't really make any sense to go any sort of further. I just sort of really, right now, I, cos I think what it was, I just pinned, pinned everything on the fact that… I'm not gonna be here forever.

It is important to note that applicant fatigue is not simply a product of individual vulnerability. As the above extract illustrates, it is exacerbated by perceived delay in, or complexity of, the bureaucratic process. The greater the length of time that the process will take, and the more complicated it seems, the more likely it is that applicant fatigue will prevent an applicant from pursuing internal review. Similarly, a failure to provide temporary accommodation during the internal review process may also exacerbate applicant fatigue and encourage an applicant to give up on a potential challenge. This point is demonstrated by the case of Interview S1 which is discussed further below in relation to our sixth reason for failing to pursue internal review: where the applicant does not 'need' the offer of housing.

'SATISFACTION' WITH DECISION

The fifth barrier to the take up of internal review is the fact that some applicants are satisfied with the decision they receive. It may seem strange to include this in a list of 'barriers' to the machinery of administrative justice. Common sense would surely dictate that applicant satisfaction is a positive situation?

This was certainly the case for some of our interviewees. Interview B11, for example, was the subject of a referral to another local authority. Brisford accepted that there was a duty to house him, but referred this housing duty to a neighbouring local authority. The applicant was very happy with this and so did not pursue internal review. Although many such referrals would count as 'negative' decisions for applicants, on this occasion it did not.

However, the literature on complaints suggests that the concept of satisfaction should sometimes be problematised. As Mulcahy and Tritter point out, satisfaction and dissatisfaction

> are not necessarily opposite ends of the same continuum but distinct phenomena. Thus, the non-expression of dissatisfaction cannot be equated with the expression of satisfaction. (1998: 827–8)

They go on to suggest (at 839) that non-pursuit of dissatisfaction should not necessarily be seen as passivity or capitulation, as this does not allow for different 'channels of expression, or that a person may make a 'rational' decision not to pursue their dissatisfaction or enter into a dispute.' Our data reflects both these assertions. There is considerable pressure on certain applicants to accept their dissatisfaction. We argue that, in both fieldwork sites, there is a distinct element of *coerced choice* in housing offers taken up by some homeless applicants which accounts both for applicants failing to enter the Refusals and internal review processes, and for them dropping out prematurely. Coerced choice may operate as a barrier to the enjoyment of rights of internal review both at the point of the offer of housing, and afterwards. At the point of the offer being made, coerced choice operates to prevent a challenge to the suitability of the offer. Coerced choice also manifests itself after the offer in applicants failing to proceed to the internal review of their offer of housing, or dropping out of that process prematurely.

The Initial Offer Of Housing

In relation to this stage, there is, of course, a methodological peculiarity underlying our thesis about coerced choice. In relation to our analysis of coerced choice at a later stage, our data emerges from the accounts of homeless applicants describing their circumstances and their reasons for failing to take up or prematurely dropping out of statutory internal review. This kind of grounded data is clearly not possible for applicants who are 'satisfied' with their initial offers of housing and fail even to challenge it at the Refusals Panel. Our interview pool was self-selected from the group of applicants who had already indicated their dissatisfaction with the offer of housing by challenging the offer at the Refusals stage. Accordingly, our thesis about coerced choice at the stage of initial offer has its source in an inference drawn from the differential rates of Refusals between single persons (and childless couples) and families in Southfield. There are significantly different rates of refusals between the singles teams and the Families Team. A far greater proportion of housing offers are challenged by families than by single applicants (or childless couples). This is a difference which requires explanation. There is nothing in the nature of the task, the homeless subjects or the nature of housing stock which can account for the difference. Instead we point to the different operations of the allocations process by the respective personnel. In particular, we suggest that the role of Southfield's Resettlement Team is influential in reducing the levels of challenge to housing offers and raising applicant 'satisfaction' (or lowering applicant 'dissatisfaction').

In our descriptions of the rehousing process for singles, we pointed to a number of factors which, we believe, explains this difference. First, the Resettlement Team conducts a 'take on' interview specifically designed to assist the applicant in choosing three areas of Southfield in which they are prepared to live. The Resettlement Team officers have more time to give information and offer advice in comparison with the Families Team caseworkers who squeeze this process into the initial homelessness interview. The Resettlement Team officers also encourage applicants, where they are in doubt about where to choose, to visit areas before selecting them. They also reinforce the one offer policy during this interview, which impacts upon subsequent behaviour. For example, Interview S21 said

> They said if you don't take your offer you have to move out of here and you're not classed as homeless no more, because you've been offered a suitable property and you've not took it. But at the end of the day it's only suitable in their eyes, not in your eyes, do you know what I mean? Suitable for them in the way they see it but not suitable for you.

Second, the Resettlement Team dampen the expectations of applicants about the likely quality of housing they may receive (in this regard, see also Atkinson et al, 1999). This reduces the scope for applicant disappointment. Third, Resettlement Team officers accompany most applicants to view their offer of housing. This affords them an opportunity to 'sell' the offer to the applicant. Part of the selling process is, as we saw in chapter three, an emphasis on the one-offer-only policy. This, we suggest, puts pressure on the applicant to accept the offer, drawing their attention away from the existence of the Refusals Panel and the opportunity to challenge the suitability of the offer.

After The Initial Offer Of Housing

Our interview data reveals a number of features of the allocations process which individually or in combination operate to create coerced choice after an offer has been made and the applicant has challenged its suitability. These are set out below.

Risk To Temporary Accommodation

Local authorities are not under a legal obligation to provide applicants with temporary accommodation pending an internal review, although they can, in their discretion, do so. Brisford did not generally provide temporary accommodation to those who were pursuing internal review, whether on entitlement or suitability. This impacted upon applicants' decisions about whether to pursue internal review. Interview B29, for example, had been advised that he would lose his temporary accommodation if he refused his offer of accommodation. Although he had sought an internal review of his offer of accommodation, he dropped out of the process prematurely and accepted the offer before receiving the result of the internal review (which, as it happened, was unsuccessful).

Substantial Delay In Being Housed

A second feature of the allocations process which contributed to coerced choice relates to potential delay in receiving a second offer of accommodation if the challenge to the initial offer is successful. Interviews B23 and B36 had both been advised by the district housing officer, to whom they had returned the keys after viewing the offered properties, about the length of time they might have to wait if they challenged the offer of accommodation and were successful. Their dissatisfaction with their temporary accommodation had, then, to be weighed against their dissatisfaction with the offer of long-term accommodation. The potential delay in receiving suitable long-term accommodation had a clear impact on Interview B23. He had originally asked for a larger property because 'he smokes and his wife's sick'. The property offered, however, was small. It was also a ten to fifteen minute walk to the nearest bus stop which was problematic as his wife required regular hospital outpatient treatment. He did not proceed to internal review because of his anxiety over the length of time he might have to wait for another offer. He explained this through an interpreter:

> she told him, it's up to you. You accept it or not. You have the right to say no... He talked about it with his wife and he said, well, he'd been forced to take it. There was no other accommodation... Cos he ask the [district housing officer] 'If I refuse there, when they gonna give me another accommodation?'... And she doesn't know when.

There is a relationship, in other words, between the desirability of the potential substantive benefit and the bureaucratic process which must unfold before it could be granted. As Harris and Eden (2000) have shown, a perceived delay in the bureaucratic process encourages potential appellants to put up with the status quo.

Risk Of Ending Up With Nothing: One Offer Policy

Both Southfield and Brisford operated a 'one offer only' policy whereby homeless applicants would be given only one suitable offer of housing. If a challenge to an offer is unsuccessful, no further offers of housing are made. The risk of unsuccessfully refusing an offer of accommodation and being left with nothing operated as a barrier to the take up of internal review. It is important to note, of course, that some applicants did pursue internal review *despite* the sense of risk. We do not suggest here that the one offer policy always prevents applicants from engaging with and completing the internal review process. Interview B63, for example, sought internal review despite an acute sense of risk: 'I caused a fuss, I did. If I was going to die I wasn't going to go quietly.'

However, our data demonstrates that for other applicants the one offer policy and the associated risk was key to their failure to take up their rights of review. The core message of the one offer policy is consistently reinforced throughout the homelessness application process both by officers and written guidance to applicants. Interview B9, for example, reluctantly accepted an offer of accommodation even though she felt threatened by her prospective neighbours. She accepted the accommodation because she felt that

> they said on the [guidance], if I refuse this place, I'd be off the housing list... I wouldn't have took it otherwise, they said if you don't take this place you'll make yourself homeless because we're not offering you nothing else.

Interview S15 had left a violent relationship, leaving one child with her parents but taking her new baby with her. She was offered a property which she felt was too far away from her support network, in an area which she had felt 'steam-rollered' into choosing during her initial application. After an unsuccessful refusal, she had been informed that she was obliged to accept the offer. She was, however, aware of her right to an internal review:

> I know that I can appeal but if the appeal failed then I would just basically be thrown out of here and I don't know what would happen if that was the case, I have a little baby to think about. ... I have been looking into private rented but I am not sure if that is feasible really and I think I am basically going to be forced to take the house on ...

Coerced choice, however, also operates to encourage some applicants to drop out of the internal review process prematurely. Interview B42, for example, had successfully pursued one internal review of an unsuitable offer. She was offered a second offer with which she was also aggrieved. However, the pressure and sense of risk had risen and she reluctantly accepted it:

> I was really devastated at first when I found out where it was... I went and viewed that, and I knew that like it or loathe it I had to accept it, because I'd already refused once, and I knew, I kind of knew that if I didn't accept this I could be on the 16th floor, cos this was a 5th floor flat, it wasn't too bad actually, when I first saw it I hated it, cos it was really dark and smelt of death, basically, so when I saw it I had..., I think my husband went with me, and so we saw the property and we thought, well, 'With a bit of polishing it will be suitable.'

Similarly in Interview S5, the interviewee had been advised to refuse a property by a member of the Resettlement Team. He understood, however, that the pressure to accept the next offer was intensified:

> it'll be the last offer I get and then I'll just have to go along with it and make the best of it. And what I can do, after a year, if I'm not happy, I can always apply for an exchange and maybe get somewhere more central, you know, in a couple of years or something.

Thus, the information he was given about the possibility of exchanging the property made the decision about whether or not to accept it more palatable and, indeed, made it a non-decision.

APPLICANT DOES NOT WANT/NEED SUBSTANTIVE BENEFIT

The final reason we discovered for failure to pursue internal review is that some applicants do not want the benefit which they applied for. There are three situations where our data indicates that the applicant does not need or want the offer of long-term housing as an outcome of the homelessness application. In all these situations, the pursuit of internal review seems unnecessary to the applicant.

Applicant Finds Other Accommodation

Where applicants find a solution to their homelessness by another route, then there is no need to pursue internal review. These situations are, like interview B35, not problematic for administrative justice. Interview B35 had made homelessness applications to both Brisford and another local authority. He was offered accommodation by the neighbouring authority and so was deemed to be not homeless by Brisford. Although there was evidence of the applicant being confused about his applications, and of being reliant on his probation officer to explain things and advise him, his failure to pursue review is explained by the fact that he had found his own solution to his housing problem.

It is possible, however, that the lack of 'need' of housing is not so simple a matter to explain and must be understood within the context of the local authority's bureaucratic practices. As we have already demonstrated, the local authority's bureaucratic operations can influence the way applicants respond to and resolve their immediate homelessness problems. The case of Interview S1 is a case in point. She had applied to Southfield for housing as she had been evicted from a previous non-Council tenancy for rent arrears. The caseworker came to the quick conclusion during the first interview that the applicant was probably intentionally homeless (an example of preliminary decision-making). Interview S1 was advised in that interview that the chances of being offered housing by the council were slim and that she should start looking for alternative accommodation herself. She immediately did so and obtained a new private tenancy two days before the formal letter of refusal of housing was delivered to her—almost two months after her initial interview. However, despite obtaining this alternative accommodation, she was still equivocal about whether she had been treated fairly by the Council:

> Interviewer: Overall, do you think you were treated fairly?
>
> Applicant: I suppose overall, yes. I mean, they found me the temporary accommodation very quickly and ... my caseworker... was lovely and he did everything he could to help me. But I think the final decision was unfair, because I mean, I've moved into here and it's great but I'm paying £125 a month more than I was before, and I couldn't manage then, so you know.

Her reason for failing to pursue internal review was that she had found her own solution to her homelessness—coupled with the fact that the Council would have required her to leave her temporary accommodation during the course of the internal review, which could take weeks to complete (her case overlaps with applicant fatigue discussed above). However, her reason for having found alternative accommodation was due to the preliminary decision-making by the caseworker.

Although she had found a solution to her homelessness, she may not have found a solution to her housing problem. As she noted, her new accommodation was going to put further financial strain on her which had been the cause of her original eviction. Council accommodation would certainly have been more affordable for her. Of course, it is unclear in this case whether or not an internal review would have reversed the initial decision of intentional homelessness. However, the case does serve to demonstrate that her action in finding her own accommodation must be understood in the context of the relationship between her and her caseworker—particularly their initial interactions—and her consequent perceptions of the limits and possibilities of her housing options.

Applicant Is Granted Discretionary Housing

We saw in chapter three that Southfield operates a discretionary housing scheme through which 'unsuccessful' homelessness applicants may nevertheless be offered long-term housing. Four of our Southfield interviewees were in this situation and saw no need to seek internal review of their negative homelessness decision. It was clear during fieldwork that applicants fail to understand the technicalities of the discretionary housing scheme and its relationship to the homelessness legislation. The only real difference in terms of the unfolding of the housing process is that those applicants are not entitled to seek internal review of the suitability of their housing offer. They may take a grievance to the Refusals Panel, but no further. None of our interviewees were aware of this. Nevertheless, the offer of discretionary housing represents a positive outcome for the applicant, and one which negates the need for internal review of the formal refusal of housing under homelessness law.

Applicant Only Sought Temporary Accommodation

Some applicants only approached Southfield's Residential Units in order to obtain temporary accommodation. However, in order to be granted temporary accommodation, they are required to be registered as a homelessness applicant. Interview S3 was such an applicant who was only seeking temporary accommodation until an opening in a drugs rehabilitation unit became available. The refusal of long-term housing, accordingly, was irrelevant to her current needs which had been met by the time of interview. Fieldwork suggested that other applicants (though none of our interviewees) sought only temporary accommodation because they were part of a transient homeless population. Internal review, similarly, is an irrelevant course of action for such individuals.

CONCLUSION

This chapter has set out our analysis of the reasons why our interviewees failed to challenge adverse decisions. Our aim has been to separate out these reasons for analytic purposes—to set out a careful conceptual structure concerning the non-pursuit of internal review which will be useful to future research on the non-emergence of disputes in the field of administrative law and social welfare. However, we recognise that for many applicants, their failure to challenge their adverse decisions is explained by a combination of reasons. Individual narratives of why people did not take up their right to internal review often touch on more than one of the 'barriers to review' outlined above.

We stated in the introduction to this chapter that we intended to contextualise the failure to pursue internal review both in relation to factors which are personal to the applicant, and to factors that relate to the applicant-bureaucracy relationship. These findings are summarised in Table 13 below.

An interaction perspective on the non-emergence of disputes in the field of administrative law and social welfare has a double advantage. It gives us deeper insights into why citizens fail to challenge adverse decisions. However, it also permits a focused and empirically based policy response to the low take up of grievance rights. This is a matter to which we will return in our concluding chapter.

Table 13: Interaction Perspective on Failure to Pursue Internal Review

REASONS FOR FAILURE TO PURSUE INTERNAL REVIEW	EXPLANATORY BUREAUCRATIC FACTORS	EXPLANATORY APPLICANT FACTORS
Ignorance of right to internal review • Didn't get letter • Didn't read letter • Didn't understand letter	• Oral communication of initial decisions • Failure to verbally inform about internal review • Complexity of decision-letters • Letters in English only • Exclusion from residential units	• Poor literacy • Language problems • General confusion • Transience • Emotional stress • Leaving interview prematurely
Internal Review Scepticism • Lack of independence • Lack of trust • Negative advice of officers	• Non-independent review • Refusal of assistance • Complexity of welfare system • Poor customer care • Advice of officers on prospects of success at internal review	• Previous negative experiences of welfare system • Unrealistic expectations • Belief that some groups (eg asylum seekers) are being prioritised
Rule-bound image of the decision-making process	• Self-confidence of officers • Oral justifications of decisions • Tone and complexity of decision-letters • Interview conflict management	• Formally rational image of decision-making process
Applicant fatigue	• Length and complexity of bureaucratic process • No t/a during internal review	• Emotional stress
'Satisfaction' with decision	• Take on interview • Dampening of expectations • Threat of losing t/a • Length of time for 2nd accommodation offer • one-offer policy	• Applicant satisfaction
Does not want/need long-term housing • Applicant finds other accommodation • Applicant is granted discretionary housing • Applicant only sought temporary housing	• 'preliminary' decision-making • Discretionary offer scheme • No t/a during internal review • Length of bureaucratic process • Complexity of bureaucratic process	• Transient population • Personal initiative

6

Understanding the Pursuit of Internal Review

INTRODUCTION

In this chapter we explore our data about why homeless applicants pursue internal review. Our analysis is divided into three sections. First, we consider the aims and motivations of applicants in taking up the right to internal review. We look at what they want, in other words. One might be forgiven for thinking that the answer to this question is obvious and not worthy of attention. Applicants, it might be suspected, would behave in a self-interested way, actively asserting their rights of citizenship (see, for example, Le Grand, 1997). However, although research on why welfare applicants pursue grievances is still fairly sparse, the clear indication is that the rationale in pursuing grievances is both complex and multi-layered (Sainsbury et al, 1995; Berthoud & Bryson, 1997; Lloyd-Bostock & Mulcahy, 1994). In particular, Lloyd-Bostock and Mulcahy's research into complaints against hospitals (1994) shows complainants acting as 'knights', altruistically wishing to improve things for others in the future—they wanted 'a satisfactory *social* response to the complaint' (original emphasis).

Further, most legal research on disputes has employed 'top-down' approaches. There has been a growing awareness that 'bottom-up' analyses provide significant ways of understanding the crystallisation of disputes (Allsop & Mulcahy, 1998). Indeed, the exploration of why our interviewees challenged their homelessness decisions permits us to critique explanatory models of disputing behaviour from an empirical perspective. Competing models have been developed in the general socio-legal literature which seek to explain disputing processes. Our data allows us to reflect on the cogency of these models for welfare applicants challenging adverse decisions.

Having explored aims and motivations in pursuing internal review, in the second section of this chapter we examine the grounds for review from the perspective of the applicants. This data provides insights into the specific criticisms which are levelled against initial decision-making processes and the bureaucracy. It permits us to reflect further on the applicability of the explanatory models to welfare applicants.

We conclude the chapter by setting our findings about motivations and grounds of review within the context of applicants' broader attitudes to internal review and their prospects of success.

In our interviews we asked a number of open questions which focused on aims and motivations in pursuing internal review. In the section below we present the range of findings on this issue. However, it must be noted that we do not presume that applicants have only one discrete aim in taking up their rights to internal review. Applicants' reasons for challenging negative decisions overlap and combine, often forming different strands of a single sense of grievance. We have separated out these different strands and present them individually for analytic purposes only. They should not be regarded as being necessarily mutually exclusive. Further, we do not seek in this section to rank motivations in terms of significance. Our data comes from a statistically unrepresentative sample of aggrieved homeless applicants. Our aim is simply to describe the range of motivations in pursuing internal review which emerged from the data.

At this stage, we should make clear that our sample of interviewees who sought internal review is skewed heavily towards Brisford. Only five interviewees from Southfield had pursued internal review. Generally, our interviews were conducted after the interviewee had submitted their review, but before they had received the result. We were, therefore, able to test their understanding of the process, a particularly important point as previous research has continually demonstrated applicant ignorance of the processes in which they are engaged (Genn & Genn, 1989; Sainsbury et al, 1995; Berthoud & Bryson, 1997). What became apparent was that the Brisford sub-sample generally had a better understanding of the process, because of the information provided with the decision-letter and by the reviewer. Even so, this understanding was often limited or lacked clarity.

Our interview data reveals three aims in requesting an internal review.

Reversal of Original Decision

The first, and perhaps most obvious aim in pursuing internal review is to secure the reversal of the original decision. This motivation was applicable to most of our interviewees. They had a need for housing and so used internal review as a further stage in the attempt to achieve this goal. The submission of the review request was often triggered by the threat of eviction from temporary accommodation. This did not always mean, however, that applicants would necessarily have pursued internal review without this threat being present. Interview B33, for example, would have preferred a more informal mode of challenging his negative decision. He was sceptical about the use of formal complaints processes and believed that their use could be counter-productive to the complainant. However, the threat of eviction from temporary accommodation precluded the luxury of proceeding in an informal fashion.

Calling the HPU to Account

The second motivation in pursuing an internal review was to call the bureaucracy to account for the adverse decision. The aim here was to complain about the nature of the decision or the decision-making process. As we explore further later in this chapter, and in chapter five, a number of our interviewees found the process of applying for housing undignifying or offensive. They expressed various dissatisfactions about their treatment as subjects of the bureaucratic process or pointed to what they felt were procedural failings. Such negative feelings could also be experienced by 'successful' homeless applicants who were upset by the nature of the offer of housing they received:

> I was quite blunt actually [in my refusal letter]. I was quite disgusted. I mean like I said, some people are different but I thought the fact that… I just, why would they offer this to a young family, a house where a woman's died under horrific circumstances and why would they offer a family that? I don't know, its just my way, my perspective on life and I felt cheapened and I felt like they were fobbing me off. (**Interview S27**)

> I felt that like I was a victim of a robot. … Something lacking humanity happened. I mean I'd been dealt with as a person up 'til that point and after that I think I was dealt with as a statistic, you know? It was cold, the letter was cold. (**Interview B63**)

For some of these applicants, the motivation in pursuing internal review was to expose this poor treatment and to call the bureaucracy to account. Rather than complain about their treatment through a complaints mechanism, they sought to expose their poor treatment through an internal review. So, for example, Interview B33 wanted an apology from Brisford for his treatment, but was told 'that's not the kind of attitude that's gonna get you help here'. He believed that the formal process of complaining,

> … from my situation on the other side of that glass, may in fact be detrimental to my case because all these people will pull together, "Hey, he's after one of ours." or something, and I feel that, you know, that they would, consciously or unconsciously, perhaps use that against me. And where it becomes personal and not just what I'm entitled to, that's all I want, right?

Interview B51 was of the opinion that his caseworker was idle. Interview B51 was a single person who had been found to be 'not vulnerable' even though he was in a wheelchair, a decision which he ridiculed. Brisford's officers had expected him to compile evidence in support of his application despite his limited resources. In his view, 'they could have had this all resolved a hell of a sight quicker than what they have done'. During our interview, he explained his desire to call the HPU to account, partly so that others in the future would not suffer in a similar fashion:

> **Applicant:** They just, they'd not done nothing, the only people that's bothered to do anything is me doctor and the solicitor. The actual housing people, the homeless unit, have not bothered to do anything whatsoever to find out that I was speaking the truth, all they tried to do is virtually put me down as a liar, of which I am not very happy about at all, and actually if it had to come to going to court for it, believe you me, I would take it to court.

> **Interviewer:** You would go to court?

> **Applicant:** Oh yes, I definitely would, I definitely would because to me, this is bang out of order, and if they're doing it with me, how many more people have they done it to, that's they way I look at it.

Delay of Eviction from Temporary Accommodation

The third motivation in pursuing internal review was to delay eviction from temporary accommodation. A number of interviewees pursued their internal review instrumentally for this reason. Thus, the identified problem was not the negative decision but the impending loss of accommodation. This was a tactic used by a number of interviewees in Brisford, though it should be noted that the usual practice of Brisford was not to give temporary accommodation pending the internal review process. Interview B1 had been through the court system to try to avoid a possession action brought by Brisford on the basis that he had fraudulently obtained council accommodation. He had been through two different hearings in a vain attempt to stop the eviction. The bailiffs, however, were scheduled to arrive shortly after our interview. He sought an internal review, not in the hope that he would be entitled to remain in the accommodation with his family (he recognised that they would have to leave) but to try and stay the eviction for a short period:

> they sent us a letter saying that the bailiffs are coming tomorrow to come and put us out, but I've been to see the bailiffs and I've told them we've got nowhere to go ... So I asked for a review, to the homelessness person, because you know, myself and my wife were talking and we said that, you know, 'If two judges have said no, you know, and we've explained everything and we go for the whole hearing, is it not the same thing they're going to tell us, just in

the whole hearing?'. So, the only thing is that they're delaying, we're delaying the process of us coming out, leaving our property, you know. ... We're trying to hold on as long as possible. (**Interview B1**)

Interview B4 similarly sought an internal review in order to extend her time in temporary accommodation provided by Brisford. Her review request suggested that Brisford had not understood the background and context to her homelessness. However, she was sceptical about her chances of success and was using the process instrumentally to secure extra time so that she could make alternative arrangements for herself:

Yeah, I've sent off my, I sent back my appeal letter. I'm hoping that will give me a bit more time to sort myself out... (**Interview B4**)

Ignorance Of Having Sought Internal Review

The above section outlined the three motivations in pursuing internal review which emerged from our data. However, we must also report another finding here which is pertinent to the question of why people take-up rights of redress. Surprisingly, some of our interviewees were either *unaware* that they were pursuing an internal review or *confused* the internal review in their case with other proceedings (such as a stay of eviction). Other research studies have found considerable levels of ignorance amongst welfare applicants about the way in which a review or tribunal conducts its business (see, for example, Sainsbury & Eardley, 1991: para 3.15; Genn & Genn, 1989: 219-21; Baldwin et al, 1992: ch 6). However, a lack of awareness of being involved in a review process was an unanticipated but interesting finding. The explanation for this situation can stem from the interviewees' level of trust and confidence in their advisers—leaving everything in their hands—and/or their level of personal vulnerability and competence (that is, they have submitted a request for an internal review but have since forgotten).

Interview B15, for example, had been evicted from supported housing for unacceptable behaviour. Brisford found her to be not in priority need. At the point of being evicted from her temporary accommodation she went to see a lawyer. She placed considerable trust in her lawyer. She seemed unaware that her solicitor had requested an internal review, confusing it with the stay of eviction from the temporary accommodation:

I went to see a solicitor and she told me to wait for the letter. So I don't know what else I suppose I've to do. *She's in charge of the case, I can do nothing about it.* (**Interview B15**, our emphasis).

The trust in the lawyer, forced by her circumstances, meant that her situation was out of her hands to the extent that she did not really know what was being done on her behalf.

The unwitting use of internal review may also, however, stem from the bureaucracy's response to a query from, or other contact by the applicant. Interview B46, for example, refused an offer of accommodation without viewing the property on the basis of a change in circumstances. She had originally approached Brisford saying that she wished to be housed near her mother in a neighbouring council. Her mother required considerable support as she suffered from arthritis and memory loss. The applicant wrote to tell the council that her circumstances had changed without consciously believing that she was participating in a refusal process:

> well they gave me a letter to say we, we accept your circumstances, the reasons have changed. That's why I won my appeal apparently, whatever appeal that I didn't even do.

The HPU was responsible here for transforming a discrete refusal of housing into a request for an internal review. In Felstiner et al's terms (1980–81) the offer of housing was an '*un*perceived injurious event'. She was unaware of the risk of not being offered another property and so had not 'named' the unsuitable offer as injurious. Had she been aware of this, then she may have consciously sought an internal review. However, her story demonstrates that some 'disputing' behaviour can involve an unwitting participant and that it is the other party, paradoxically, who is the transformative agent in the process.

Conclusions About Motivations In Pursuing Internal Review

Our data seems to confirm the findings from the limited research which exists on why welfare applicants pursue redress mechanisms (Sainsbury et al, 1995; Berthoud & Bryson 1997). This research indicates that in appealing against, or seeking review of, an adverse welfare decision, claimants want the substantive benefit originally applied for. However, the research goes on to indicate that they *also* want to be heard, understood, responded to and treated with respect. This is consonant with our findings that interviewees sought the reversal of the original adverse decision, but also sought to call the HPU to account for their treatment as subjects of the bureaucratic process. At this stage we should consider the implications of these empirical findings for the cogency of the explanatory models of disputing behaviour which exist in the general socio-legal literature.

We saw in chapter one that Felstiner et al's (1980–81) conceptual framework of naming, blaming and claiming, although highly influential, has been the subject of some criticism (Lloyd-Bostock 1984, 1991; Merry 1990). Lloyd-Bostock and Mulcahy (1994) have suggested an alternative model of complaining behaviour. They set up a theoretical framework for understanding complaining behaviour which they call an 'account' model

(1994:141). Under this model, initial complaining is better conceived as being an event in and of itself—a non-instrumental event calling someone to account for the failure to meet the complainant's normative expectations. They distinguish this model from what might be called a 'redress' model which stresses the purpose of complaining (broadly conceived) as the seeking of redress (compensation, restitution or some other substantive benefit). The 'naming, blaming and claiming' framework fits this model. Lloyd-Bostock and Mulcahy's work shows the limitations of the 'redress' model. Their 'account' model clearly has relevance for complaining behaviour and must be given proper recognition as an alternative explanatory model, though Genn's research (1999:180) suggests that, empirically, the redress model is by far the more pertinent. It would be a mistake, however, to see these models as mutually exclusive. Neither set of authors discount alternative propositions, that of Lloyd-Bostock and Mulcahy being particularly reflexive. Our finding that our interviewees were motivated by the desire to be granted housing, or suitable housing, fits squarely with the 'redress' model of disputing behaviour. However, our additional finding that some of our interviewees also wanted to call the HPU to account for their treatment of procedural failures falls squarely within the 'account' model. Further, Genn's research (1999) also suggests that the type of problem is significant for the motivation(s) of citizens in pursuing 'justice'. Where the problem is of a serious personal nature (as in Lloyd-Bostock and Mulcahy's study of hospital patients) or where the citizen is the subject of an imposing bureaucratic process in relation to deeply felt need (as in our study of homelessness applicants), it is perhaps to be expected that an 'account' model will feature more prominently in explaining motivations in pursuing grievances. Indeed, this finding injects an additional layer of interest into the study of citizens' challenges to adverse welfare decisions. As Allsop and Mulcahy (1998: 803–4) point out in their research on complaining behaviour in doctor-patient relationships,

> Complaints from patients and carers are of interest because of the way in which they change the usual rules of the doctor-patient relationship. Typically doctors control interactions as they determine the knowledge and flow of resources over time and space in the encounter. ... By voicing their dissatisfaction, people attempt to hold a doctor to account. We suggest this has a transformative effect on the doctor-patient relationship. A response is required from the doctor who may well have to justify, or at least explain, their decision making and in so doing may well be called upon to articulate what is involved in their work and answer questions different from those posed by fellow professionals.

We have already noted how decision-making practices and processes are controlled by the HPUs in our study and are usually kept secret, emphasised by the practice of HPU officers completing application forms themselves which applicants then sign *without* reading. An applicant who seeks an internal review similarly transforms that hierarchical relationship, and the HPU is required to justify itself. This requires the HPU either to defend its decision or to accept it is wrong. Ultimately, the applicant may want long-term housing, but the act of requesting an internal review may also in itself be an 'account episode' (Lloyd-Bostock & Mulcahy, 1994).

The implications of these combined findings is that much welfare disputing is perhaps better understood within a hybrid explanatory framework which spans both the 'redress' and 'account' models. However, our separate findings about the instrumental use of internal review and the unwitting use of internal review expose some further weaknesses in the existing models. Our interviewees who pursued internal review in order to delay eviction from temporary accommodation demonstrate that neither the redress nor account models apply. Both models presume some kind of conscious act on the part of the citizen which was missing in relation to our interviewees who pursued internal review unwittingly. Similarly, both models envisage there being a coherent relationship between the spirit and the letter of the claim or complaint. This was missing in relation to our interviewees who pursued internal review as a disguised means of delaying their eviction from temporary accommodation.

GROUNDS OF REVIEW

A number of different justifications for the internal review request emerged from the data. Some interviewees regarded the decision as being inaccurate in some way. Others were less specific in their criticisms, but nonetheless regarded the decision as unfair. In this second situation, the adverse decision offends their own, often unarticulated, sense of desert or need. Others' sense of unfairness was based on comparisons between their treatment and that of others. As with the reasons for non-pursuit of internal review, applicants' sense of grievance is better understood within the context of the interactions between applicant and bureaucrat, and the expectations engendered by the application process. These situations are examined in turn.

Inaccuracy

Most interviewees believed that the decision in their case was inaccurate. Inaccuracy is a matter of some importance for administrative justice theory. Sainsbury, for example, notes:

> I consider accuracy to be the primary demand of administrative justice because, no matter what other desirable attributes a decision-making process

might embody, its decisions are unlikely to be acceptable if they are wrong. (1992: 302)

Sainsbury (1992; 1994a) distinguishes accuracy—the substantive outcome— from fairness—the process itself. However, he makes the point that, although analytically separate, the two concepts are closely linked as fair treatment during the process is a means of promoting and demonstrating accuracy. The significance of accuracy to procedural fairness has become the subject of some strong debate within socio-legal studies. Galligan (1996) advances a detailed argument that the principal role of procedures is to produce accurate outcomes. In setting out his thesis, he subjects the social psychological literature on procedural justice (in particular, the work of Tyler, 1987; 1988 and 1990) to some robust scrutiny:

> Something is seriously wrong with an account of procedural fairness which emphasises the inherent value of procedural rules about hearing and bias to the almost total neglect of their instrumental role in upholding normative expectations relating to outcomes. This is not to deny that the hearing and bias rules may have value independently of outcomes; but it is to insist that whatever non-instrumental value they have is subsidiary to their instrumental role. (1996:93)

Galligan's engagement with the social psychological literature has in turn been criticised by Adler (2001). Our empirical data is unfortunately ill-equipped to shed light on this debate, though it supports the view that applicants care both about the effect of inaccuracy on the substance of decision outcomes and about its effect on their dignity. The criticism of inaccuracy precipitates a sense of unfairness and, from the perspective of the applicant, constitutes a ground of internal review. In the section below we present our data about inaccuracy as a ground for internal review. We follow the schema of Sainsbury who suggests that accuracy relies on the twin tasks of 'collecting information and of applying the relevant decision-making criteria' (1994a:303).

Collecting Information

A number of our interviewees believed that the HPU had failed to understand the facts of their cases. Different explanations for such inaccuracy were offered. These constitute specific accusations of procedural or other failures and are set out below.

Language Barriers Some applicants for whom English was not their first language, suggested that language difficulties had led to a misunderstanding of their cases. Interview B28, for example, made the following observation (through an interpreter) about her assessments interview in which she had not been provided with an interpreter:

The thing is the whole thing rushed. She didn't understand the process what they've asked her and that and also she thinks that what she said they didn't understand either the caseworker. ... Because she speaks one or two English but not really and you can see now she understands bits, but to express sometimes she may not be able to you see?

The internal review offered an opportunity to be able to communicate her circumstances and needs properly, moving beyond the barriers created by language.

Inadequate Applicant Participation In Application Process Some applicants suggested that the failure to permit their greater involvement in the application process had led to inaccuracies. We noted in chapters three and four that the interviewing styles of officers in both Southfield and Brisford was often 'authoritarian'. So, for example, application forms are signed by the applicant before they are completed. Officers themselves complete the application forms in their own words. In this way, applicants' participation in the process is, to use Arnstein's phrase (1969), a 'degree of tokenism'—they are treated as passive within the application process. Although the decision was about them, their felt need had been marginalised within the process. Use of the formal review process was an explicit means of resisting that marginalisation, and an assertion of self against the assumptions and interpretations of the caseworker and bureaucracy. Thus, the internal review is a way of reinserting themselves into the process. As Sainsbury (1992: 304) argues, participation in the process 'can enhance the quality of evidence and also serve to convince individuals that a decision is accurate in their particular circumstances (ie increase the 'acceptability of the decision process')'.

Interview B40 illustrates these points well. She had lost her tied accommodation on health grounds, as a result of severe tinnitus. Her son sat in on her interview and helped her throughout the application process. She was found not to have a priority need. They felt that the caseworker had misunderstood the nature and severity of tinnitus, a fact confirmed to them by it being misspelt on the decision-letter. They believed that this lack of understanding could have been rectified during the interview if the caseworker had simply let them read the application form:

Son: we have one major complaint with all this ... At the end of [the interview] I said or you said 'You know could we have a look at the form'. And he said there was no need to look at the form because he had filled in everything as obviously it's his job. And I remember saying 'Well it's your job so you should know how to fill the form in for us, that is your job'. But as it turns out he has inadequately filled the form in, very inadequately because due to the letter we had back from them he obviously he didn't understand the problem between tinnitus and hearing aids as an example because he's more or less said 'Well you've got a hearing aid, that's it you've combated it'. He didn't have full understanding and should have asked us for more details. ... [I was] a bit annoyed about [not being able to read the form] because I don't really see why we couldn't have read the form and also you're asked to sign the form when you haven't read it, but he did say he's only writing down what we said but then again he didn't because he didn't write down enough points of what we said to him. So I think he basically didn't do his job, he did not provide his boss who makes the decisions with the facts clearly because when the facts are clearly set we have a case, and I know we do.

Here the son's position that the interviewer 'didn't do his job' is clearly linked to that person's failure to complete the application form correctly. The poor quality of the applicant's participation in the fact-finding process—reduced to a passive role—was, in his view, instrumental to the inaccurate decision. The decision-maker, functionally separated from the interviewer by this interviewee, was rendered incapable of making the right decision.

Restrictive Methods Of Proof Other applicants were critical of the limited means by which Brisford would regard a fact as having been 'proved'. The formal rationality of Brisford's bureaucracy inclined it towards the routinisation of its operations and procedures. The 'facts' of cases had to be established by standard methods of proof which were sanctioned by Principal Assessment Officers. Some applicants, however, noted that the production of such 'proof' was not always possible and that its absence did not negate the existence of the fact. In many cases this meant that proof was confirmed not by the oral narrative of the applicant, but by formal texts. Textuality, as Ewick and Silbey (1998: 100) suggest, has a central significance in the organisation of a 'modern legal-rational society' as texts 'can be preserved, retrieved, inspected, and interrogated'. The texts themselves are privileged over the oral narrative and confirm or deny that narrative. As Interview B33 put it, 'without paperwork we sort of don't exist, our story doesn't hold true'.

In other situations, certain 'texts' are privileged by the HPU over others as constituting proof of a fact. For example, Interview B49 applied for housing for himself and his child. Brisford required him to prove the dependence of the child by Child Benefit claim book. The physical presence of the child and the submission of the birth certificate was insufficient to prove the child's dependency on the applicant:

Applicant: I think one of the things that they do wrong is that, not only that their staff is not trained properly enough, is that they don't know how to, they don't look at every individual case on its merits...

Interviewer: did you understand what they were saying in this letter when you read this letter basically?

Applicant: It's just all waffle, I mean I don't understand. If you're to read back what you say, you have to have a child, what did you say?

Interviewer: I mean, it just says that you don't fall into these following groups, you know, the criteria,

Applicant: Yeah, go on.

Interviewer: you know, dependent children living …

Applicant: Stop there. Don't I have my son? There is his birth certificate, there is the school where he goes, you get me? I mean to me that is a start only, you know, nobody is gonna want to make that kind of forgery or that lying information, you know? You know, it's just, that's why I said lack of training, do you get me? The staff don't understand these things. You probably understand this more than they do, you know.

Interviewer: Right, OK.

Applicant: No, I'm just saying, you've seen my son, and I brought this, I also brought his school thing, you get me? And they insisted on this benefit book, you know, child benefit book, you know. I mean it's not by law that you have to claim it, you don't have to claim that, it's your wish, you get me. OK, every child must have that but if I didn't claim it or if I didn't wanna claim it, you get me? There is no law.

The incredulity of this interviewee at his treatment ('Don't I have my son?'), and the writing out of his son, are indicative of the subjection of interviewees to bureaucracy. It is the assumed and imposed expertise of the bureaucracy (a contrast with the rhetorical turn towards consumerism) which is being resisted by reference to the obviousness—the fact—that his son lives with him.

Limited Ability To Appreciate Complex Circumstances Others were critical of Brisford's inability to comprehend complex circumstances. Another aspect of routinisation in bureaucratic operations is a narrow construction and acceptance of the 'normal' to the exclusion of more complicated circumstances. The bureaucracy's constructions of 'normality' are demonstrated to applicants in their interactions throughout the application process, leaving applicants feeling aggrieved.

Interview B33, for example, was a single man with two dependent children. Like Interview B49 above, the issue in his case was whether the children were dependent on him rather than his ex-partner. Brisford issued a decision that he was not in priority need. He believed that his interviewing officer approached the investigatory process with a limited sense of what was 'normal' and, consequently, true. He felt on the defensive during his interview as his caseworker did not seem to accept that he, a white man, could have black-African children:

> Yeah, my case worker, didn't seem particularly interested in the sense that, you know 'All right, another person comes in, tells me their story.' I felt straight away that I was on the defensive, like that I was looked at as guilty of something, you know, because the story is quite convoluted and complex and to some people who expect things to happen this way and this way unless you're abnormal, if you don't it sounds, ooh, a bit, maybe suspicious, I don't know, but. So I basically told her what the story was and they said, 'We'll look into it.'

The complexity of this interviewee's story is, then, interpreted as suspicious by the bureaucracy, a fact which is communicated to him during the opening stages of the interview.

Failure To Take Account Of Relevant Information Some applicants criticised the HPU's failure to take account of relevant information which had been supplied. This criticism related in particular to what applicants regarded as unsuitable offers of housing. Some of our interviewees focused on a break in the information flow within the HPU which meant that allocations decisions were being made with an incomplete set of notes about applicants' needs and preferences. The information deficit at the allocations stage was particularly pertinent in Brisford where the allocations team was divorced from the assessments team.

Interview B34, for example, suffered from Parkinson's disease and was a recovering alcoholic. He had told various officers that he did not want to be offered sheltered housing or a ground floor flat (on the basis that they could be easily burgled). Despite this, however, he was offered sheltered housing and ground floor properties:

> how can they refuse me [through the one offer policy] when they've been giving me places I told them I don't want? I told them directly I don't want these places. I don't want to live away down the other side of [the city], I don't wanna live in .. if I was telling you, as an intelligent person, are they dim, are they thick or what? You know, there can't be no brain up there, I'm saying to you I don't want a ground floor flat, I don't wanna live in a housing trust, like a sheltered housing place, and they offer me two or three of them, I don't wanna live away down [the city], what would you do, would you offer me them places?

A similar information deficit occurred in the case of Interview B57 who complained that the accommodation offered was near to a major traffic intersection which posed a health problem for his son:

It just happens and, and there you are, Mr Innocent in a situation made by two people who haven't communicated through the department and they can't, you know what's going to happen if they uphold my offer. Their supervisors will go "Well why did you offer it? Why didn't you check his notes?" and so you know I just feel there's a miscommunication within all the departments that puts people in this situation.

In Southfield, the information collection process stalled most often when applicants wished to change their proposed areas of choice. This particularly affected those who made an application through the Families Team (as they had to make this selection when they initially made their homelessness application). For Interview S18, who left a violent relationship by making her homelessness application, that time was particularly difficult:

> I put, when I first went, I had some areas down and er, I put really far areas away for the simple reason my head was messed up, I was on anti-depressant tablets and I was just, my head was just not there. I actually phoned him up and says to him, look, I am alright I have been to the doctors, things like that, and I am getting myself on track now, er, I need to change my areas, because I picked really far areas and he said well what are you phoning me for, you just write in. He was just not helpful at all ... I got offered [area X], which is rough, er, run down and basically well too far away. I actually put, I put [area X] down as one of my areas and I actually wrote them a letter and I told them to change it but that is how bothered my caseworker is because he didn't actually change it ...

The Southfield interview data suggest that caseworkers or other officers sometimes steered interviewees to particular areas. Interview S15, in particular, described herself as being 'steam rollered' into her choice of areas, noting

> but I had so much on my mind I didn't really think it through and [I didn't have] an opportunity to say 'wait and hang on a minute'.

Incorrect Application of Decision-Making Criteria

The second strand of inaccuracy relates to the proper application of the decision-making criteria. It was evident that a number of applicants believed that the decision-making criteria had been incorrectly applied. Interview B59, for example, was found not to have a priority need. The decision-letter recited the relevant sub-paragraphs of the definition of priority need. The interviewee went through these and showed how she felt that there had been an incorrect application of the law to her situation:

> [he says] I'm not vulnerable as a result of old age, mental illness, handicap, physical disability or for any other special reason. But again I've already

mentioned, because of the pain, painkillers I actually fall into the group. ... So, and also I suffer from depression, so I do fall into the mental illness category as well, suicidal depression is one of the most serious. And [he says] I'm not homeless or threatened with homelessness as a result of an emergency such as fire, flood or other disaster. Attempted murder [by my Mother], I class as this other disaster. So I fall into a basically, all of those categories but one, cos I'm not pregnant, but I can't get pregnant cos of gynaecological conditions anyway. So, it's like 3 out of 4 categories, and he's made a decision and said that I don't fall into these categories.

Other applicants had a clear sense that the local authority had failed to offer them a 'suitable' property. The property factors which rendered the offer unsuitable in the perception of our interviewees included size, positioning (relative to ground) and decoration. For some interviewees, however, it was the location of the property which made it unsuitable in their eyes. It might have been too far away from their support network or the area might have been one which had a reputation. Interview B20, for example, was a pensioner who looked after her grandchild during the day while her ex-daughter-in-law worked:

how can they entertain the idea of putting people who are only going to get older, in areas like that, you know. I mean, after three o'clock in the afternoon, this time of year, I wouldn't have gone out [laughs], forget it, I'm not that brave. ... But also, for practical reasons. It's not an easy area to get to, there isn't an awful lot of transport, and then it wasn't, it was making it difficult for me looking after her, you know.

Unspecific Sense Of Unfairness

Although many of our interviewees pinpointed particular failures of the bureaucratic process which led to what they regarded as an inaccurate decision, others simply expressed a dissatisfaction with the substantive unfairness of the result. This position is often adopted where there is limited or no understanding of the provisions being applied by the HPU in coming to the adverse decision. Quite often, the adverse decision simply offends the applicant's sense of their own desert or need. Interview B39's challenge to the original negative decision resulted from his desperation. He could not articulate how Brisford had erred in its original decision. However, the decision simply failed to acknowledge his self-evidently obvious need for accommodation. Internal review afforded another chance to get somewhere to live:

Interviewer: Do you agree with this decision in the letter?

Applicant: It's not question agree, not agree. Of course, I don't agree. I need somewhere to stay.

Interviewer: What do you think is wrong with this decision?

Applicant: I dunno if it's wrong or right. I need somewhere to sleep, this is what I know...

Interviewer: How do you think you have been treated by the council?

Applicant: Of course, if they give me somewhere to stay, I would say yes, they've treated me well. If they don't give me, I will say no.

Adverse decisions generally, and bureaucratic assumptions about interviewees' need in particular, can trigger an emotional response in applicants. Emotions were strongly expressed even amongst 'successful applicants' who pursued a grievance in respect of their offer of housing. The offer of accommodation is a matter of considerable importance to applicants and, as we saw in chapter two, is the subject of much internal review activity. A considerable number of our interviewees expressed their dissatisfaction about housing offers in quite emotive terms:

> I mean there's this letter in your one hand saying if you don't take this you're in the street virtually, and it's extremely unlikely that they'll ever give you anything again, and then on the other hand you're standing in this place and you're shaking because you know, I mean I knew I couldn't live there... actually I basically said that, you know, you might as well have put out a syringe and a bottle of meths for me to drink and said 'with compliments of Brisford'. I just felt that, you know, there was no way you could live there and not despair. (**Interview B63**)

> I don't want to feel that I'm a reject of society and I'm shoved in a cupboard because I'm over sixty and I've lost my money and nobody wants to know about me. (**Interview B20**)

In both study areas officers believed that many clients had unreasonable expectations of the type and standard of property available. One might anticipate, then, that our interviewees would raise their failed expectations as a reason for pursuing their refusal. Certainly, there was evidence that some of our interviewees did have such expectations, apparently derived from informal assertions by friends and others, and not dampened by the assessment process. However, this was not a uniform view. Others expressed the sanguine view that resources were being stretched (particularly amongst the Southfield sample). The contradiction was best expressed by Interview B46, who made the following observation:

> I think, I mean I understand that they are limited in what they've got and what they can offer you. ... I understand they are limited but then I sort of contradict myself, because there's a hell of a lot of empty properties. So, but I do understand they are limited erm and I think it's probably easier for them to get you in a box or a place, get you off and move on to the next one.

Nevertheless, the strength of feeling about the nature of the housing offer was such that internal review was often pursued regardless.

Adverse decisions, then, can trigger deeply felt emotional responses which can fuel and inform the internal review request. However, the assumed emotions of the reviewing officer can also have a role to play in fuelling the review request. Where an adverse decision offends an applicant's sense of felt need, faith in the humanity of the reviewing officer and the hope of an appropriate emotional response from him or her can form the basis of an internal review request. Interview B43 provides an illustration. He was a Kosovan asylum-seeker who had been referred to a neighbouring local authority under the local connection provisions. His grounds for a review were that he wished to stay in Brisford to offer support to his family and his wife who were housed in Brisford:

> Interpreter: I can't leave them, they are my life, I have to be close to them, both of them, because only me I was in the war, I'm not under stress but all of them they are now because we want to be together, close to each other part of this reason you understand that.
>
> Interviewer: can you ask him does he know what happens in the appeal process? Does he have any idea? ...
>
> Interpreter: They took that appeal under consideration and they read very carefully and they feel something, they some have some emotional feelings, of course they're going to make the right decision for him.

Thus, the unspecific sense of unfairness may lead to appeals to emotion.

Comparative Sense Of Unfairness

Other interviewees relied on their knowledge of how fellow applicants had fared to determine whether the decision in their case was 'right' or 'wrong'. They constructed a case of comparative substantive unfairness. Interview B36, for example, sought asylum in the UK having come from Somalia. He could not understand why he had been referred to a neighbouring authority under the local connection provision when others had not:

> Interpreter: Because they say that a lot of people like us they apply and they get a positive decision. We're normal people, our case is special, it is different, and we receive a negative decision, that's the point that we can't understand.

He was seeking a 'humane' response to his family's problem as the neighbouring authority's social services had proved less accessible and less willing than Brisford's social services.

As with decisions about entitlement to housing, comparisons with other homeless applicants fuelled our interviewees' perceptions of the fairness of housing offers. Interviewees often disclosed a powerful sense of injustice that others had been offered accommodation of better quality ahead of them. The comparators used tended to be either those subject to asylum and immigration policies or single mother stereotypes. Interview B14, for example, conducted his own 'personal research' on re-housing options:

> I did a personal research myself and I actually found that people, a teenage girl whose pregnant, who has no disability, you know, they can offer her a whole house and live in [Brisford] whereas somebody who has a severe disability and he's black they would put him on the sixth floor estate you know and so to me that didn't make sense, you know, because pregnancy is not really a disability, you know, I felt that disabled people should be more, should have more priority than pregnant people because you hear this story about people who get pregnant just to get a council flat.

Pursuing Internal Review with No Grounds of Review

The above sections have described the grounds of review which emerged from our data. Our interviewees believed that the decision was unfair either because of some form of inaccuracy, or through a comparative sense of unfair treatment, or they simply regarded the decision as substantively unfair without particularly being able to articulate why this was so. However, a fourth finding emerged which also relates to the grounds for seeking internal review, though, paradoxically, it involves the situation where applicants felt that they had no particular grounds for review per se.

Interview B23 believed that all requests for assistance are refused initially as a rationing technique by public sector agencies. She saw the application process as a staged process whereby only those who sought internal review would obtain a proper consideration of their case. Her previous experience of having successfully appealed against a refusal of a bus pass suggested to her that blanket initial refusals were standard practice amongst local authority offices:

> with my past experiences of appealing, like for my [bus pass] and things like that, I thought that'd be my best bet and, you know, maybe they do that to everyone and people who don't appeal, then they've got an easy, like, case to wrap up and say, 'right, that's it. That's another one out.'

Conclusions About Grounds Of Review

Our findings about our interviewees' grounds for pursuing internal review have an intrinsic interest. Data about the criticisms levelled against welfare agencies by applicants is, relatively speaking, still quite rare. There is a tendency within legal studies to focus on criticisms of the administrative process only after they have been examined and distorted through the lens of administrative law. Many of the criticisms which emerged from our data are easily recognisable as aspects of the doctrines of due process within administrative law. However, it should not be surprising (except to the most out-of-touch lawyers) to discover that welfare applicants' complaints are often less developed or articulated, particularly where the substance of the decision-making process is confusing or mysterious to them.

Adverse welfare decisions quite often simply offend the citizen's intuitive sense of justice, or fail to appreciate their needs and so seem unfair. Applicants' own sense of marginalisation, potentially through the distortion of one's needs and their re-interpretation into bureaucratic categories, may become apparent during the initial interview process through the interaction between applicant and bureaucrat. Decisions generate emotions which can then be re-inserted in the application process by reference either to the lack of emotion in the bureaucracy or the common humanity of the reviewer. Whilst disputes are social constructs (Felstiner et al, 1980-1: 631), one should not dissociate emotions from them.

The data about grounds of review also permits us to reflect further on the applicability of Felstiner et al's explanatory model of disputing behaviour (1980–81). Our interviewees were a particular and perhaps unusual group of disputants. They were generally poor, marginalised, and desperate—desperate for what might be considered to be a basic human need: housing. The fact that most of our interviewees were driven by need interrupts the naming-blaming-claiming sequence. The extent of need expands the significance of 'claiming' to the disputing process, and minimises the significance of 'blaming'. A number of interviewees who pursued internal review did so without 'blaming' the local authority. They believed that the local authority had done its best within limited resources, or had no particular view on the issue. Nevertheless, they felt compelled to seek internal review because they needed the substantive benefit. It is possible, in other words to proceed directly from 'naming' to 'claiming' while by-passing 'blaming'.

CONFIDENCE AND SCEPTICISM IN PURSUING INTERNAL REVIEW

Having examined applicants' motivations in pursuing internal review, and their perceived grounds of review, we conclude this chapter by examining our interviewees' broader attitudes towards the internal review process. In chapter five, we discussed one cause of the non-pursuit of internal review as scepticism of the process. We drew attention to our interviewees' belief that it lacked independence, their mistrust of the system, and officers' own negative advice about the value of pursuing a review. In particular, we argued that scepticism was often a product of our interviewees' perception of a breach of trust. Scepticism was equally evident amongst most of those interviewees who *did* pursue an internal review. We begin, however, with the contrasting situation of those interviewees who, in fact, had confidence in the process.

Confidence

Some interviewees entered the internal review process with confidence that it would produce the 'right' result. Previous positive experiences with the welfare system can be significant in fuelling such confidence. As we have already seen above, Interview B23 had in the past successfully appealed against a refusal of a bus pass. This experience gave her confidence in her chances of success at internal review in relation to her homelessness application.

   Confidence in the ability of internal review to produce the 'right' result was particularly pertinent where applicants felt that the initial decision-making process had failed to capture the accurate account of their circumstances. Internal review, then, promised the opportunity for the full facts to be properly understood. Interview B40 (discussed above), for example, was confident because she felt that Brisford had not understood the nature of her illness. She believed that internal review would rectify those inaccuracies and produce a reversal of fortune. The confidence of some applicants was fuelled by the advice of advisers, or friends, or, sometimes, officers. Their expectations had been raised at some stage that their application should be accepted and they would be rehoused by the local authority. Interview B40, for example, had been advised that she had a 'strong case'. Similarly, Interview B59 had been advised by a caseworker that she would be in priority need. Her caseworker had apparently told her and her partner that they were a 'lovely couple' and, unlike his other clients, he wanted to help them.

Scepticism

Within our sample, however, the more usual attitude was not confidence but scepticism. Such applicants pursued internal review *despite* scepticism. Internal review here is an action of last resort, sometimes born of desperation or requested for instrumental reasons. Scepticism about the internal review process can come from a number of different sources, or may be focused on a number of different fears. Previous negative experiences can be significant in creating or fuelling mistrust which leads to scepticism. As we have seen in chapter five, prior experiences of being turned down by welfare agencies and other failures in the relationship of trust, can lead to scepticism and fatigue which militate against the exercise of one's rights of grievance.

Scepticism may also focus on the prospect of ethnic discrimination, a broader mistrust of society:

> To be honest, I don't know [what the result will be], cos of all the bureaucracy and I'm just thinking probably, you know, because, cos all the bureaucrats and red tape and it's a black man, even though we're British, we contribute to the society here, we've paid our taxes and dues and you're just a name on a piece of paper and stuff like that, you know, and they just don't care about us, they just don't care. You know, it's just, you're just cut off from the system. (**Interview B1**)

The scepticism of others, by way of contrast, rested on the view that certain groups were being privileged under the system. As we saw above, some interviewees' sense of grievance is defined by their belief that others are being treated more favourably. Interview B59, for example, believed that he would be by-passed in favour of asylum-seekers:

> I'm by no means racist, or anything like that, but you know, I do think that we should help our, our own country before we start helping, I mean our country's in turmoil, you know what I mean. I think, you know, we should help all our people and then help other people, but we've still got homelessness and things like that, because we're trying to do other things. And this is what's, this is what's worrying, you know, they should be offering the [poorest quality hostel] to the people who come from crisis, from war, because at the end of the day, if they have come from war and they're that desperate then go (...) you know, then they can all stay there. You know, but first things first, we haven't, we should've sorted our own problems before we started sorting other country's problems out.

Interview B33 believed that the review process may just be a bureaucratic method of gleaning further information in order to justify the original rejection:

> my assumption is that they're going back over everything again, see how it all fits together, see if they've made any errors. Well, they're probably not looking for their own errors, but finding out more about me again and finding out what I'm getting from the social security, checking it out with them—is this guy claiming, is he genuine, bla, bla, bla, ... Right, but it seems to me that that's why they keep going back, they're trying to find a way to not realise their duty of care.

Interview B58's scepticism was grounded in his understanding that there were insufficient resources—'there are too many people to house'. However, as a comparative exercise he noted that 'many people who deserve a house, they don't get [anything]. I can see many people ... lot of lies, they get everywhere.' His understanding, then, was that the system was a 'lottery'. His internal review request, accordingly, was an exercise in 'trying his luck'. Fairness was not a bureaucratic priority:

> everybody's polite and everything is incredibly good, but once you look inside a system, once you are inside a system, once you are on the list, I know a few homeless person, I have a friend who works with homeless drug addicts, so I know perfectly well that the system is far from fair, (laughs) but they're trying to be, everybody's trying his best but you cannot be fair because there are too many, too many of us, too many homeless and not too many people working for us and the provisions are not there.

Confidence Coexistent With Scepticism

Although some interviewees seemed to be either confident or sceptical, others displayed both attitudes during interview. The case of Interview B61 illustrates that applicants may retain quite conflicting attitudes towards the internal review process. On the one hand, he believed that one result of the review might be that they refuse to rehouse him on the basis of reasons not originally set out:

> You know, ... if .. what they said, the grounds that they haven't re-housed me on, is what they said and the grounds that I've appealed on ... are correct, they can't really refuse me, by law they can't refuse me. They can't change their mind later and say, 'No, we didn't re-house you because of this, that and the other'. No, you didn't re-house me because of what it states in that letter, don't go making up any more excuses. I've appealed on what you said in that letter.

On the other hand, he remained confident of his chances of success, although his comment on this was tinged with a degree of uncertainty ('if there's any justice')

> I am optimistic, you know what I mean. I'm about sixty-forty optimistic, yeah. If they take into consideration, I mean, if there's a justice and they, and they do you know, they do look into what I've said, they can look into it, yeah, they're gonna have to say, 'Well, this man is right', you know.

Subsequently, however, he described what happened in the review process in the following way:

> Probably the other person, probably Mrs [Assessments Officer] works on this side of the table, and he works on that side of the table, you know what I mean. Yeah, that's my, that's my view of an assessment officer, and he says, 'Hello, Theresa, do you fancy a cup of tea?', and she says, 'Yeah', and he goes, 'What do you think of this fucking idiot, he's sent me this back'. And she says, 'Yeah, I refused him', 'What shall I do? Shall I refuse him too?', 'Yeah,

well you might as well, we've got other things to do. I've got a relative here who needs a flat'.

CONCLUSION

Apart from the intrinsic interest in knowing why interviewees pursue their dissatisfaction—both in terms of their motivations and their criticisms of the adverse decision—this data has permitted us to test the explanatory models of disputing behaviour which exist in the general socio-legal literature. In this chapter we have assessed the applicability of these models to the situation of welfare applicants challenging adverse decisions. The 'account' model of Lloyd-Bostock and Mulcahy (1994) was proposed to highlight the fact that a redress model does not capture the totality of disputing behaviour. It demonstrates that the naming, blaming and claiming sequence (Felstiner et al, 1980 81) is not inevitably tied to the seeking of redress. It alternatively may be a discrete exercise in calling a party to account. Our data demonstrates that these explanatory models should not be regarded as mutually exclusive. There was evidence of both models in the disputing behaviour of our interviewees. Most of our interviewees were seeking redress—the offer of accommodation, or suitable accommodation—but some were additionally calling the HPU to account for poor treatment or procedural failings. This finding confirms that of other research in the field of social welfare (Sainsbury et al, 1995; Berthoud & Bryson, 1997) and suggests that much welfare decision-making is best understood within a hybrid explanatory framework which spans both the redress and account models.

However, we also found anomalous situations which expose the weakness in the ability of even a hybrid framework to capture all disputing behaviour comprehensively. Our data shows that some disputes fall outside both models—either where applicants were unaware of the internal review request, or where internal review was used instrumentally for ends other than the granting of the substantive benefit.

Our data on our interviewees' perceptions of the grounds of internal review also suggest that the 'redress' component of a hybrid framework is, at times, problematic. An embryonic dispute may proceed from naming to claiming without going through the stage of blaming. This interruption in the sequence is, we believe, a product of the desperate plight of our interviewees. The extent of their need propelled them to seek redress even in the absence of blame. The lack of blame might, of course, be explained by a 'false consciousness', but nevertheless these interviewees still pursued their internal review. This finding suggests that analyses of disputing behaviour must be context-specific. Overarching theory must be sensitive to the substance of disputes, the individuals concerned, and the different sequences which may follow.

We have also drawn attention in this chapter to the importance of emotions in understanding the pursuit of grievances. The account model of disputing implicitly acknowledges the emotional dimension of the pursuit of grievances, as does the Felstiner et al model explicitly. The social psychological literature on procedural justice also implicitly relates to emotions. However, an explicit focus on emotions and their significance for understanding disputing behaviour is still substantially missing from administrative justice research, and would, we suggest, prove a fruitful avenue for future research. This is a point which Lange has made in relation to regulation studies. She observes (2002: 197) that studies of regulation have been 'limited by focusing on cognitive aspects and by neglecting emotional dynamics of social action'. Legal processes tend to sideline emotions, in favour of cognition, without accepting their interaction (*ibid*: 198–200). We do not suggest that emotions by themselves can explain the reviewing behaviour of aggrieved welfare applicants. Similar emotions were evident in the language employed both by interviewees who did pursue review and by those who did not. However, the emotional dimension is indispensable to a full understanding of disputing behaviour. The development of an account model in particular is testament to the importance of emotions, and the data presented in this chapter demonstrates the impossibility of divorcing emotions from motivations in pursuing internal review and from the sense of grievance itself. The emotions of the applicant together with the assumed emotions of the reviewer *are* employed and relied upon in fleshing out grievances.

Finally, it is a finding of some interest that our interviewees sought internal review both with confidence and scepticism. We have seen in chapter five that scepticism may prevent some but not all applicants from taking up the right to internal review. What is clear from our data is that those who pursue their internal review share characteristics of those who do not. Our data in this chapter demonstrates again that a focus on scepticism or confidence in isolation is insufficient to explain the take up of rights of internal review. There is also an interesting and related question of why applicants pursue internal review when they are so sceptical about the 'system' or process. Sarat (1990: 359–365) has suggested in his work on welfare claimants' use of legal services, despite scepticism about their independence from the welfare bureaucracy, that 'given the prospect of starvation, real or imagined, there was no other choice'. Our view, however, is that applicants do exercise choice in applying for housing and in pursuing internal review. However, that 'choice' is heavily influenced by a sense of desperation. Indeed, the case of Interview B61 who articulated the co-existence of confidence and scepticism is perhaps particularly pertinent to our understanding of the decision to pursue internal review despite scepticism. Desperation unsettles the hold of scepticism and forcibly injects a weak form of hope into the consciousness of the applicant. Some form of hope co-exists alongside scepticism because the consequences of pure scepticism are too unpalatable given the extent of need.

7

Lawyers and Other Coping Strategies

INTRODUCTION

Much important socio-legal research has concentrated upon the effect which legal advice has upon particular disputes as well as the conditions under which such advice should be available. Despite the assertion that informal dispute resolution should be conducted without the need for lawyers, it is indubitably the case that such representation often makes a difference to the outcome of many disputing processes. In litigation, lawyers obtain better results because they themselves often have the advantage of being 'repeat players' (Galanter, 1974: 114–9). Research in the field of social welfare has repeatedly demonstrated that legal representation can make a positive differ- ence to an applicant's chance of success when challenging adverse decisions (Genn & Genn, 1989; Sainsbury & Eardley, 1991; Baldwin et al, 1992; Berthoud & Bryson, 1997; Seron et al, 2001; cf Davis et al, 1998). Given the demonstrated significance of legal advice and representation to the workings of the administrative justice system, and the historical interest which lawyers and legal representation has had for socio-legal studies, we were interested in why and how our interviewees accessed legal assistance, and the effects of legal representation on the practice of internal review.

However, our data indicates that lawyers were not the only 'audience' to which our interviewees told their story. The 'audience' can be any person or persons who are told about the dispute or from whom one of the disputants seeks advice. As Mather and Yngvesson (1980–1: 782) suggest, 'mobiliza- tion of a particular audience ... might be a crucial strategy in the manage- ment of a dispute'. They note the way in which the audience can shape, transform, and crystallise a matter into a dispute through broadening or narrowing it. Within our interview sample, many of those who pursued internal review sought the attention of a non-legal audience. It is important to stress from the outset that the use of alternative (ie non-lawyer) strategies was quite prevalent amongst our interview sample. Further, although our sample is statistically unrepresentative, our national survey data outlined in chapter two suggests that the use of legal representation in internal review processes is fairly small. As we will see in the sections below which explore the various coping strategies employed, several 'audiences' existed in relation to our interviewees who pursued internal review. In addition to lawyers, applicants also spoke to family, friends, community members, fellow applicants, doctors, councillors, MPs and caring agency workers.

Significantly, however, one of the most important audiences in disputing can be the other party itself. Our data discloses the importance to applicants of discussing their decision with the caseworker or of making contact within the bureaucracy. The parties—applicant and bureaucracy—are central players in the formation of a grievance. Often complainants seek to resolve their problem by initially voicing their complaint about their treatment to the person responsible (Genn, 1984; 1999; May & Stengal, 1990; Mulcahy & Tritter, 1998). Merry (1979) refers to this as a process of 'dyadic confrontation with the offending party', although for our sample it is often an attempt to challenge or change a decision through ordinary conversation. Felstiner et al (1980–1: 640) refer to the parties to disputes as 'central agents ... in the transformation process. Their behavior will be a function of personality as it interacts with prior experience and current pressures'.

One way in which this further interaction might be important is in defining down a grievance: rather than pursuing an internal review, a grievance might be passed through an alternative system. Internal reviews operate within a complex 'accountability space' (to adapt the terminology of Hancher & Moran, 1989). Grievances may, for example, be diverted into complaints processes rather than internal review systems, particularly where the recipient of the grievance is less knowledgeable about internal review. Equally, complaints about process may be dissociated by the recipient from complaints about inaccuracy and, thus, interpreted as a complaint rather than an incipient grievance. For example, in discussing the reason for the low take-up of internal review in Southfield a Team Leader of one of the residential units made the following point about his staff's ignorance (whilst at the same time highlighting his own):

> I don't think the review process is widely known even amongst staff. What tends to happen, if someone doesn't like a decision they tend to make a complaint using the complaints procedure rather than the judicial review procedure. That comes through a different process and that's generally around the way they were treated or the way they were spoken to or the type of accommodation that was arranged for them. Very rarely is the actual decision challenged.

On the other hand, some interviewees, like Interview B33 discussed in chapter six, pursued an internal review rather than a complaint as the latter might be held against them by the bureaucracy.

More generally, though, the bureaucracy was for many the first port of call to discuss their decision. This is an equally important interaction in that the caseworker can influence the trajectory of the problem, transforming it into something else. Earlier chapters have discussed this interaction. As we have seen in chapter five, some of our interviewees were informed by caseworkers that their chances of success were low in an internal review. This was identified as a reason for not pursuing their application. Some caseworkers refused to discuss negative decisions once they had been communicated. We discuss later in this chapter one knock-on effect on our interviewees of a caseworker's refusal to enter into discussion about the decision—the interviewees' decision to seek legal advice. Failure to discuss the decision might equally be a factor leading the applicant to voice their grievance through the formal internal review structure. Yet a number of our interviewees, when asked what an ideal system of internal review might be, wanted dialogue or re-assessment rather than the prospect of formal challenge.

Interview S11 had been offered a property with a shower, not a bath. Her son suffered from impetigo and cried so much that he vomited in a shower. She adopted a number of different strategies to challenge this accommodation, one of which involved telephoning her caseworker daily:

> I'm never off the phone to him, because you've got to be though because they just forget about you. You know like...Its like the council I was on the phone to [my caseworker-] everyday 'Is anything been done about [the property]?' 'He's in a queue, get off the phone. I'll phone you back.' That's all I kept getting. My mate said to me 'phone um' and I said 'you know what Marie, I am sick of phoning of them, they can phone me now'. I am absolutely sick to death of phoning them, wasting my credit on them, and putting me on hold. It just got to the stage that they can phone me now, I got absolutely fed up of phoning them it was just getting beyond a joke, me phoning them every day, every day because I just wanted to move out.

For many applicants, then, the first 'audience' is the bureaucracy itself. Their first port of call is to try to enter into a dialogue with the agency about the adverse decision. There is some evidence, however, that a simple dialogue with an HPU is generally less likely to result in an informal reconsideration of an adverse decision, than is, for example, some form of representation from a councillor, MP or adviser (Halliday, 2001). This perhaps explains why many of our applicants additionally, or subsequently, told their stories to other audiences. Their aims in doing so, and the strategies they adopted are explored below.

ALTERNATIVE COPING STRATEGIES

We have already noted that the use of legal representation in internal review is atypical on a national scale. Within our sample also, there were many applicants who developed coping strategies other than seeking legal assistance—what we have termed 'alternative coping strategies'. In this section we explore these alternative ways in which our interviewees who pursued internal review responded to the adverse initial decision and what coping strategies they employed to assist their cases. We recognise that a distinction exists in the literature between a 'strategy' and 'tactic' (de Certeau, 1984; Quinn, 2000). Our analysis seeks to build on the understanding of the frame of 'coping strategies' developed within the housing studies literature, particularly in the context of home ownership failures. Croft (2002) helpfully identifies a coping strategy as 'any preventive or reactive action taken to correct or mitigate the effects of contingent or crystallised risk'. Forrest and Kennett, drawing on Becker (1960), suggest that a strategy

> indicates a degree of conscious planning in adverse circumstances ... Coping strategies are specific and usually short-term adaptations to contingencies, with little reference to longer-term plans. (1996: 373)

We identified three different alternative strategies.

Advice And/Or Information

Many of our interviewees sought advice or information from non-lawyers. This group of information or advice givers can be sub-divided into two types of 'audience': (1) informal networks; and (2) formal agency workers.

Informal Networks

Informal networks may comprise various actors including relatives, friends, community members, even fellow applicants. Statistical studies of disputing have noted that informal networks can be 'extremely important in providing or reinforcing the incentive to claim' (Genn, 1984: 65; also May & Stengal, 1990). Our data demonstrate this point further. For example, Interview S11 decided to challenge the offer despite concerns about the one offer policy. Her mother (incorrectly) advised her that she should not withdraw her refusal:

> Yes that's what my mum said when I got offered at [district A] and I refused it and I was crying because I was upset thinking they are going to throw me out. My mum said 'don't [...], they can't throw you out. Where you going to go?

Back to square one, back to the town hall, to the homeless'. She said 'they can't throw you out of there, stop worrying.' 'Cause I was in a mess. I was a mess.

Indeed, the informality of much of the advice received by our applicants is reflected in the importance given to advice received from others waiting in reception areas or HPU canteens. So, for example, Interview S28 described his choice of temporary accommodation being affected by the conversations he had in the canteen prior to his assessments interview:

Information such as, I was told about that [bed & breakfast], there was people there that point blank just told me 'if you hear that name, just say no.' And believe me that was the first place they offered me and believe me I said 'no'.
...
And there was loads of people who had been waiting in the canteen down there and its like, you just hear all these different stories everybody's telling you of their dissatisfaction of how they are being treated.

Interview B48's expectations were derived from his conversations with others at a day centre for those with mental health issues. Others received informal advice from hostel residents or street homeless persons. People who had been through the system before, particularly where they had got what they wanted, were regarded as important sources. Interview B42's partner persuaded her to take the risk of going through the refusals process in part because of a friend who had successfully refused a property.

Informal networks were particularly important for those who spoke little or no English. Assistance might comprise the translation of letters or just general advice. Interview B36 were a family of Somalian asylum-seekers who had been successful in their asylum application. Having been placed in a neighbouring authority by Brisford's Social Services, Brisford's HPU sought to make a local connection referral to that neighbouring authority. Our interview was conducted through an interpreter, during which they made their reliance on informal networks apparent:

The system was complicated for them ... So I understand that they don't understand that much ... except for the few things that they get from friends, people tell them they have to apply for this, you have a right for this, you're accepted this, you're not accepted. (**Interpreter for Interview B36**)

Formal Agency Workers

Applicants often sought advice or information from formal agency workers who were assisting them in other aspects of their lives. For example, Interview B48 depended upon a bed and breakfast project worker believing that person to have a greater knowledge of the workings of the council. Interview B48 consulted this person when he received his eviction letter:

> He has actually worked for the Borough Town Hall so he knows about paying the money and you know paying rent so he has, he did all, all the form and everything anyway ...
> I meant to take the letter to him on, on time sort of thing cos I don't usually open the letters, I gave it to him to open it and see because I see I mean, I can't really do much about it when, when I'm writing letters because I, I don't know how to really to deal with these things you know, you know. So he opens the letter and he says that they want you to, I was a bit worried, they want you to move, they want you to go because you're not such-and-such a, because I have heard people who lived there also there were one or two of them has, has left so I wasn't, I was a bit worried also because I was worried all the way through. Then he said that so what he could do is that, then he gave me the suggestion that you go back to the doctor and tell them about it and also go back to the homeless unit.

Similarly, Interview S18 was helped by her carer. This relationship had developed to the extent that the interviewee referred to this person as her 'housing officer':

> [Southfield's caseworker] was just not helpful at all and its like I actually did ask, I always ask the woman who comes here, I just call her me 'Housing Officer', I always ask her when she comes, either leave a letter for her. She is dead nice, she always replies to my letters and she always puts on them 'I hope you are alright' and things like that, it is like I'm more drawn to her helping me, which is not her job, than I am me caseworker because she is more help. She phones through the Housing, and things like that for me. You know and she actually told me to go over the Housing and tell them and she actually phoned the Housing up for me and the Homeless Housing and things like that so that's what I did.

Other interviewees, however, went to their caseworker as a source of advice. Caseworkers may also actively influence on their own initiative the type of coping strategies employed by applicants. It was noted in chapter four that caseworkers in Brisford advised certain clients of their right to request an internal review or to seek advice about their application. So, for example, Interview B3, a former businessman who had been street homeless for seven years, was advised by his caseworker as follows:

> and she said, ' if you want a review *you just write it*'. *She bring the pen for me*. I write this thing. (emphasis added)

The caseworker facilitated the review request but, through her advice (or the way in which it was interpreted by the interviewee), also determined that the interviewee did not use third party advice. The substance of a negative decision-letter can also have the same effect. As we saw in chapter four, Brisford encloses an information pack with its negative decision letters. This includes a form on which clients provide their reasons for requesting a review. Some clients complete this form immediately without further ado and without considering the prospect of third party advice: 'I just filled in the bit at the back of the page. It all come with the same letter' (**Interview B23**).

Non-Legal Representation/Support

Interviewees also sought to enlist the support of various actors in relation to the internal review request. This generally constituted an attempt to get the 'representative' to influence the HPU towards changing its decision. However, as one might expect, these representatives brought to the process expertise or interests which were different to those of a lawyer. Their engagement with the HPU, then, did not concern the legality of the adverse decision. Some representation was quite specific, for example, where a doctor was asked to write a letter of support in relation to a particular medical complaint. Interview S11 sought support from a wide range of sources in relation to challenging her offer of housing, though placed particular reliance on her doctor:

> I wrote them a letter. I got on to my MP to write them a letter, the [health worker] a letter. I had to write a letter to my doctor or get in touch with me doctor to get the doctor to write me a support letter, then my case worker then got in touch with my doctor for more information, and, like I say, I got it on medical grounds ... I've been every day more or less at the doctors for something...

Other representation was quite general in scope, for example, from MPs or local councillors. Some interviewees were keen to receive as much of such support as possible in order to break through bureaucratic barriers. Interview B14, for example, explained why he went to his MP and three different Councillors:

> I wanted to have more people behind me you know, because I felt I had, I felt that Brisford was at fault which they were, you know, yeah, so I just wanted more people to know about it and if the case had gone to court you know I would have probably put in for, for some compensation for what they put me through, you know.

Similarly, Interview S29 did not consult a lawyer 'because this is a simple procedure but it's just that they are bringing all their bureaucracy into it, its such a simple thing'. Instead, she invited her local MP to view the property she was offered 'with his own eyes'. Having waited a whole week for him to come, however, she regarded him as relatively useless:

> [he] couldn't be bothered to come out and see me... I mean if you're going to be an MP I think at the end of the day, you've got these flash cars, at least show something for it.

Her attempts to enlist political support, however, did not stop there. She simply moved up the chain and contacted Tony Blair's office.

Going It Alone

A few interviewees negotiated the internal review process without seeking any assistance. Such applicants, however, were very much in the minority within our sample. Some of these applicants sought no assistance as an expression of their own sense of power in relation to the bureaucracy. Such confidence could be the result of prior experience. Interview B41, for example, was a 'repeat player' having been to a number of HPUs and 'knew all the tricks'. Others, however, did not know who to seek assistance from or were unaware that assistance was available. In this sense, 'going it alone' may not denote an active strategy, but rather an absence of strategy.

WHY AND HOW DID APPLICANTS ACCESS/FAIL TO
ACCESS LEGAL ASSISTANCE?

The above section explored the actions of those who sought assistance from persons other than lawyers. However, a number of these and other interviewees did seek legal representation, formally and informally, as part of the review process. We focus on this process in this section. First we explore their motivations in enlisting the assistance of lawyers.

Motivations In Seeking Legal Assistance

The motivations in seeking legal assistance were clear and perhaps unsurprising. First, applicants sought legal help to increase their power in relation to challenging the HPU. Second, they sought legal help to increase their understanding of the legal aspects of the homelessness application process.

Counteracting Powerlessness

A number of our applicants sought the help of lawyers because they felt powerless relative to the HPU. We should be careful, of course, not to regard the position of such applicants as one of powerlessness in an absolute sense.

Rather, they perceived a distinct power *imbalance*. The decision to seek legal assistance can be an act of resistance. As Sarat notes

> While the welfare poor are surrounded and entrapped by legal rules as well as by officials and institutions which claim authority to say what the law is and what the rules mean, they are not ... transfixed or paralysed. (1990: 346)

Our interviewees who experienced relative powerlessness often expressed it in terms of desperation. Applicants who received eviction notices from temporary accommodation were particularly affected here. In the case of Interview S14, an eviction notice was faxed through to the temporary hostel provider after a negative decision had been made in relation to their homelessness application. The fax conveyed the sense of immediacy and desperation to the applicants. They recognised that they had 'no chance of fighting [the council] themselves'. Seeking advice was their 'last resort'. As they put it, 'it was our last desperate place to go, we didn't know what else to do'.

Another cause of feelings of relative powerlessness amongst our interviewees was the failure of the bureaucracy to communicate with them. Thus, the notion of the 'faceless bureaucracy' proved to be a particular driver for applicants to seek legal advice. Interview B33 expressed his frustration after he was found not to have a priority need despite having two children. He initially tried to persuade Brisford of his perspective but found that they would not listen to his reasons why the children were living with him:

> Then I went straight to the lawyer because I found that going [to the HPU] I would just be fobbed off. The decision seemed final, they weren't gonna listen to me, doesn't matter what I said, I mean that's why I kept trying to get a duty manager instead of talking to that woman because I knew that they would just give me that case worker again. So I thought all right, as far as I'm concerned, talking to them, they're not listening to me any more, I'd better get someone who they're gonna listen to, so they can do it officially through the channels that they do, send each other faxes and official letters and bla, bla, bla.

Interview B21 similarly went to a lawyer when she failed (after repeated attempts) to get the HPU to change its mind. Brisford had offered her a property which she had failed to respond to within the allocated time period. Although she had not received her offer letter on time, Brisford failed to accept this. She described her frustration at trying to sort out the problem herself which prompted her eventually to seek legal assistance:

> what was I going to do? I couldn't argue with them, because I wouldn't have got anywhere, you know, they discharge duty, they discharge duty, what could I do? The problem was that they refused to accept the fact I hadn't got the letter on time. They said I was, they told me, they called me liar on the phone.

> I couldn't talk to anyone, they kept passing me on from one department to another. In the end, I didn't know who I talked to.

The act of not going to a lawyer, of course, may be an expression of self-empowerment (cf Genn, 1999). As Interview B18 put it, 'I always do everything myself'. Indeed, these two aspects of power in relation to the seeking of legal assistance is evidenced clearly within the single case of Interview B9. She had an alcohol dependency problem and lived a chaotic lifestyle. Originally, she had been deemed by Brisford not to have a priority need and her ex-husband had advised her to seek legal advice to stop her impending eviction. She did so by looking through the telephone directory. The solicitors successfully sought an internal review of her decision 'I felt helpless because I'm usually quite good at things but I let the solicitor deal with it cos I was cracking up.' She was offered a property and felt compelled to take it because of the one offer policy. She did not seek legal advice at this stage, though: 'I'm a bit proud, I won't ask for help, you know what I mean? ... I'm that sort of person, but I should have done really.' Various expressions of her own power and powerlessness infuse the approaches adopted by this interviewee at the different stages in her application. Originally, she had to let the solicitor deal with the priority need issue (explained by her as stopping her eviction from the accommodation) because of her mental state; however, when offered the property her pride stopped her from seeking advice which, in retrospect, she wished she had done.

Further, we do not wish to suggest that legal assistance always increased the applicants' sense of power. It could have the opposite effect. Some applicants experienced an increased sense of *powerlessness* as a result of using a lawyer. This happened when they felt excluded from the interactions between the lawyer and the HPU:

> I haven't got a clue what's happening, you know, it's in the hands of the solicitor, and it's down now to what she can do and what she can't do, because there's nothing I can do, like I say, as you can see yourself, I'm stuck in a wheelchair, I can't just get from A to B willy-nilly, and it's very hard for me to get down there ... (**Interview B51**)

> But it was as though you didn't exist really, everybody was doing everything for you but you didn't exist (**Interview S19**)

Counteracting Ignorance Or Confusion

Some applicants sought legal help because they were confused about the legal aspects of the homelessness application process. Although a number of interviewees were 'repeat players' in that they had made homelessness applications before, parts of the process in which they became engaged sent them to a lawyer's door. Interviewees felt most out of their depth when dealing with law. Thus, Interview B33 said,

> basically I believe, because the law is a very complex thing and I certainly don't read on it or know about it, I do tend to go to professionals who can.

The decision to seek legal advice, of course, requires the prior recognition that it is a *legal* process in which one is involved. Interview B54 clearly made this identification as a result of his dialogue with the HPU. He felt he needed someone with a 'clear head' to handle the internal review request:

> simply because they kept harping on about the legal side of it and everything is so strict on the government act, 1996 or whatever it is, we decided we would just get a lawyer involved, which was the correct thing to do. ... at the end of the day neither of us were in a mental state to want to deal with it. It's easier for someone with a clear head who knows exactly what's going on.

This suggests that interviewing styles may have a bearing on whether applicants seek legal advice. In previous chapters, we noted the different styles adopted by caseworkers in our study areas. It may well be that informing applicants of the legal basis for the assessment, during the interview, has the effect of pushing some applicants towards legal advice.

Conditions Affecting The Seeking Of Legal Assistance

Throughout this book, we have acknowledged that our sample of unsuccessful applicants in the two study areas is statistically unrepresentative. Nevertheless, even a casual observation of that sample would note that there is a sizeable difference between the two areas in terms of those interviewees who sought legal advice. Just three applicants sought legal advice in our Southfield sample, including those who refused properties; in our Brisford sample, 19 unsuccessful applicants sought advice and all bar one applicant who sought an internal review on the suitability of a housing offer obtained legal advice at some stage. This limited snapshot raises the suspicion that Brisford and Southfield experienced very different rates of the take up of legal assistance.

Previous research has noted geographical unevenness in the distribution of advice, particularly housing advice (see Genn & Genn, 1989: 223; Nixon et al, 1996). It was certainly true that Brisford was well-serviced by law firms with reputations for housing and low income work, legal advice centres, and Citizens Advice Bureaux ('CABx'). However, it was also the case that Southfield had similarly high levels of housing advice through law firms, a local branch of a national charity, legal advice centres and CABx. Thus, the distribution of housing advice was about on a par between the two field-work sites.

In this section we set out the conditions which both hindered and facilitated the seeking of legal advice. Our data is ill-equipped to explain the seeming disparity between rates of legal assistance in our two study areas. However, by setting out the 'push' and 'pull' factors which emerged from our interview data we hope that some insights may be gleaned in relation to accounting for the take-up of legal assistance. Our findings certainly resonate with those of other research (Genn, 1984; 1999; Genn & Genn, 1989).

Push Factors: Conditions Which Facilitated The Seeking Of Legal Assistance

Recommendations To Seek Advice Genn has observed that a significant proportion of those who sought legal advice on personal injury issues had done so on the advice of a third person:

> the informal discussions which took place before they sought formal legal advice were extremely important in providing or reinforcing the incentive to claim. (1984: 65)

A similar effect, albeit not as significant, was evident in our sample. Friends and hostel workers were particular sources of the advice to seek legal assistance. The former were particularly important where English was not the first language of interviewees. In such cases, friends and relations might introduce the interviewee to a lawyer.

Previous Positive Experience A further reason for going to lawyers relates to interviewees' previous experience with, and use of, lawyers (see May & Stengel, 1990: 112-3). It was no coincidence that many clients returned to lawyers who had helped them in the past with family, immigration, personal injury, or other housing matters. Previous experience of law may also be a factor in leading clients to identify the process as legal. Indeed, this might be particularly the case where recent housing problems, possibly causing the current incidence of homelessness, lead to some engagement with law. Thus Interview B3 used a lawyer, who had previously won his immigration appeal, to deal with an impending eviction from temporary accommodation for rent arrears. In fact, he wrote his internal review request himself but subsequently received advice about the review from the same solicitor.

Pull Factors: Conditions Which Militated Against The Seeking Of Legal Advice

In her detailed public survey of the resolution of justiciable problems, Genn found the following influences on those people who sought their own resolution of problems without legal advice:

inaccessibility of good quality advice about legal rights; fear of legal costs; previous negative experiences of legal advisers or legal processes; a sense of powerlessness about certain types of problem; and in some cases a sense of alienation from the legal system. (1999: 76)

Our findings, set out below, seem consonant with Genn's data.

Perceived Cost Interview B61 exercised his right to an internal review but did not seek legal advice because he believed that he could not afford a solicitor. He expressed feelings of powerlessness:

> When you're homeless and you have no economic means, its not much steps or routes you can go down, you know, you're limited to what you can do. (**Interview B61**)

Ignorance Being ignorant of the existence of legal help is a clear barrier to the take-up of legal assistance. The content of HPU's decision-letters may affect access to advice. Brisford's negative decision letters contained details not only of how to exercise a right to review but also of the providers of legal advice on housing issues. Southfield's decision letter was at one stage accompanied by details of appropriate sources of legal advice and what happened in an internal review but, at the time of our fieldwork, this practice had been withdrawn. Genn and Genn (1989:221) note that the degree of understanding of what happens in tribunals impacts upon whether clients seek legal advice. It might be that this is also a factor in relation to internal reviews. Certainly, Brisford interviewees were more knowledgeable about how the review would be conducted, many citing the information provided with the decision-letter.

Previous Negative Experience We noted above that previous positive experience of lawyers was a push factor which could encourage the use of lawyers in relation to internal review. However, previous negative experiences of law and lawyers could just as easily encourage non-use. Interview B1 did not seek legal advice for this reason. He had been evicted from a Brisford property on the basis that it had been obtained by deception, a finding which he vehemently denied. He described his experience of court proceedings:

> a barrister just went in there and just mumbled a bit and the judge said, 'No, we're going to order the property to [Brisford]', and that was it. And he refused for me to appeal.

Interview B1 wrote his internal review request himself because he felt that 'it's best to hear it from the horse's mouth'. His negative view about lawyers was reflected in his expression that 'it's my words and it's probably as good [as] what the solicitor might say'.

Language Difficulties There was some evidence from our interviews that applicants for whom English was a second language felt that it was difficult to access legal services:

> Our problem is that I am not speaking good English so I don't know, I don't know where to go. (**Interview B2**)

Disorientation Finally, there was also evidence that some of our sample were so disoriented at the time of their application and afterwards that the prospect of seeking legal advice was not considered.

It is important to note, however, that not all people who seek legal advice end up getting it. A small number of our interviewees who tried to obtain legal assistance failed to do so. There was evidence that certain solicitors were unable to take on new cases as they were so busy. CABx were also singled out as being particularly difficult to contact. Interview B61 actually went to four different CABx before finding one which was open. Other interviewees were not so successful:

> I have been to citizens' advice but every time I have been it's shut so no, I've not really had any advice from anybody. (**Interview S11**)

> [Citizens' advice] are just very difficult to get hold of and I am not quite sure where there is one. (**Interview S15**)

Another applicant had left his telephone number with advisers but had not been called back. Interview B18 was referred to a local branch of a national charity by another council, which described him apparently as having been 'stitched up' by Brisford:

> it's a free phone number, it cost me twelve quid on my mobile to phone it for five minutes. It wiped out my credit call. ... I haven't phoned them back cos I can't afford to and I can't really be standing around in the cold at a phone box, for as long as it's going to take to ... they have my number to contact me and they haven't. (**Interview B18**)

Finding a Lawyer

It has already been noted that those persons with previous experience of lawyers tended to revisit those persons, or accept referrals on to different specialists. For others, however, the experience was rather different, a surprising number of interviewees saying that they sought legal advice or found a particular lawyer by luck or chance rather than design. Given the effect particular lawyers have upon reviewers (discussed below), this experience was interesting.

For example, Interview B51, who was in a wheelchair, was informed by

his hostel manager that he could obtain legal advice. Luck played a significant role in choosing an adviser:

> I didn't have a telephone card, and the only telephone here is a telephone card
> phone, they wouldn't let me use the office phone, so there was no way I could
> phone them, and I was going into the city one day with a young man that
> helped with me application, and I spotted it, I just spotted it from the bus, so
> I found out where it was, so the following day I managed to get down to the
> law centre.

Interview B59 equally described luck as playing a role: 'luckily enough, the
housing specialist was in at the law centre the same day [as he went]'. More
than this, though, the law centre was actually closed when he went there, but
the receptionist opened the door for him: 'she let us in when she wasn't
supposed to and gave us all this information ...' Subsequently, however,
research played a role in his choice of lawyer. He eventually chose a well-
known local specialist on the following basis:

> Through Joe, and also through the fact that people have said to me since 'Oh
> yeah, yeah, I've got awarded my council flat', 'Who helped you then?',
> '[Solicitor X]', [Solicitor X, Solicitor X, Solicitor X, Solicitor X]. Again and
> again and again, Solicitor X. Yeah, anyone that's fallen into the same circum-
> stances as me, you know, and there are a fair few people that we know, that've
> been screwed over, and they have actually helped them. Between that and the
> one's that are down the way, the [Solicitor Y] ... It's a bit too coincidental ...
> there's gotta be some sort of method or some sort of equation that they used
> to get people out of the system.

At What Stage Was Legal Assistance Sought?

Although it might reasonably be expected that clients seek specialist advice
after receiving their decision-letter, that is not necessarily the case amongst
our sample. Some, for example, explained that they sought legal advice
before making their application as part of personal research about what
might be expected and/or what sort of information would be required. A
small number sought advice *during* the application process. Even those who
sought advice *after* the decision letter had been received did so, as has
already been noted, much later when they were about to be evicted from
their temporary accommodation. Only a small number of interviewees
actually sought legal advice with plenty of time to spare.

THE EFFECT OF LEGAL REPRESENTATION ON THE PRACTICES OF
INTERNAL REVIEW

Having noted that legal representation in internal review processes is atypical, and having considered why and how the minority who do enjoy legal assistance go about getting it, we move on to consider in this section its impact on the practice of internal review. Due to the fact that Southfield conducts very few statutory internal reviews, much of our discussion in this section focuses on Brisford, though, where appropriate, reference to Southfield is also made.

Although there is no quantitative data to support this view, our qualitative data about the conduct of internal reviews within the HPUs suggests that legal representation makes a positive difference to applicant's chances of success. It certainly affects the way in which the internal review is handled. There are two aspects to this, we suggest. The first relates to the substance of the internal review request. The second relates to the reaction of the reviewing officer.

Most of the solicitors we interviewed expressed the view that homeless applicants understand very little of homelessness law, of what an internal review involves or of how to mount a 'proper' challenge to a homelessness decision. Certainly, a number of our applicant interviewees expressed such uncertainty about how internal reviews were conducted. The solicitors' view was that applicants without legal representation are at a disadvantage. It is perhaps unsurprising that solicitors should hold this view. However, more significantly, this view was also held by the officers within Brisford who regularly carry out reviews.

> a major difference [is that] the information a solicitor is going to ask you to take into consideration pursuant to the review is going to be quite specific. You know, and they're going to give an argument as to why they feel that this person is vulnerable or not intentionally homeless or whatever. An independent review, not all of them because some of them are very detailed as well, but a lot of them are not going to give that information. They're simply going to say to you 'I don't think that I am intentionally homeless cos I had to leave there cos of violence.' (**Principal Assessments Officer 1**)

> [lawyers] know all the legal jargon and they know the Act, and a normal lay person probably don't understand anything (**Support Manager**)

Legal representation, generally speaking, is said to improve the quality of the challenge to the original decision from the perspective of the reviewing officers in both study areas. There is, however, an additional reason why legal representation may make a difference to the applicant's chances of success. The reviewing officers in Brisford noted that the involvement of a legal representative signals the potential for county court litigation. The threat of further litigation encourages Brisford's officers to be more careful about the conduct of the internal review and the wording of the review determination. The threat of being challenged in court is taken seriously within Brisford, and the prospect of losing a case is one which it is keen to avoid. Greater caution is exercised, accordingly, when the threat exists. This is not just to do with professional pride. There is also a financial aspect to it in terms of meeting legal costs:

> I have sole responsibility for everything, when that invoice comes at the end of the financial year that says this is all the legal costs, it's mine, it's something I have done or failed to do that's led to that. That is very, very stressful. Because every single time you make a decision you wanna be sure you're doing exactly the right thing, right down to the T. (**Principal Reviews Officer**)

Similar levels of caution occurred in Southfield, although the threat of county court litigation was not as intense. It was suggested that use of a lawyer often meant that case law would be considered, and therefore would lead to communication with the local authority's legal advisers. The existence of legal representation was said by one reviewer to improve the quality of the case being put forward by the applicant and so increase the possibility of a positive outcome. The officer added that legal representation may have an impact upon her decision-making:

> I personally wouldn't treat them any differently, but I know we do feel under a bit more pressure from one that's [represented] ... I know it's wrong, but it probably makes you think 'There's more weight behind this' (**Principal Officer**).

In Brisford, reviewers of suitability issues had an informal hierarchy of legal advisers, particularly where the law firm was known for its housing expertise ('when I see one from [Firm A] or [Firm B] I just think 'oh goodness'': Principal Allocations Officer). Within firms, some advisers were regarded as providing better quality advice:

> quality differs ... maybe the older partner in the firm will provide more detailed additional information so that you do have to do, you know, look in depth and follow up some information and stuff like that. (**Principal Rehousing Officer**)

It is important to stress that the effects of legal representation on the decision-making of the Principal Reviews Officer and other reviewing officers are, as one might expect, not uniform. Halliday (2000a) has described how judicial review acted as a double-edged sword in relation to homelessness decision-making. Experiences of judicial review could be used positively to infuse decision-making with legal values and norms, but could also be used defensively to mask adherence to non-legal values. A parallel finding can be made in relation to legal representation and internal review in Brisford. Legal representation certainly urged greater caution on the part of reviewing officers. However, such caution might relate to the substance of the decision or the procedures adopted to arrive at the substantive outcome, or it may simply relate to the wording of the decision. For example one of the Principal Assessments Officers suggested that legal representation would have a greater impact on how she worded her decision-letters:

> I don't think we're short changing anybody in the way that we're dealing with the reviews or the decisions, I think they do get sort of you know a clear explanation as to why a decision's been upheld and things like that, whether it's through a solicitor or not, but I guess with a solicitor what you're being more careful of I guess is that anything that you might say you know they twist it another way (**Principal Assessments Officer 2**)

To this extent, legal representation would not increase the chances of success for the homeless applicant. In effect, the decision remains the same but the packaging of the decision is specially tailored for the legal representative. However, there is also evidence of caution which makes a difference to the substance of the decision-outcome or the decision-making processes leading up to that outcome.

The perception within Brisford's HPU was that legal representation was an increasing feature of the internal review process. Given the increasing involvement of legal representatives, it appears that internal review has now become both a specialised and adversarial enterprise. Indeed, in Brisford, this situation has been enhanced by the creation of a Principal Reviews Officer. Often in Brisford, internal review is the locus of highly specialised legal debate between the Principal Reviews Officer and legal representatives. Where, however, internal review requests lack legal representation, the internal review is much more likely to take the form of a simple administrative review. The quality of the participation of the homeless applicant by herself is notably lacking in comparison with that of the legal representative. The introduction of internal review in Brisford, therefore, has intensified the level of legal involvement in the administrative process. It also operates as a formal platform for the introduction of legal adversarialism into homelessness decision-making. This point is explored further in the following section which concerns the juridification of homelessness decision-making.

Juridification Of Homelessness Decision-Making

Juridification has been a prominent theme of socio-legal research in recent times. It is associated with normative and strategic critiques of public law's penetration into private domains through the expansion of the regulatory welfare state (Cooper 1995; Loughlin, 1996). More modestly, however, it has been used descriptively to chart an increasing prominence of law in the structuring of social, political and economic relations. In this short section we discuss the function of internal review in facilitating the increased significance of legality—substantive legal concepts and legal procedural requirements—to decision-making within the administrative arena. This, we suggest, is one (perhaps small) aspect of the juridification thesis, akin to Bridges et al's (1987) discussion of the 'judicialisation' of local government whereby local authority actors internalise the 'judicial gaze' and carry out their operations under the shadow of litigation.

Brisford had for many years prior to the introduction of internal review been involved in defending legal challenges. We are not suggesting, accordingly, that internal review has heralded external legal representatives into its administrative arena for the first time. Our claim is more modest. Prior to the introduction of internal review the debate regarding the legality of a decision was formally held in court—that is, outside the administrative arena—although clearly there would be informal correspondence and discussions preceding judicial review litigation. Internal review, however, has now provided a *formal* space *within* the administrative arena for legal debate, and given the use of legal representation by many of Brisford's internal review applicants, the enterprise of internal review has substantially increased the scale of legal debate as an integral part of the administrative process. The discourse of legality has, accordingly, been intensified within Brisford's homelessness decision-making in the sense that it is more frequent, more visible and more pressing as a practical matter to which decision-makers must attend.

Of course, we are not proposing as a generalisable finding that internal review necessarily *will* increase the juridification of homelessness decision-making. Rather we are suggesting that internal review *may* provide a platform for juridification, subject to other conditions being met. We would suggest that there are two other basic conditions. First, there must be a take-up of internal review by applicants. Clearly for internal review to act as a conduit for juridification, it must be used by applicants in the first place. Second, legal representation must be sought by the applicants. Where internal review requests are made without legal assistance, as we have argued above, internal review takes the form of a simple administrative review rather than being an instance of legal adversarialism. Where these two conditions are met, internal review facilitates the injection of legality into the administrative arena in a new and increased way. Thereafter, the significance of juridification to the practical routines of homelessness decision-making and the substance of decision-outcomes is dependent on the strength of a pre-existing legality discourse within the organisation and the structure of the organisation whereby legal knowledge is disseminated and a commitment to legality is applied in the making and checking of decisions (see Halliday *forthcoming*). Nevertheless, it is interesting to note that the experience of internal review in Brisford has had the effect of juridifying routine administrative decision-making—at least at the internal review stage.

Shifting The Character Of Administrative Justice

Another way of describing Brisford's experience of juridification is to suggest that the character of the administrative justice inherent in the administrative process has shifted with the introduction of internal review. Mashaw's (1983) celebrated typology of administrative justice is helpful here. He sets out three models of administrative justice: bureaucratic rationality, professional treatment and moral judgement. These models are competitive rather than mutually exclusive: 'the internal logic of any one of them tends to drive the characteristics of the others from the field as it works itself out in concrete situations' (1983:23). Internal (or 'hierarchical') review is characteristic of the bureaucratic rationality model of administrative justice. Under this model the values of accuracy and efficiency are privileged. The function of internal review is to check on the accuracy and efficiency of initial decisions. This is precisely the role of internal review in Brisford where there is no legal representation. Although the internal review is requested by the applicant, the process is controlled internally and functions to review the quality of the initial decision according to the internally generated notion of accuracy.

However, when an applicant's legal representative is involved, the character of administrative justice is shifted towards Mashaw's moral judgement model. Under this model 'the traditional goal of the adjudicatory process is to resolve disputes about rights.' (1983:29) The paradigm situations are the civil and criminal trial. The essence of the moral judgement model is that parties to a dispute are placed on an even playing field and given equal opportunities to make out their claim to entitlements. As we noted above, the intrusion of a legal representative into the administrative arena through internal review brings with it a sense of adversarialism. Rather than the internal review being a simple internal check on the accuracy of an initial decision, it becomes the locus of legal debate (between the local authority and the external legal representative) about the applicant's entitlements under homelessness law. Although the dispute is not being heard before an independent tribunal, the character of administrative justice in the internal review process has nevertheless shifted. The value of accuracy (internally generated) has been displaced (at least partially) in favour of the value of fairness, in the sense of the applicant being granted the opportunity to present his case and enter into a dialogue and debate about the basis of his entitlements. There has been a move, to use Galligan's conceptualisation of procedural fairness (1996), along the continuum from bureaucratic administration to fair treatment. Or, to use Sainbury's terms (1994), the process of internal review shifts away from the administrative towards the adjudicative realm.

CONCLUSION

In this chapter, we have sought to capture the different responses of our interviewees to the negative decisions in their cases. Our survey data in chapter two suggests that the use of legal representation in internal review is atypical on a national scale. Our interview sample contained examples both of applicants who did seek legal help and those who did not. A number of our interviewees engaged with other techniques and tactics beyond legal advice designed to cope with their housing situation and their negative decision. Other applicants, however, did seek legal advice and our interview sample, particularly in relation to Brisford, was sufficient for us to gain valuable data about why and how this occurs. Our data gives us insights into applicants' motivation in seeking legal help and into the barriers to the take up of legal services. These findings are consonant with larger quantitative projects which have sought to examine these questions in depth.

Importantly, also, we have been able to chart the effects of legal representation on internal review. Without wishing to enter the debate about the desirability of legal representation in internal review processes, we have nevertheless been able to assess its impact. The perceptions of officers who carried out reviews was that legally represented applicants had a greater chance of success. This claim must rest at the level of suggestion only and requires testing with quantitative methods. However, our data certainly demonstrates that the practice of internal review changes with legal representation. Greater caution is exercised over an internal review where a lawyer is involved. The implications of this, we suggest, is that internal review may act as a conduit for the juridification of homelessness decision-making in general, and certainly shifts the character of administrative justice being practised in those specific cases where there is representation. Rather than the internal review being a simple administrative check, it shifts towards the adjudicative realm and becomes a dress rehearsal for full-blown external review in the courts.

8

Conclusion

We began this book with the story of Andrew Holt and his surprising failure to challenge a refusal of help by Brisford Council, despite his desperation for a solution to his homelessness. His story captures the basic conundrum which first fuelled our interest in internal review: why do so few welfare applicants challenge refusals of help despite a continuing sense of need? Our data has afforded us the opportunity to develop a list of barriers to the pursuit of administrative grievances. We set these against the background of the social reality of the applicant-bureaucracy relationship which is played out in the homelessness application process. Where pertinent, we have situated our empirical analysis within broader theoretical debates in law, socio-legal studies and sociology.

In this concluding chapter we summarise and discuss our main findings about the (non-)emergence of disputes. However, we also reflect on some of our other findings. Although our project began as an enquiry into the (non-) pursuit of internal review, it developed into a wider project which examined welfare decision-making, internal review, the role of lawyers and administrative justice. Additionally, we consider the implications of our findings for policy development and for the continuation of the research agenda. We begin, however, with a consideration of our findings about homelessness decision-making in our two case study authorities.

DECISION-MAKING IN SOUTHFIELD AND BRISFORD

In chapters three and four we presented our ethnographic data about decision-making in the two local authorities which took part in the research—both at the initial and internal review stages of the overall administrative processes. Existing research about homelessness decision-making has shown that, in common with other aspects of welfare, the bureaucratic process is complex, subject to competing pressures and multi-faceted (Loveland, 1995; Cowan 1997; Halliday, 2000a; 2000b). Our findings confirm this pattern. Indeed, we have employed various heuristic devices to describe the decision-making process and applicant-officer relationships to show variations within bureaucratic practices. Our data also demonstrated how a competition between internal organisational discourses can produce different results at different moments or at different stages of the bureaucratic process. Whilst resisting the temptation to describe our case study authorities too simplistically, we have nevertheless portrayed Southfield as the 'risk authority' and Brisford as the 'audit authority' in order to distinguish the respective *dominant* ethos within each. This categorisation allows us to contrast the general prevailing concern of Southfield as a single organisation with that of Brisford.

Scott (2000) has made the point that there is a plurality of accountability mechanisms which bear down on the day-to-day business of government. This plurality of mechanisms permits the administration of homelessness law to manifest broadly distinguishable characteristics in different locations. The substance of routine decision-making, in other words, looks different in various agencies according to what the agencies care about most. This is not to suggest that agencies care only about one thing, or about one accountability pressure. The truth, of course, is that the business of government is a juggling act (and often not an impressive one, as the case of Southfield shows). However, we should not shy away from distinguishing one act from another as privileging, broadly speaking, some concerns over others.

Moreover, this is not just a truism about the existence of discretion in bureaucratic decision-making. It is possible to trace the links between accountability pressures and bureaucratic practices. The links may not be perfect, nor do they necessarily tell the whole story, but by examining the case studies of Southfield and Brisford we can certainly observe distinguishable patterns of the influence of different accountability pressures on routine decision-making on the ground.

Southfield, as the 'risk authority', was notably pre-occupied with the task of risk management. The risk in question concerned tenantability: the prospect of bad tenants and anti-social neighbours. The risk management strategy was to separate the wheat from the chaff at the gateway to its housing—the implementation of homelessness law and the operations of its general housing register. Its principal techniques were the maintenance of an exclusions database, focusing on previous rent arrears together with histories of anti-social and criminal behaviour, and a self-declaration of past 'serious' offences. The HPU, in its routine operations, had internalised the risk management discourse. The source of this prevailing discourse was external to the HPU, however. It lay in local political initiatives to stem the problem of anti-social behaviour in the community. We saw in chapter two that anti-social behaviour has been a concern which has informed the development of homelessness law and policy at a national level. The history of Southfield as a community, however, meant that anti-social behaviour was a particularly local and prevailing concern. Equally, housing management and maintenance budgets have been the subject of funding cuts since the mid 1970s and impose financial constraints on how local authorities can react to the risk of anti-social behaviour. It is cheaper to try and exclude 'risk' tenants than to manage anti-social behaviour once in existence. The chain of accountability can be traced from the HPU to its local political masters, and from there to Southfield's community—the local electorate. The accountability mechanism, then, which prevailed upon the substance of routine homelessness decision-making in Southfield was old fashioned local democracy.

Brisford, by way of contrast, has been characterised as the 'audit authority'. Whereas Southfield was preoccupied with risk management, Brisford was pre-occupied with performance management. Performance 'quality' was reduced to a quantifiable calculus defined according to the Best Value regime. Although Best Value was the engine driving the HPU, the outward façade was derived from the Charter Mark regime and its concern for 'customer' service. This too was defined according to quantifiable criteria. However, the discourse of customer care was ultimately subject to the concerns of economic efficiency. The Charter Mark regime may have provided the trimmings of the HPU's service, but the Best Value regime provided the direction. The day-to-day work of the HPU was fashioned around meeting these targets and thereby the demonstration of 'quality'. The HPU had internalised this 'audit' discourse, but the source of the discourse was in central government's regulation of local government bureaucracy. The chain of accountability in Brisford is perhaps starker than that in Southfield and can be traced from the HPU to its local political masters, then to its central government regulators—and from there to New Labour itself.

Although we have distinguished Southfield from Brisford in its homelessness decision-making, there is a common feature which unites them—the fact that a discourse of welfarism has been effectively silenced in their operations. In both sites we saw pockets of resistance where individual low-level officers expressed frustration at the dominant ethos within their organisations and tried (usually unsuccessfully) to counter it. However, despite local resistance, welfarist discourse was overwhelmed in both authorities by the 'common sense' approaches of risk and consumerism, reflecting broader trends within government generally (Dean, 1999). Nevertheless, the existence of such discourses suggests that the path to strategies and techniques of advanced liberalism, or neo-liberalism, is incomplete, and punctured at the 'street level' by opposing forces.

EXPLAINING AND PREDICTING DISPUTING BEHAVIOUR

In chapters five and six we set out our findings about why some of our interviewees failed to pursue internal review and why others did request a review.

Chapter five contains a list of the various barriers to take up which emerged from our data. We have been careful to stress that these barriers are presented individually for analytic purposes. We hope that this analytic framework on the non-emergence of disputes in welfare will complement the small amount of existing research in this area and provide a useful foundation for taking the research agenda forward. However, it is important to stress that individual narratives of applicants failing to challenge adverse decisions often (perhaps usually) involve some combination of these barriers applying.

In chapter two, we asked whether there were any conditions under which we should expect to see an increase in the take-up of internal review. Clearly, if the barriers which we have set out in chapter five disappeared, then we would expect the take up to increase substantially. If every applicant knew about the right, had faith in the integrity of the process, had the energy to go through with the challenge, recognised the existence of discretion in the process, was aggrieved at the adverse decision and continued to need the substantive benefit, then we should expect to see a much greater incidence of requests for internal review. As we have said throughout this book, we cannot claim that our list of barriers is exhaustive. We would expect future research to shed light on other barriers to the challenge of adverse decisions—particularly in relation to tribunals where research has already highlighted the barriers of cost, complexity and physical access (Adler & Gulland, 2002). Nevertheless, to posit our list as one of 'barriers' to the take-up of internal review is to suggest that their absence should increase take up.

However, this is not to say very much. It simply begs the question of when we might expect there to be less ignorance, fatigue, scepticism, rule-bound legal consciousness, satisfaction and a greater incidence of genuine and/or continuing need. Although we have demonstrated that the applicant-bureaucracy relationship is important to our understanding of why these attitudes exist, our data demonstrates that other contexts also fuel their existence and influence their form. Previous experiences, negative and positive, are important. Comparisons with the (presumed) fate of other individuals or other groups can be significant. The concept of 'audience' is also important here as we demonstrated in chapter seven. The advice and support of informal networks, or formal advice or agency workers can be influential. As Felstiner et al (1980–81) have pointed out, disputes are social constructs. Our data suggests that the process of social construction takes place within these various contexts. Neither applicants' senses of grievances, nor the attitudinal barriers to the take up of internal review, emerge inside a social vacuum. Rather, they come to life by applicants talking to other people, by comparing themselves with others, and by comparing their current circumstances with their past.

Our data in chapter six also demonstrates that those who *do* pursue internal review often nevertheless suffer from scepticism and fatigue. We have noted that there are similarities between aggrieved applicants who challenge decisions and those who do not. This re-emphasises the point that understanding individual micro decisions about whether to engage in a dispute is a complex business. As we highlighted above, many of our interviewees' decisions not to pursue internal review was the result of a combination of barriers. Our data is incapable either of weighting the significance of individual barriers relative to each other, or of understanding the complex relationships between barriers where they co-exist inside individuals' consciousnesses. Individual stories of why people did and did not challenge adverse decisions demonstrate a complex constellation of factors that push someone to challenge or pull them back from doing so. The existence of a single factor, then, does not produce a uniform outcome. Similar experiences can push an applicant towards pursuing their grievance, or pull them back from doing so, as is demonstrated by the 'problem' of scepticism. The focus on a single factor to explain or predict disputing behaviour can be very misleading, accordingly.

All of this makes it impossible to predict on the basis of our data when there might be an increase in challenges to adverse welfare decisions. Although there are some policy initiatives which might militate against the barriers arising within the applicant-bureaucracy relationship, it is more difficult to account for the external contexts which influence the existence and application of the barriers (or combination of barriers) to individual aggrieved applicants. Our data is incapable, then, of predicting macro trends in the behaviour of aggrieved applicants. It is, however, capable of revealing some of the difficulties of such a task, and of providing some foundational qualitative data which could inform future quantitative studies which seek to move towards a better macro understanding of the failure to take up grievance rights against welfare agencies.

Nevertheless, our stress on the interaction perspective—the importance of understanding the existence of the barriers to internal review within the context of the applicant-bureaucracy relationship—has provided some important data which could feed into policy developments intended to reduce the barriers to the challenges of adverse decisions. These are discussed in the following section.

THE INTERACTION PERSPECTIVE AND POLICY

Our ethnographic data about decision-making in Southfield and Brisford, together with our interview data about the (non-)pursuit of internal review, have shown that the applicant-bureaucracy relationship is an important context for understanding the (non-)emergence of disputes. We have been able to locate applicants' senses of grievance in their experiences of the application process, and we have located various 'attitudinal' barriers to the take up of internal review in the applicant-bureaucracy relationship. Although, as we have just noted, the interaction perspective is insufficient to explain the (non-)emergence of disputes comprehensively, some potential policy developments can be suggested. These should militate against the existence of barriers to the take up of grievance rights within bureaucratic practices. However, it is important to be cautious in suggesting potential policy developments beyond our subject area (as we suggested in chapter seven). Our analysis of homelessness law may not effortlessly translate, for example, to the administration of social security, or other aspects of administrative law. Accordingly, in this section we highlight a number of themes which we believe are suggested by our data as being pertinent to the existence of the various barriers to the take up of internal review. We suggest them at a sufficient level of generality for them to be able to be applied in different contexts.

Communication

Genn and Genn (1989) suggest that some agencies are more successful than others in communicating the existence of a right of redress. Our data certainly points to the significance of poor communication between the bureaucracy and the applicant as a cause of ignorance of rights of internal review. This perhaps is most clearly seen in relation to formal decision-letters. Formal correspondence can often be bewildering for an applicant; and the decision-letter is often one of many formal letters which may become lumped together, or only surface-read. This is made worse when decision-letters are legalistic in tone—as we noted in chapter four, our field-worker had difficulty understanding Brisford's decision-letters. Our data suggests that correspondence can be a very ineffective way of communicating with applicants. Even the location of information about grievance rights within a letter may be important. There was evidence to suggest that Brisford's method of communicating the right to review in a separate information pack which contained a review request form was a more successful method of communication than Southfield's method which involved burying the information at the end of a complicated letter.

Our data also suggests that oral communication is as important, if not more so, than written communication. In Southfield, in particular, there was a notable mismatch between messages conveyed orally and messages conveyed formally in writing. For many applicants, the complicated process of welfare application is more easily understood in spoken interactions. This raises the importance of consistency between spoken and written messages. Although 'textuality' may have taken on a privileged significance in modern legal-rational society as Ewick and Silbey have noted (1998: 100), this is perhaps not true from the perspective of individual welfare applicants. Applicants' understanding of the processes in which they are involved may be derived as much from the way in which the local authority officer conducts the interview. For example, some styles of interview identify the administrative process with law and legal process, thus shifting the terrain of grievances about procedure and decision-making.

Trust, Faith and Scepticism

We saw in chapter five that a breach of trust between applicant and bureaucracy can trigger a loss of faith in the integrity of an internal review process. It may also, we suggest, cause a lack of faith in the integrity of tribunal processes, as research has demonstrated that citizens often fail to recognise the distinction between agency and tribunal (see, for example, Genn & Genn, 1989; Sainsbury et al, 1995; Harris & Eden, 2000). In chapter six, we noted that many of our interviewees pursued an internal review *despite* considerable scepticism and mistrust. Our data suggests the importance to trust of integrity, transparency, responsiveness, competence and efficiency on the part of the bureaucracy—particularly the front-line workers (who, unfortunately, are often the worst paid and most demoralised). Faith in the integrity of a review process could also be promoted by some form of publicity about the rates of success for applicants. Publicity has recently gained considerable importance in systems of housing allocation as a result of a shift to 'choice-based lettings', but it is equally prevalent in areas in housing and beyond, such as the local publication of performance statistics. Such a development would be particularly pertinent for an agency like Brisford which is particularly 'consumer friendly' and 'audit conscious' and regularly provides public information about other aspects of its services.

The lack of independence of the internal review process caused some (though by no means all) of our interviewees to doubt its integrity. An internal review is by its nature not independent. However, as Sainsbury (1999) has noted, independence is increasingly a relative concept and becomes a matter of the distance between initial decision-maker and reviewer (rather than a complete institutional break). There is, perhaps, some scope for increasing the distance between reviewer and initial decision-maker which may mitigate applicants' concerns about potential overlap between independence and impartiality. Some intra-organisational distance between decision-maker and reviewer may also promise additional benefits in relation to the quality of the reviewing process as Baldwin et al (1992) have demonstrated. Alternatively, distance might be achieved by seeking reviewers from outside the organisation, but this carries with it certain problems such as the lack of exposure to the organisational priorities of the local administration.

Our data demonstrated that the applicant-bureaucrat relationship was important here in one other way. Advice of officers about an applicant's prospects of success at review can trigger a loss of faith in the internal review mechanism. Although such advice may be given out of a concern for the applicant, it does what it sets out to do—encourages the non-take up of grievances—which, in turn, suggests to applicants that the internal review system is worthless to them.

Image of Decision-Making

Certain bureaucratic practices may contribute to a distorted image of bureaucratic decision-making which may militate against the take up of internal review. What we have termed a 'formally-rational' image of decision-making may be encouraged by officers in face-to-face encounters—either through self-confidence or to deflect conflict—or in formal correspondence. Southfield's correspondence about an applicant's ability to challenge an offer of housing at the Refusals Panel provides an example of a letter which appropriately stresses the discretionary nature of the initial decision-making task. However, the negative assessment decision-letter, by contrast, suggests that there has been the application of unchallengeable, general legal rules. If the discretionary nature of the scheme being applied was stressed, applicants might have a better appreciation of the flexibility of the regime.

Length and Complexity of the Bureaucratic Process

The length and complexity of the bureaucratic process can contribute to or exacerbate an applicant's fatigue. Our data demonstrates that the welfare application may be but one of many difficulties being faced concurrently by applicants. The shorter and easier an appeal or review process is, the less likely it is to contribute to an applicant's sense of fatigue. Even so, a quick process can produce procedurally and/or substantively unfair results. Our discussion of the 'refusals' processes of both case studies demonstrate the inherent problems in quick adjudication of a grievance. The drop out rate between the informal refusal and the formal internal review suggests that a quick, intermediate process is not necessarily 'better' justice.

Schemes designed to control who is and is not entitled to certain benefits often have a complexity which is both counterproductive and hardly amenable to simple interpretations. The homelessness legislation is no different in this respect—despite being relatively short and supplemented by a Code of Guidance, its interpretation is shrouded by obscure language in its formulation and supplemented by convoluted judicial camouflage. To really know homelessness law, then, requires considerable expertise. However, our case studies provide evidence that even amongst those in the know, some advisers are better than others. This means that in the pursuit of their grievance, some applicants have a head-start over others. The geographical unevenness of legal advice across the UK, combined with declining levels of legal aid, mean that those who might be expected to know it may not be available. In Brisford, for example, there was evidence that certain advisers had a moratorium on new cases. Yet, geographical unevenness does not provide the whole picture for, as we noted in chapter seven, both Southfield and Brisford are well-served by legal practitioners who have proficiency in homelessness work. Access to quality legal advice clearly assists the individual but, in Brisford, also impacts on the decipherability of decision-letters themselves. As we have noted, the audience for the decision-letter becomes the lawyer and not the applicant; yet we know that not all applicants seek legal advice and, indeed, an indecipherable decision-letter can be off-putting. It follows from this that the ready availability of legal advice should not be regarded as a panacea—it can be both individually productive, but collectively problematic.

Coerced Choice

Our data in relation to Southfield showed the potential for the creation of coerced choice in relation to the acceptance of housing offers. This finding has particular pertinence to the field of housing, but it demonstrates a wider ability of bureaucracies to exert a degree of control over applicants' expectations. Such control is often exercised in order to assist the bureaucracy to meet its own objectives. To limit such control as a barrier to the take up of grievance rights, welfare agencies should be reflexive about their influence on applicants' constructions of 'satisfaction' and about why such influence is exerted. They should be open and welcoming to competing influences from, for example, interest groups.

INTERNAL REVIEW AND ADMINISTRATIVE JUSTICE

One of the main concerns over internal review and its relationship to administrative justice has been whether, when it is a compulsory step before external review is allowed, it would act to deter applicants from pursing external review. Sainsbury (1994b) has argued that it would. Harris (1999) has contested this view. Focusing on the problem of 'appeal fatigue', Harris suggests that this could be overcome by clearly pointing out to applicants that they have a right to external appeal. It should be clear by now that our data demonstrates that such a view is problematic. The empirical reality of applicants' engagements with the administrative justice system, as we showed in chapter five, is more complicated. Our findings about the limited effectiveness of 'clear' information about subsequent rights to review or appeal, and about applicant fatigue, support Sainsbury's fears. They offer some important qualitative insights into why drop out rates after initial forms of redress are so high.

Our data, however, offers additional insights into the relationship between internal review and administrative justice. Sainsbury (1994a) has set out the distinction between the ideal types of internal review and appeal, but notes that in reality the distinctions can be blurred, and that internal review can occupy an uneasy space which straddles both the administrative and the adjudicative realm. Our data sheds new light on this point. Our case studies demonstrated that the presence of legal representation in internal review can cause internal review to be shifted from the administrative towards the adjudicative realm. Our data showed that the presence of legal representation impacted on how a reviewing officer would conduct the internal review. When no legal representation was present, internal review took the form of a simple administrative check, consistent with Mashaw's (1983) model of bureaucratic justice. However, when an applicant was legally represented, internal review provided a formal space within the administrative arena for adversarial legal debate. It took the form of a rehearsal for external review in the courts. In doing so, the character of administrative justice being played out had moved towards Mashaw's moral judgement model. This means that in assessing the character of administrative justice being practised in internal review, we must not only have regard to its place within the overall architecture of the administrative justice system, but we must also give close attention to the micro-social reality of particular practices.

Our research findings further suggest that internal review has an ambivalent relationship to initial decision-making. On the one hand, we saw in Brisford that internal review offered an educative potential in relation to ongoing initial decision-making. Brisford's Principal Reviews Officer used the experience of internal review to discuss cases with junior officers, to point out deficiencies in their practice, and to inform them about case law developments. On the other hand, we also saw that the possibility of internal review acted as a security blanket when officers were tempted to make an initial decision of poor quality. In Brisford, the discourses of efficiency and legality were in competition with each other. Internal review offered a security blanket and calmed officers' nerves about sacrificing legality to efficiency by making a decision which they felt was rushed or of otherwise poor quality. Concerns with legality and welfare had to be sacrificed at times in order to meet casework targets. The existence of the right to internal review, however, offered the false security that the HPU could always get the decision right at review stage. The difficulty is that such security is premised on the notion of the rational aggrieved applicant who will pursue all his/her options for redress. Our data has demonstrated the considerable weakness of this image.

There was also evidence that internal review could be used defensively to bolster decisions before the onslaught of external review, or could be used positively to re-examine an applicant's claim to housing. The review could focus, then, on the substance or merely the articulation of the initial decision. Accordingly, like judicial review, it acted as a double-edged sword (Halliday 2000a). These contrasting findings about the relationship between internal review and the substance of decision-making demonstrate that internal review does not have a pre-determined relationship to administrative justice. It forms just one part of the overall picture. Its role in the justice of the bureaucratic process must be understood alongside the other contingencies that make up the fabric of the overall bureaucratic environment.

THE RESEARCH AGENDA

It is appropriate for us to finish this book by thinking about the future research agenda. Internal review has been a much neglected topic of administrative justice research. Similarly, too little research has been undertaken on the issue of the (non-) emergence of disputes in social welfare in particular and in relation to administrative grievances in general. We hope that this book makes significant contributions to both areas. Nevertheless, we should be careful to reflect on the gaps in our knowledge which remain. This is not simply because good empirical research, by its nature, is focused, thereby making a particular and bounded contribution to academic knowledge. It is also because research often raises as many questions as it answers. In this final section, we set out some general questions that either remain to be answered, or must be asked in light of our findings.

What Configurations of Factors Facilitate the Take-up of Grievance Rights?

We have tried to stress the difficulty of answering this question. We have carefully set out the barriers to the take-up of internal review which existed within our sample. However, at the same time we have also pointed to the various contexts within which disputes are socially constructed and emphasised that our data is ill-equipped to map out the configurations of relevant factors/contexts which would facilitate the take-up of grievance rights. To move towards a better understanding of variations in take-up rates, we must carefully combine qualitative and quantitative methods. We believe that our findings in this project make an important contribution to this end. Our qualitative data may feed into larger and more ambitious projects with a quantitative element which could seek to explain differential rates of take-up according to, for example, geographical location and social group. Such an alliance of qualitative and quantitative methods would promise significant advances to our understanding of the conundrum of non-take up.

The Importance of 'Audience'

One important element of the above agenda is the issue of 'audience'. Our data demonstrated that many potential audiences exist. These audiences constitute some of the contexts within which disputes and barriers to disputes are socially constructed, and advice and support about challenging adverse decisions may be given. Although the role of lawyers as an audience has traditionally been a major concern of socio-legal studies in relation to the emergence and management of disputes, there is much to be gained, we suggest, in systematically enquiring into the role played by family, friends, fellow applicants, and so on, despite the difficulty of such a task.

Impact of Legal Representation

This is not to say, of course, that further research into lawyers and their influence on the emergence of disputes is not important. For those who use legal representation there is a question, for example, about whether applicants seek legal help because of their desire to pursue internal review, or whether they pursue internal review because of their preliminary contact with lawyers. The answer suggested by our data is that both propositions are true, but more systematic data on this issue would be welcome. Research has repeatedly demonstrated the positive impact which legal representation can have on applicants' chances of success at tribunals. Our data suggests that the same may be true at the internal review stage. However, this requires proper quantitative testing.

Interaction Perspective

Further work on the implications of the interaction perspective is required. We have tried to show in this chapter how an interaction perspective on the (non-)emergence of administrative disputes can feed into policy developments. However, such policy developments need to be carefully researched and tested in different contexts. This would lead to both greater subtlety and refinement in policy responses. It would also shed further light on the (non-)emergence of disputes.

The interaction perspective equally raised questions about the significance of the applicant-bureaucracy relationship to the legal consciousness of applicants. We pointed to various aspect of bureaucratic practice which, we suggested, might contribute to, or encourage, a 'formally rational' image of legal decision-making within the agency. We recognise, however, that proper systematic enquiry is required in order to situate legal consciousness pertaining to prospective challenges to adverse decisions within the applicant-bureaucracy relationship. This, too, would be a fruitful area of future research.

The Emotional Dimension

Finally, more research is required about the emotional dimensions of administrative and welfare disputes. Unsuccessful applications for assistance and interactions with bureaucracies do not always yield 'rational economic' responses but they do generally generate emotions. Our data has demonstrated the significance of emotions to applicants' motivations in seeking internal review and their grounds for doing so. Equally, however, our data in chapter five demonstrates that there is an emotional dimension to the failure to pursue internal review. Our list of the barriers to the pursuit of internal review reveals the substance of emotions in applicants' reactions to adverse decisions, even though we have not explicitly framed our analysis in this way. An exploration of emotions is necessary, then, for a full understanding of disputing behaviour. It is a matter to which insufficient attention has been paid in administrative justice research and about which more research would be welcome.

Bibliography

Adler, M (2001) 'A Socio-legal Approach to Procedural Justice' unpublished seminar paper presented to Centre for Socio-Legal Studies, Oxford University

Adler, M and Gulland, J (2002) *Tribunals for Users' Programme: Literature Review of Users' Experiences, Perceptions and Expectations* unpublished report for Lord Chancellor's Department, London

Administrative Review Council (2000) *Internal Review of Agency Decision-Making: Report to the Attorney General*, Report No 44 (Administrative Review Council, Canberra)

Allsop, J and Mulcahy, L (1998) 'Maintaining Professional Identity: Doctors' Responses to Complaints' 20 *Sociology of Health and Illness* 802

Anderson, I and Tulloch, D (2000) *Pathways Through Homelessness: A Review of the Research Evidence* (Scottish Homes, Edinburgh)

Arden, A and Hunter, C (1997) *Homelessness and Allocations* (Legal Action Group, London)

Arnstein, S (1969) 'A Ladder of Citizen Participation' July *Journal of the American Institute of Planners* 216

Atkinson, R, Buck, T, Pollard, D, and Smith, N (1999) *A Regional Study of Local Authority and Court Processes in Homelessness Cases* Research Series No 9/99 (Lord Chancellor's Department, London)

Bailey, R and Ruddock, J (1972) *The Grief Report* (Shelter, London)

Baker, T (2000) 'Insuring Morality' 29 *Economy and Society* 559

Baldwin, J, Wikeley, N and Young, R (1992) *Judging Social Security* (Oxford University Press, Oxford)

Beck, U (1999) *World Risk Society* (Polity, Cambridge)

Becker, H (1960) 'Notes on the Concept of Commitment' 66 *American Journal of Sociology* 32

Berthoud, R and Bryson, A (1997) 'Social Security Appeals: What Do the Claimants Want' 4 *Journal of Social Security Law* 17

Blandy, S, Cole, I, Hunter, C and Robinson, D (2001) *Leasehold Valuation Tribunals: Extending the Remit* (Centre for Regional Economic and Social Research, Sheffield Hallam University, Sheffield)

Bridges, L, Game, C, Lomas, N, McBride & Ransom (1987) *Legality and Local Politics* (Gower, Aldershot)

Bridges, L, Sunkin, M and Meszaros, G (1995) *Judicial Review in Perspective* (Cavendish, London)

Bridges L, Meszaros G & Sunkin M (1998) *Dynamics of Public Law Litigation, Report of Research Activities and Results to ESRC* (Grant R00023554301)

Bumiller, K (1988) *The Civil Rights Society: The Social Construction of Victims* (Johns Hopkins University Press, Baltimore)

Butler, S (1998) *Access Denied* (Shelter, London)

Carlen, P (1994) 'The Governance of Homelessness: Legality, Lore and Lexicon in the Agency-maintainance of Youth Homelessness' 41 *Critical Social Policy* 18

Cohen, S (2001) *Immigration Controls, the Family and the Welfare State* (Jessica Kingsley, London)

Cooper, D (1995) 'Local Government Legal Consciousness in the Shadow of Juridification' 22 *Journal of Law and Society* 506

Cowan, D (1997) *Homelessness: The (In-)Appropriate Applicant* (Dartmouth, Aldershot)

—— (1999) *Housing Law and Policy* (MacMillan, Basingstoke)

Cowan, D, Gilroy, R, and Pantazis, C (1999) 'Risking Housing Need' 26 *Journal of Law and Society* 403

Cowan, D with Fionda, J (1998) 'Homelessness Internal Appeal Mechanisms: Serving the Administrative Process' 27 *Anglo-American Law Review* 66 (Pt I) and 169 (Pt II)

Cowan, D and Marsh, A (2001) 'There's Regulatory Crime and Then There's Landlord-Crime: from "Rachmanites" to "Partners"' 65 *Modern Law Review* 831

Cowan, D, and Pantazis, C (2001) 'Social Housing as Crime Control' 10 *Social and Legal Studies* 435

Croft, J (2002) *Risk Crystallisation, Housing Debt and Social Division*, Unpublished PhD Thesis (University of Bristol, Bristol)

Dalley G, and Berthoud R (1992) *Challenging Discretion: The Social Fund Review Procedure* (Policy Studies Institute, London)

Damer, S (1974) 'Wine Alley: The Sociology of a Dreadful Enclosure' 22 *Sociological Review* 221

Davis, G, Wikeley, N and Young, R, with Barron, J and Bedward, J (1998) *Child Support in Action* (Hart Publishing, Oxford)

Dean, M (1999) *Governmentality: Power and Rule in Modern Society* (Sage, London)

De Certeau, M (1984) *The Practice of Everyday Life* (University of California Press, Berkeley)

DETR (2000) *Best Value in Housing Framework* (London, DETR)

DoE (1994) *Access to Local Authority and Housing Association Tenancies* (HMSO, London)

—— (1996) *Code of Guidance on Parts VI and VII of the Housing Act 1996* (London, DoE)

DTLR (2002) *Tackling Anti-Social Behaviour*, A Consultation Paper (DTLR, London)

Dummett, A and Nicol, A (1990) *Subjects, Citizens, Aliens and Others: Nationality and Immigration Law* (Weidenfeld & Nicolson, London)

Engel, D (1998) 'How Does Law Matter in the Constitution of Legal Consciousness' in B Garth and A Sarat (eds), *How Does Law Matter?*, Fundamental Issues in Law and Society Research Volume 3 (Northwestern University Press, Evanston)

Ericson, R, and Haggerty, K (1997) *Policing the Risk Society* (Oxford University Press, Oxford)

Ericson, R, Barry, D, and Doyle, A (2000) 'The Moral Hazards of Neo-liberalism: Lessons from the Private Insurance Industry' 29 *Economy and Society* 532

Ewald, F (1991) 'Insurance and Risk' in G Burchell, C Gordon and P Miller (eds), *The Foucault Effect: Studies in Governmentality* (University of Chicago Press, Chicago)

Ewick, P and Silbey, S (1992) 'Conformity, Contestation, and Resistance: An Account of Legal Conscionsness' 26 *New England Law Review* 731

—— (1998) *The Common Place of Law: Stories from Everyday Life* (University of Chicago Press, Chicago)

Felstiner, W, Abel, R and Sarat, A (1980-1) 'The Emergence and Transformation of Disputes: Naming, Blaming, Claiming …' 15 *Law and Society Review* 631

Forrest, R and Kennett, P (1996) 'Coping Strategies, Housing Careers and Households with Negative Equity' 25 *Journal of Social Policy* 369

Forrest, R and Murie, A (1990) *Selling the Welfare State: The Privatisation of Council Housing* (Routledge, London)

Franks, O (1957) *Report on the Committee on Administrative Tribunals and Enquiries*, Cmnd 218 (HMSO, London)

Fukuyama, F (1995) *Trust: the Social Virtues and Creation of Prosperity* (Free Press Paperbacks, New York)

Galanter, M (1974) 'Why the "Haves" Come Out Ahead: Speculations on the Limits of Legal Change' 9 *Law and Society Review* 94

Galligan, D (1996) *Due Process and Fair Procedures: A Study of Administrative Procedures* (Oxford University Press, Oxford)

Gandy, O (1993) *The Panoptic Sort: A Political Economy of Personal Information* (Westview, Boulder)

Garland, D (1996) 'The Limits of the Sovereign State: Strategies of Crime Control in Contemporary Society' 36 *British Journal of Criminology* 445

—— (2001) *The Culture of Control: Crime and Social Order in Contemporary Society* (Oxford University Press, Oxford)

Geary, R and Leith, P (2001) 'From Operational Strategies to Serving the Customer: Technology and Ethics in Welfare Law' 15 *International Review of Law, Computers and Technology* 213

Genn, H (1984) 'Who Claims Compensation: Factors Associated with Claiming and Obtaining Damages', in D Harris et al (eds), *Compensation and Support for Illness and Injury* (Clarendon Press, Oxford)

—— (1994) 'Tribunal Review of Administrative Decision-making' in G Richardson and H Genn, *Administrative Law and Government Action* (Clarendon Press, Oxford)

—— (1999) *Paths to Justice: What People Do and Think about Going to Law* (Hart Publishing, Oxford)

Genn, H and Genn, Y (1989) *The Effectiveness of Representation at Tribunals*, Report to the Lord Chancellor (Lord Chancellor's Department, London)

Giddens, A (1990) *The Consequences of Modernity* (Polity Press, Cambridge)

Glaser, B and Strauss, A (1967) *The Discovery of Grounded Theory: Strategies for Qualitative Research* (Weidenfield and Nicolson, London)

Greve, J (1964) *London's Homeless* (Bell, London)

Greve, J, Page, D and Greve, S (1971) *Homelessness in London* (Scottish Academic Press, Edinburgh)

Hacking, I (1986) 'Making Up People' in T Heller (ed), *Reconstructing individualism* (Stanford University Press, California)

Halliday, S (1998) 'Researching the "Impact" of Judicial Review on Routine Administrative Decision-making', in D Cowan (ed), *Housing: Participation and Exclusion* (Dartmouth, Aldershot)

—— (2000a) 'The Influence of Judicial Review on Bureaucratic Decision-making' *Public Law* 110

—— (2000b) 'Institutional Racism in Bureaucratic Decision-making: a Case Study in the Administration of Homelessness Law' 27 *Journal of Law and Society* 449

—— (2001) 'Internal Review and Administrative Justice: Some Evidence and Research Questions from Homelessness Decision-making' 23 *Journal of Social Welfare and Family Law* 473

—— (forthcoming) *Judicial Review and Compliance with Administrative Law* (Hart Publishing, Oxford)

Hancher, L and Moran, M (1989) 'Organising Regulatory Space', in L Hancher and M Moran (eds), *Capitalism, Culture and Regulation* (Oxford University Press, Oxford)

Harlow, C and Rawlings, R (1997) *Law and Administration*, 2nd edn, (Butterworths, London)

Harris, M (1999) 'The Place of Formal and Informal Review in the Administrative Justice System' in M Harris and M Partington (eds), *Administrative Justice in the 21st Century* (Hart Publishing, Oxford)

Harris, N and Eden, K (2000) *Challenges to School: Exclusion, Appeals and the Law* (Routledge/Farmer, London)

Heimer, C (undated) *Solving the Problem of Trust* (American Bar Foundation Working Paper #9804)

Hoggett, P (1996) 'New Modes of Control in the Public Service' 74 *Public Administration* 9

Hood, C, Rothstein, H, and Baldwin, R (2001), *The Government of Risk:*

Understanding Risk Regulation Regimes (Oxford University Press, Oxford)

Hood, C, Scott, C, James, O, Jones, G, and Travers, T (1999) *Regulation Inside Government: Waste-Watchers, Quality Police, and Sleaze-Busters* (Oxford University Press, Oxford)

Huby, M and Dix, G (1992) *Evaluating the Social Fund* (HMSO, London)

Hunter, C, Nixon, J and Shayer, S (2001) *Neighbour Nuisance, Social Landlords and the Law* (Chartered Institute of Housing, Coventry)

Jacobs, K, Kemeny, J and Manzi, T (1999) 'The Struggle to Define Homelessness: a Constructivist Perspective' in S Hutson and D Clapham (eds), *Homelessness: Public Policies and Private Troubles* (Cassell, London)

Jacobs, K and Manzi, T (2000) 'Performance Indicators and Social Constructivism: Conflict and Control in Housing Management' 62 *Critical Social Policy* 85

Lange, B (2002) 'The Emotional Dimension in Legal Regulation' 29 *Journal of Law and Society* 197

Law Commission (2002) *Renting Homes 1: Status and Security*, Consultation Paper No 162 (Law Commission, London)

Le Grand, J (1997) 'Knights, Knaves or Pawns? Human Behaviour and Social Policy' 26 *Journal of Social Policy* 149

Levene, K and Mellema, V (2001) 'Strategizing the Street: How Law Matters in the Lives of Women in the Street-level Drug Economy' 28 *Law and Social Inquiry* 169

Lewis, N, Seneviratne, M, and Cracknell, S (1987) *Complaints Procedures in Local Government* (Centre for Criminological and Socio-Legal Studies, University of Sheffield, Sheffield)

Lipsky, M (1980) *Street Level Bureaucracy: Dilemmas of the Individual in Public Services* (Russell Sage Foundation, New York)

Lloyd-Bostock, S (1984) 'Fault and Liability for Accidents: the Accident Victim's Perspective' in D Harris et al (eds), *Compensation and Support for Illness and Injury* (Clarendon Press, Oxford)

—— (1991), 'Propensity to Sue in England and the United States of America: The Role of Attribution Processes – A Comment on Kritzer' 18 *Journal of Law and Society* 428

Lloyd-Bostock, S and Mulcahy, L (1994) 'The Social Psychology of Making and Responding to Hospital Complaints: An Account Model of Complaint Processes' 16 *Law and Policy* 185

Loughlin, M (1996) *Legality and Locality: The Role of Law in Central-Local Government Relationships* (Oxford University Press, Oxford)

Loveland, I (1995) *Housing Homeless Persons* (Oxford University Press, Oxford)

Luhmann, N (1988) 'Familiarity, Confidence, Trust: Problems and Alternatives' in D Gambetta (ed), *Trust: Making and Breaking of Co-operative Relations* (Blackwell, Oxford)

Mashaw, J (1983) *Bureaucratic Justice* (Yale, New Haven)

Mather, L and Yngvesson, B (1980-1) 'Language, Audience, and the Transformation of Disputes' 15 *Law and Society Review* 775

May, M and Stengal, D (1990) 'Who Sues their Doctors? How Patients Handle Medical Grievances' 24 *Law and Society Review* 105

Merry SE (1979) 'Going to Court: Strategies of Dispute Management in an American Urban Neighborhood' 14 *Law and Society Review* 895

—— (1990) *Getting Justice and Getting Even: Legal Consciousness Among Working-Class Americans* (University of Chicago Press, Chicago)

Miller, P (2001) 'Governing Numbers: Why Calculative Practices Matter' 68 *Social Research* 379

Mulcahy, L, and Tritter, J (1998) 'Pathways, Pyramids and Icebergs? Mapping the Links Between Dissatisfaction and Complaints' 20 *Sociology of Health and Illness* 825

Mullins, D and Niner, P with Marsh, A and Walker, B (1996) *Evaluation of the 1991 Homelessness Code of Guidance* (HMSO, London)

Murie, A (1997a) 'The Social Rented Sector, Housing and the Welfare State in the UK' 12 *Housing Studies* 437

—— (1997b) 'Linking Housing Changes to Crime' 31 *Social Policy and Administration* 22

Nielson, L (2000) 'Situating Legal Consciousness: Experiences and Attitudes of Ordinary Citizens about Law and Street Harassment' 34 *Law and Society Review* 1055

Niner, P (1989) *Homelessness in Nine Local Authorities* (HMSO, London)

Nixon, J, Smith, Y, Wishart, B and Hunter, C (1996) *Housing Cases in the County Courts* (Policy Press, Bristol)

Office of the Deputy Prime Minister (2000) *Best Value Performance Indicators for 2001/2002* (ODPM, London)

O'Callaghan, B and Dominian, L (1996) *Study of Homeless Applicants* (Department of the Environment, London)

O'Malley, P and Palmer, D (1996), 'Post-Keynesian Policing' 25 *Economy and Society* 137

Page, D (1994) *Building for Communities: A Study of New Housing Association Estates* (Joseph Rowntree Foundation, York)

Parker, C (1999) 'Compliance Professionalism and Regulatory Community: The Australian Trade Practices Regime' 26 *Journal of Law and Society* 215

Parton, N (1996) 'Social Work, Risk and the "Blaming System"' in N Parton (ed), *Social Theory, Social Change and Social Work* (Routledge, London)

Power, M (1997) *The Audit Society: Rituals of Verification* (Oxford University Press, Oxford)

Quinn, B (2000) 'The Paradox of Complaining: Law, Humor, and Harassment in the Everyday Workworld' 27 *Law and Social Inquiry* 1151

Ravenhill, M (2000) *Routes into Homelessness* (London Borough of Camden, London)

Robson, P and Poustie, M (1996) *Homeless People and the Law* (Butterworths, London)

Robson, P and Watchman, P (1981) 'The Homeless Persons Obstacle Race' *Journal of Social Welfare Law* 1 (pt I) and 65 (pt II)

Rose, N (1993) 'Government, Authority and Expertise in Advanced Liberalism' 22 *Economy and Society* 283

—— (1996) 'The Death of the Social? Re-figuring the Territory of Government' 25 *Economy and Society* 327

—— (1999) *Powers of Freedom: Reframing Political Thought* (Cambridge University Press, Cambridge)

Rose, N and Miller, P (1995) 'Political Power Beyond the State: Problematics of Government' 43 *British Journal of Sociology* 173

Sainsbury, R (1992) 'Administrative Justice: Discretion and Procedure in Social Security Decision-making' in K Hawkins (ed), *The Uses of Discretion* (Oxford University Press, Oxford)

—— (1994a) 'Internal Reviews and the Weakening of Social Security Claimants' Rights of Appeal' in G Richardson and H Genn (eds), *Administrative Law and Government Action: The Courts and Alternative Mechanisms of Review* (Oxford University Press, Oxford)

—— (1994b) 'Administrative Review or Tribunal?' *Conference of Tribunal Presidents and Chairmen, 22nd April 1994* (Council of Tribunals), cited in M Harris 'The Place of Formal and Informal Review in the Administrative Justice System' in M Harris and M Partington (eds), *Administrative Justice in the 21st Century* (Hart Publishing, Oxford), footnote 24

—— (1999) 'The Reform of Social Security Adjudication' in M Harris and M Partington (eds), *Administrative Justice in the 21st Century* (Hart Publishing, Oxford)

—— (2000) 'Social Security Decision-making and Appeals' in N Harris (ed) *Social Security Law in Context* (Oxford University Press, Oxford)

Sainsbury, R and Eardley, T (1991) *Housing Benefit Reviews* (HMSO, London)

Sainsbury, R, Hirst, M and Lawton, D (1995) *Evaluation of Disability Living Allowance and Attendance Allowance*, Department of Social Security Research Report No 41 (HMSO, London)

Sarat, A (1990) '"The Law is All Over ...": Power, Resistance and the Legal Consciousness of the Welfare Poor' 2 *Yale Journal of Law and the Humanities* 343

Sarat, A and Kearns, T (1993) 'Beyond the Great Divide: Forms of Legal Scholarship and Everyday Life' in A Sarat and T Kearns (eds), *Law in Everyday Life*, The Amherst Series in Law, Jurisprudence and Social Thought (University of Michigan Press, Ann Arbor)

Scott, C (2000) 'Accountability in the Regulatory State' 27 *Journal of Law & Society* 38

Seligman, A (1997) *The Problem of Trust* (Princeton University Press, Princeton)

Seron, C, Frankel, M, Van Ryzin, G, with Kovath, J (2001) 'The Impact of Legal Counsel on Outcomes for Poor Tenants in New York City's Housing Court: Results of a Randomized Experiment' 35 *Law and Society Review* 419

Sheppard, C and Raine, J (1999) 'Parking Adjudications: The Impact of New Technology' in M Harris and M Partington (eds) *Administrative Justice in the 21ˢᵗ Century* (Hart Publishing, Oxford)

Social Exclusion Unit (1999) *Anti-Social Behaviour*, Report of Policy Action Team 8 (Social Exclusion Unit, London)

Somerville, P (1994) 'Homelessness Policy in Britain' 22 *Policy and Politics* 163

—— (1999) 'The Making and Unmaking of Homelessness Legislation', in S Hutson and D Clapham (eds), *Homelessness: Public Policies and Private Troubles* (London, Cassell)

Stenson, K and Watt, P (1999) 'Crime, Risk and Governance in a Southern English Village' in G Dingwall and S Moody (eds), *Crime and Conflict in the Countryside* (University of Wales Press, Cardiff)

Sunkin, M (1987) 'What is Happening to Applications for Judicial Review?' 50 *Modern Law Review* 432

Sztompka, P (1999) *Trust: A Sociological Theory* (Cambridge University Press, Cambridge)

Taylor-Gooby, P (ed) (2000) *Risk, Trust and Welfare* (MacMillan, Basingstoke)

Taylor-Gooby, P, Dean, H, Munro, M, and Parker, G (1999) 'Risk and the Welfare State' 50 *British Journal of Sociology* 177

Tyler, T (1987) 'Procedural Justice Research' 1 *Social Justice Research* 41

—— (1988) 'What is Procedural Justice' 22 *Law & Society Review* 103

—— (1990) *Why People Obey the Law* (Yale University Press, New Haven)

Vincent-Jones, P (2000) 'Central-local Relations under the Local Government Act 1999: A New Consensus' 63 *Modern Law Review* 84

—— (2001) 'From Housing Management to the Management of Housing: the Challenge of Best Value' in D Cowan and A Marsh (eds), *Two Steps Forward: Housing Policy into the Millennium* (The Policy Press, Bristol)

—— (2002) 'Values and Purpose in Government: Central-local Relations in Regulatory Perspective' 29 *Journal of Law and Society* 27

Walker, R (2000) 'The Changing Management of Social Housing: The Impact of Externalisation and Managerialisation' 15 *Housing Studies* 281

Webb, J and Nicholson, D (1999) 'Institutionalising Trust: Ethics and the Responsive Regulation of the Legal Profession' 2 *Legal Ethics* 148

Yngvesson, B (1988) 'Making Law at the Doorway: The Clerk, the Court and the Construction of Community in a New England Town' 22 *Law and Society Review* 409